EVERY SCAR
A TREASURE

Wisdom for Life's Journey

DR. T. S. WISE

Every Scar a Treasure: Wisdom for Life's Journey

Scripture quotations taken from the New American Standard Bible®,
Copyright © 1960, 1962, 1963, 1968, 1971, 1972, 1973,
1975, 1977, 1995 by The Lockman Foundation
Used by permission." (www.Lockman.org)

ISBN: 978-0-9860613-3-2

Published by
Dr. Terry S. Wise
With kind assistance from Servant Communications, Inc.
Kirksville, Missouri 63501

Cover picture © Lekcej | Dreamstime.com – Dry Tree Silhouette.
Used with permission.

Flourishes: Bergamot Ornaments font by Emily Lime Design @
http://www.fontspace.com/emily-lime-design/bergamot-ornaments.
Licensed as Freeware for personal and commercial use.

Cover & Interior Design: Lissa Auciello-Brogan

Printed in the United States of America.

14 13 12 11 10 / 10 9 8 7 6 5 4 3 2 1

Dedication

This book is dedicated to my father, Phillip Craig Wise, who passed away on November 19, 2009 at the age of seventy-one. "You can't put an old head on young shoulders," he used to say, and I have a sneaky suspicion that he was referring to me! He would have enjoyed conversing about the contents of this book, and it would have been delightful to sit at his feet and hear the trove of treasure from his own scars.

When I think of my father, I am overwhelmed with pleasant thoughts. We watched the *Lawrence Welk Show* together as a family. He coached my youth baseball teams, fished with me at Lake Wapello, bought me my first shotgun, dialogued with me about God, supported my singing groups, allowed me to work in his shop to earn a few extra dollars, and saw me off for my first year of college. He had shortcomings like all of us, but He was kind, gentle, loving, and smart, with a wonderful sense of humor. People liked him. I liked him. Each night he tucked us kids into bed and kissed us goodnight. He was a dedicated husband, father, and employee. Though he never made much money, he gave me a priceless gift—the gift of love.

At the young age of forty-three, dad underwent five-way heart bypass surgery—and years later, a second one. In addition to severe heart problems, he would later develop Parkinson's disease and lung issues from his years of working around chemicals. Each day was a precious gift to my father, who stared down death on a daily basis. You can never love those closest to you too much, and it is only now, in my older age, that I realize what a gift I had been given in my father.

My father made one decision that forever altered the trajectory of my life—he began taking his family to church. I was introduced to God while in the sixth grade, became heavily involved in youth group, and eventually sensed a call to kingdom service. I have been a devoted God-follower ever since. Amazing the life-altering influence fathers can have upon their children with just one decision!

I still talk to my father, though the conversation is one sided these days, and tears fill my eyes when I think of him. I miss him dearly. Dad was a repairman—a skilled craftsman of musical instruments with a high school education. I would grow up to earn three doctorates, become a senior executive, and write numerous books. The foundation of my life was laid by my father, and he deserves credit for all that I have become. I hope my life is a reflection of the fine man that he was. Not only do I miss him, but I strive to be more like him, and that is the affirmation of his influence upon me. With deep gratitude, this book is lovingly dedicated to my father. I am proud of you, Dad, and proud to be your son. Thank you for being my father.

Contents

Preface

This night was like most other nights—wide-awake at odd hours of the morning. Early morning awakenings have been a faithful friend of mine over the years. When the kids were little, I rose at three o'clock in the morning to write, work on doctoral studies, or simply stare at the walls in deep thought. I returned to bed at six o'clock for another hour of sleep before heading off to a full day of work and family activities in the evening. To be up in the middle of the night was nothing new to me.

In fact, I enjoyed being undisturbed at this time of the day, or should I say night? With others soundly tucked in bed, the peaceful morning hours were all mine. As soft music played in the background, powerful thinking processes were unleashed. After a full day of external stimulation and a mind constantly in motion, these early morning hours were pure bliss. These precious "alone" hours helped to quietly recharge my batteries and allowed my mind to engage the world of inner thought. What more could a thinking introvert ask for!

This night, however, was a bit different. I didn't feel like researching, reading, or studying. Instead, I began to freestyle—that is, unleash a written stream-of-consciousness. I have learned a great deal from the bumps and bruises of life, and my heart was longing to express these insights. This was fun writing. No agenda and no outline—just releasing the overflow of a full heart. Let it rip. Emancipate each thought. Let it flow like a raging river about to overcome its banks. It was emotional writing accompanied by a plethora of memories, both good and bad. This book was birthed in the middle of the night—in solitude, with nothing but a full heart, a laptop computer, and soft blues music.

As I finished one chapter, another came to me. The floodgates opened, and a torrent of new chapters kept bursting forth. They are still clamoring to get out, but I must stop somewhere, and though this book doesn't begin to scratch the surface of all that life has taught me, it is a start. I maintain a list of additional chapters I hope to write, but they must wait for other volumes to follow. Rather than a psychological self-help treatise, this is a book of wisdom—insight gleaned from my own journey through life that I gladly share with those who are inclined to listen. I am hopeful, however, that my work will both uplift your countenance and benefit your own journey.

For some folks, it is important to maintain an ivory-tower image of picture-perfect living. They wish for us to believe that they have arrived, all things are in alignment, and they are the consummate image of success. In reality, it is nothing but an image they purposefully project and work hard to protect. All we have to do is scratch the surface of their lives and like Humpty-Dumpty, the image comes tumbling down. Projecting this kind of façade doesn't interest me in the least. I just want to be me, and I want to be real—warts and all. I have yet to meet a perfect person in this life, and let me be clear at the onset that I am lucky most days just to make it through without too many blunders. This life is a journey of becoming and transforming, and whether we take two steps forward or one step back, we always strive for progress in becoming all that God intends for us.

In those early morning hours when my heart yearned for expression, I pledged to be genuine with my stories, my failures, and my learnings. There is no ivory-tower bone in my body as I seek only authenticity. I am what I am and want to be the way God made me. As a fellow sojourner on the road of life, I walk beside you and picture us engaging one another in great conversation. At times, I imagine, we stop, put our arms around each other and pray together, cry together, and encourage one another. My life is not perfect, and I have no illusion about yours, either. But, since we are on this path together, let me share my harvest of learning and gleanings from God. Take what is helpful and discard what isn't. At the end of the day, know that I praise God for you and wish you the very best on your journey through life. If we are lucky, we will meet again and pick up where we left off—great conversation and mutual uplifting. Godspeed!

TSW
Kirksville, MO 2018

chapter one

Every Scar a Treasure

s a young kid, I ran fast. I could smart off to the older boys and get away with it since they were unable to catch me. With the agility of a rabbit, I weaved in, out, and around. Every once in a while I stumbled and fell, like the time my knee collided hard with the pavement and scraped a good section of skin off. I thought the scab would never heal. I remember it as though it happened yesterday, and I have the scar to prove it.

Stories hide behind our scars, and life is like that, too. We go about our business hopping to and fro, and then down we go. We get all banged up, maybe not physically, but emotionally. Healing, if it ever fully comes, seems to take forever, and when it does, we never quite heal the same as we were before. Every scrape leaves behind its mark, accompanied, of course, by a story.

My father underwent open heart bypass at the age of forty-three to clear multiple clogged arteries. The surgery was brutal, and my mind still conjures up images of his ordeal that I just can't seem to shake. Years later, he would undergo a second bypass surgery that was just as difficult. I admire his courage in the face of such difficulty. The incident not only changed him physically but emotionally, as well. He had the scars to prove it; one right down the middle of his chest, and another one on the inside revealing his emotional wound.

Scars are symbols with a story to tell. Some we love to share because they make us laugh, especially at ourselves; we all do foolish things now and then worthy of a good chuckle. Other stories aren't as easily articulated because of lingering pain. Scars can point to trauma and loss, and the emotional wounds are hard to bear. While the outside may have healed, the inside can still be tender. That's what symbols do—point to something other than themselves. What do the scars in your life point to? Do they look backward to the pain you once endured or forward to your resulting transformation? Every scar is a treasure, if we allow it to symbolize our new, different, and transformed self.

Wounded Reactions

When we become wounded, several responses are possible. First, we can fight. You hurt me, so I hurt you back, two-fold. An eye for an eye, or as some would have it, two eyes for one eye. Sometimes we respond to God like this. When something happens to us that we feel He should have prevented, we fight Him, not physically, but emotionally and spiritually. We want Him to hurt like He hurt us.

Secondly, we can run. Instead of fighting back, we simply hide, or ignore the situation altogether. With this response, the best defense is to retreat and nurse our wounds so we can live to fight another day. After all, fighting is hard work, emotionally and physically draining, and who knows, losing the battle may be a real possibility. In a spiritual sense, we can run from God, too. When the Spirit leads in a direction we don't fancy, we simply flee like Jonah. Adam and Eve took this approach in the Garden of Eden, and when God came to visit, they hid.

Often, a third alternative is chosen, and instead of fighting or running, we simply acquiesce. Sometimes we become battle-weary souls who can no longer stomach the war zone. It is easier to give up and give in. When the pit bull growls at us, we roll over on our back in complete submission, too tired to do anything else.

A final way of licking our wounds is to learn from them. This perspective rises above the incident itself and asks what positive gain can come from it. Life is really a great big classroom where many lessons are learned. It hurts to be wounded, and sometimes it really, really hurts to the point where we question whether life is even worth living, but if we pay attention and open our heart and mind, we will learn a great deal. Life can be an amazing teacher if we allow ourselves to be educated under its tutelage. Every scar can be a treasure, if we are willing to see the symbol from a fresh perspective.

A Fresh Perspective

What do you do with what's been done to you? That is the gist of it, isn't it? All too often, instead of allowing our wounds to heal, we keep ripping the scabs off which delays or prevents proper healing. The problem is that we keep bringing the past into the present, allowing it to impact our life in negative ways. When this occurs, anger, resentment, stress, grudges, blaming, and victim mentality become the basis of our life in the here and now. By constantly looking backward, we take our eyes off the ball and stumble in our present life.

Past hurts are like cancer cells that love to feed on sugar. With the necessary sustenance upon which to gorge itself readily available, cancer multiplies and spreads. Since past hurts function in a similar way, it is imperative that we stop feeding the monster of the past. It is high time we take responsibility for our own happiness and quit playing the blame game. Our past doesn't change. It cannot change. What happened, happened. It is over and done with, and we have scars to prove it. But when we feed the monster of the past, we give it power over us. Negativity, anger, resentment, blame, and the like provide the necessary fuel it needs for lingering in our life and growing to portly proportions. Before long, we walk around life with an emotional goiter the size of a watermelon that interferes with our happy, normal functioning self.

In no way am I trying to marginalize the past or gloss over past wounds. Sometimes what has been done to us is so atrocious, it is beyond words. My comments are not meant to minimize the egregious hurt, but rather, to help us move forward. Neither am I implying that we should wound others, or seek out scars, in order to create a treasure. This warped perspective is similar to Paul's own thoughts in Romans 6:1–2: "What shall we say then? Are we to continue in sin so that grace may increase? May it never be!" What we do with our past from here on out is up to us. It is a decision only we can make. Will we continue feeding the deadly cancer or cut off its food source?

Professional athletes are trained to keep a short memory so that poor past performance doesn't affect their current play. Former Minnesota Vikings kicker Blair Walsh had a measly 27-yard field goal to kick with 26 seconds remaining to win an important 2015 NFC playoff game against the Seattle Seahawks. What was a mere chip-shot hooked left of the goalpost, and Minnesota's season abruptly ended. The 10-9 loss had far-reaching implications for Walsh as he was later cut during the 2016 season.

The ordeal must have weighed heavily upon his shoulders as both the media and fans voiced outrage. His failure could have defined both him and his NFL career, but it didn't. He could have easily given up, blamed others or become stuck in a depressive funk for the rest of his life thinking of what might have been, but he didn't. Did he miss an easy field goal? He sure did. Did his failure cost the Minnesota Vikings a coveted playoff win? It sure did. Just ask Blair Walsh—he has the scar to prove it. But instead of feeding the monster in his past, he focused on the present, kept his memory short, and began kicking for a new team. He refused to allow old wounds to define him by not bringing the past into the present.

Think about it—life is always lived in the present moment. Since the past is nothing more than water under the bridge, our thoughts *about* the past actually occur in the present—the here and now. If memories are merely present thoughts about the past, as some claim, then overcoming the past isn't about going back to a place and time of yesteryear; rather, healing comes from living in the present moment and controlling our thoughts in the here and now. When our present thinking harbors negative self-talk about what happened back then, our current energy is reflected backward. The only power our thoughts have over us is the power we give them. It is essential that we *not* feed the monster of the past.

The words of Paul in Philippians 4:8 come to mind, "Finally, brethren, whatever is true, whatever is honorable, whatever is right, whatever is pure, whatever is lovely, whatever is of good repute, if there is any excellence and if anything worthy of praise, dwell on these things." We find Paul "taking every thought captive to the obedience of Christ" (2 Cor. 10:5) and "forgetting what lies behind and reaching forward to what lies ahead" (Phil. 3:13). It seems clear that focusing our attention on past wounds does not effectively help us run the race of life.

This is where choice comes into the picture. How will you choose to live in the present moment? Will you emulate Blair Walsh and move on to the next chapter, or will you expend precious energy on water that has already moved downriver? What will you do with what has been done to you?

What is Healing?

If healing is what we seek, what does it actually mean to heal? In our attempt to move beyond pain, we often try various options in our search for wholeness. We could try to forget about our past wounding as though it was a light switch we simply flick on and off. But that is futile. Forgetting is not only impossible, I don't believe we are supposed to forget, for our experiences in life allow us to weave a tale of God's transformative power.

We could sit back and hope that time dulls the pain. After all, doesn't time heal all wounds? Time is certainly a helpful factor, but healing isn't really a matter of minutes, weeks, or years. In fact, healing often takes a lot more than mere time, such as dealing with our own behavior, working on forgiveness, and learning to harness our own thoughts.

We could simply ignore our feelings, deny our wounds, and bury our hurts way down deep. The problem with this approach, however, is that sooner or later we are bound to explode. If we stuff the pain deep enough and long enough, we become an unstable stick of dynamite ready to blow at the slightest bump. In the end, nothing gets resolved, and an entirely new set of problems crops up in addition to the mess that already exists.

We could wait around for the other party to make the first move, apologize, or initiate evidences of changed behavior. Unfortunately, we may be waiting a very long time. Some folks could care less how we feel, that we were wounded, or that they were the ones who wounded us. Besides, why place our contentment in the hands of others? We need to take charge of our own happiness.

Instead of doing anything at all, some choose to preserve the hurt by wallowing in their pain. As a result, the embers never die down. By remaining frozen in the grip of raw emotions, we become like a record player stuck in the same groove. The emotional hijacking weighs us down and produces painful and annoying despair. In the end, it accomplishes nothing of value, and we never seem to get past it.

Finally, we could simply dwell on the past, wishing things were different, or live with underlying guilt at our inability to turn back the clock. Unfortunately, this is wishful thinking. Deep regret makes us yearn for a do-over, but alas, it cannot be undone, and the day burns long with continued pain.

None of the above thought patterns work. They all come up short and are doomed for failure. Healing isn't forgetting, ignoring, wallowing in, or redoing the past. Healing isn't waiting on others to apologize or constantly wishing we could go back in time. Healing is active. It is something we do, something we pursue, and something we choose.

Healing from past wounds is about releasing their power over us, of neutralizing their effect upon us, and no longer allowing unpleasant memories to master us. Though it seems counterintuitive, we overcome the past by focusing on the present. Old wounds can become thieves that steal our peace of mind, but we were made for freedom—freedom from the encumbrances of the past. According to John 8:36, "if the Son makes you free, you will be free indeed." Galatians 5:1 notes, "It was for freedom that Christ set us free; therefore keep standing firm and do not be subject again to a yoke of slavery." In John's gospel, we find Jesus saying, "The thief comes only to steal and kill and destroy; I came that they may have life, and have it abundantly" (Jn. 10:10). It is challenging to experience the abundant life Jesus speaks of when we are tethered to past wounds.

Though we try, we are unable to remove the scars in our lives, for they actually become individualized markings that chart our life's journey. Instead of trying to perform plastic surgery to cover them up, we should allow them to stand as elements of beauty. Beautiful scars? It is not that we try to collect them like tattoo markings, but that our journey through life, no matter how painful it may be, is about becoming, transforming, and renewing. It is this resulting effect that radiates the beauty of our Creator. When present thoughts focus on the hurtful past, our freedom to become all that God desires is thwarted or delayed. Instead of experiencing freedom, we become enslaved, and the abundant life portrayed in Scripture vanishes like the morning fog. We certainly acknowledge our scars, but healing comes when we alter our relationship to the past.

Have You Had Enough?

We have a better chance of healing when we become sick and tired of being sick and tired. When we say, "Enough is enough. I won't live like this anymore," we have come to a place of inner desperation. At this juncture, we become serious about change and begin seeking new ways of living. The habits of old thought patterns die hard, and we realize afresh that something has to change. What we focus on consumes our energies, our thoughts, and our time, and it becomes our daily reality. By casting our past into the spotlight, we merely cultivate sadness and depression, allowing a victim mentality to flourish. When we arrive at the doorstep of "enough is enough," however, we become open to change and are willing to not only see things differently, but to feel differently about the past, as well. Isn't it time you begin living with joy and peace? If so, then you are at the right place at the right time.

Take Responsibility

Realizing that our relationship to the past must change if we desire inner peace, taking responsibility for our thoughts and actions from this moment forward is imperative. Releasing past hurt isn't easy, but it will not happen—in fact, it cannot happen—without taking responsibility for making it happen. Our happiness is no one else's responsibility or problem. Lying in wait for someone else to cure our internal heartache simply doesn't work. Friends, family, and significant others can be wonderful support systems, but our own happiness falls squarely upon our own shoulders. By seizing ownership of what we can control, rather than fretting about what we can't, the release of past hurt is more likely to occur.

Responsibility entails an awareness of our internal surroundings and turning that awareness into positive action. Are we cognizant of the feelings that make us sad? Do we know what prompts us to dwell on the past? Do we recognize the negative thoughts that constantly cycle through our mind and cause suffering? New realities come about because we open up areas of our heart that was once closed by pain.

Jesus set his face to the wind and moved toward the pain of Jerusalem, not away from it. He knew what he was in for, as Matthew 16:21 notes, "From that time Jesus began to show His disciples that He must go to Jerusalem, and suffer many things from the elders and chief priests and scribes, and be killed, and be raised up on the third day." Jerusalem would be a troublesome place, for his message of internal transformation infuriated the contemporary religious leaders. Viewed as a threat to the religious establishment, he was also portrayed as a revolutionary against Roman rule. There is irony in the very name of Jerusalem, which means "city of peace," for Jesus experienced the very opposite—death by crucifixion as a common criminal.

Jesus seized control of his own self-awareness, and he even reconfirmed his Jerusalem path by praying in the Garden of Gethsemane, "My Father, if it is possible, let this cup pass from Me; yet not as I will, but as You will" (Mt. 26:39), and, "My Father, if this cannot pass away unless I drink it, Your will be done" (Mt. 26:42). He moved toward the bumps and bruises of his life, and in the end, we are told of his resurrection. Unless we are willing to travel to Jerusalem, that is, move toward the tender places of the heart, we forfeit our own transforming resurrection in this life. In other words, we never come out on the other side, better, stronger, and happier. Past wounds never fully heal without intentionality, and that takes responsibility, awareness, and a generous dose of courage.

Change Your Story

One way we take control of our peace journey is to change our story, our inner dialogue. Our minds are bombarded with self-talk. We relive the past, recycle the hurt, and the needless drama of mind-chatter keeps stirring the pot. By retelling the same hurtful stories, we become lost in their pain. But what if we told different stories? What if we reframed our story and began looking at it from a different perspective? What if we didn't allow our mind-chatter to go unchallenged, but instead, harnessed those thoughts so the focus of our narrative was different? What if we lost interest in the stories we tell ourselves and did away with their negative fascination? Would their power over us diminish?

Much of the time our selective memory tells us lies and half-truths that cause us to dwell on our pain. What if we didn't just *tell* the story but instead saw *through* the story to something far more glorious? By looking *through* our stories, we acknowledge the painful past and still come out on the resurrected side. By taking responsibility for our own happiness and being aware of our negative storytelling, we are able to cast aside our morbid interest in the stories themselves and see beyond them. When painful adventures of the past no longer take center stage, we become keenly aware of our constantly shifting emotions, feelings, thoughts, and sensations.

By loosening the grip of negative narratives with which we have framed our experiences, we become alert to our own awareness. This means that we are alive. It means we have lived, and are living. We feel, we emote, we think, we sensate. In other words, our feelings, emotions, thoughts, and sensations are not locked in the prison of the past. We experience them as part of life and as part of being alive. We don't ignore them or bury them deep inside, but we acknowledge them with full awareness that they are part of what it means to be human. All of our thoughts, feelings, and emotions have the freedom to be, and we have the freedom to move forward in spite of their presence.

No longer will the stories of the past define us, influence us in negative ways, or take up precious real estate in our mind. No longer will we be emotional hostages in the grip of destructive mind-chatter. Though tempted to suffer under the pain of past wounds, we will now acknowledge the full array of life's constantly shifting sensations, while continuing to chart our path forward. While our emotions and sensations have the freedom to exist, they do not have the right to capture and hold us hostage. When we take charge of ourselves and willingly choose to create our own story, we write one that is positive and honorable. If you don't like the last chapter of your life, then quit reading it. Move on to the next chapter.

Waiting around for our happiness to unfold is a waste of time. By looking beyond our negative self-talk, we choose to see things differently; and instead of the constant mind-chatter capturing our attention, we begin anew with a fresh start. Life is lived in the present, moment by moment. Each moment is a precious opportunity to be you, to be happy, and to pursue life with full abandon, uninhibited by past wounds. The present moment is all we have, so let's make the most of it. And remember, there is a place within you that no one can harm. It is a sacred space where God communicates with your soul. It is you at the core of your being. No person or circumstance can steal that away from you, and nothing can tarnish its beauty. Go back to that sacred place of wholeness as often as you need to and begin writing a new chapter for yourself. Allow the light from within this most holy place to shine forth, moment by moment, and permeate your entire being.

Name Your Fears

Another way of taking control of our happiness is to name our fears. We allow past wounds to haunt us, and by naming our fears, we expose their dirty work accomplished in the dark recesses of our mind. By naming our fears, we shine a spotlight upon them so we can expose, identify, and destroy their stronghold. We don't want to merely be the product of our past or the sum total of our experiences; instead, we desire to see beyond our past and our experiences to become the kind of person we want to be. In a sense, we must detach from those things and use them to form a new, transformed self.

Moving from our past to living each moment with freedom—freedom to be, do, live, enjoy, and become, takes brave determination. Painful past experiences cause much heartache for us. Our self-esteem can be challenged because of past rejection from parents, spouses, or meaningful others. We sometimes fear commitment because of painful relationships with others we cared about. For some, the need for control, attention, or approval often relates to negative experiences. Others pursue an opposite direction, such as isolation, withdrawal, or lack of trust.

This demonstrates how powerful the present moment can be. It has the potential to empower and propel us farther along life's journey, or it can become a hurtful memory that stifles our growth and inner freedom. Living positively in the here and now produces untold benefits for ourselves and others.

Now is the time to unravel the spaghetti junction of fears and hurts chaining us to the past. It is this moment, and every moment from this one on, that must be seized by the collar and controlled by our own responsibility. Our contentment is up to us, and no one else. We will no longer wait for our circumstances to change before we are happy or delay our joy by waiting on others to apologize. Instead, with full responsibility, we will take the bull by the horns, name our fears, expose their dirty deeds, and choose to live in the moment, seeing through our hurtful stories and writing a new chapter.

Get to Know You

Who are you? I am not asking your name, where you live, what job you hold, or some other superficial identifier. I want to know how you see yourself. Deep down, how do you perceive your worth and your identity? Do you see yourself as a victim of the past? Do you view yourself as someone who has been wronged, someone who has been abused, someone who has been treated unfairly, or someone God is punishing?

Defining ourselves by what has happened to us is problematic. Unhelpful and inaccurate, it confines our thinking to the past while our untold potential is never fully tapped. It is a suppression mentality that holds us back. We shuffle around life with our arms handcuffed, our feet shackled, all connected to the chain around our waist. As prisoners, we scoot one shuffle at a time, and at the end of the day, we don't get very far, only to be locked back into our cell at night so we can begin the whole routine over again the next day. Pretty exciting life, isn't it?

In reality, we yearn to walk about freely and go wherever our interests take us. We long to break free of our bonds and take big steps, in any direction we choose. If we desire to run, we can. Skip? Yes, we can do that. Walk while holding the hand of another? Absolutely! And, most importantly, we are free to walk or run wherever the Spirit leads. No more returning to the prison cell every night only to shuffle around the next day. We can be free, and freedom is always better than confinement.

The freedom we long for, however, isn't obtained by defining ourselves according to what has happened to us. That is a fatal mistake, and we easily fall prey to mistaken identities and lies about ourselves. Even our surrounding culture can become a pack of wolves, waiting for us to slip up while howling out lies about who we are. But, we are more than the sum of our parts. We are more than our failures. We are more than our thoughts and emotions. Life is a series of experiences, good and bad, of thoughts and feelings that go up and down, and of diverse people and circumstances. We feel all of these things, and by doing so, we experience the living of life. This means that we are alive and consciously aware. Because we possess awareness, we are able to rise above what has been done to us. We recognize that just because we *feel* these experiences doesn't mean we *are* the experience. In other words, what happens to us does not become us. This is an important distinction worth remembering.

This "awareness" is what separates us from the animal world and makes us unique. Animals know, but they don't know that they know. Humans also know, but they are aware of their awareness. They know that they know. This enables us to ask deep questions like, "Why am I here? Why is there something rather than nothing? Is there a God and if so, what does He want from me?" Humans have the capacity to not only ponder their experiences, but they can also rise above their circumstances. We realize that self-identity is distinct from the incidents that happen to us. It is this ability that helps us understand that we are bigger, better, and more than the trials of our life.

When we focus on our identity way down deep, an identity of significant worth, we can separate ourselves from what happens to us. We no longer perceive ourselves as mere products of our past, locked in the shackles of old wounds, but begin seeing ourselves as the Creator's unique work of art. We realize that what happens to us does not become us. We are deeper, more complex, and far more valuable than to merely be identified with our past, much of which we couldn't control anyway.

Become an Example

Looking back over my life, I can easily name experiences that would have made my journey less complicated. I wish I had a mentor early in my life to provide guidance and direction, but I didn't. That would have been so beneficial. Had my parents been educated and attained a greater socio-economic status, my adjustment into the real world may have been smoother. These backward-looking thoughts are fruitless endeavors of the mind. Instead of wishing that certain things could have been different, I work to become an example to others. I want their experience of me to be the very kind of encounter I also yearn to experience. The better I heal, the better I can help.

Instead of wallowing in the negatives, I took responsibility for my own happiness and plowed a path that led me to now. I have had positive experiences that lifted my soul and negative experiences that nearly did me in. I have experienced both the thrill of victory and the agony of defeat. But, whether good or bad, they were merely things that happened to me; they were not me. I am aware of my experiences, and I am aware that I am aware of them. That means that I can separate my experiences (the awareness) from me (the one who is aware).

Now that I am farther down the road, I seek to be an example to others of the things that would have made a difference in my own life. In traveling through this desert, I stop for water to nourish my soul, but I refill the bottle left for travelers so others may experience an oasis moment in their own journey. In the end, I strive to become an example to others of how scars can become treasures. Living in the present and responding positively to the wounds of the past become both a healing balm and a positive example to fellow sojourners. I don't want to become another person's scar, so I refill the water bottle for others trekking through the desert.

❦

Wisdom for the Journey

Life's journey contains its share of pain. Life happens, and sometimes it happens badly. Some sorrow is due to our own stubbornness and bad choices, and other difficulties are simply beyond our control, let alone comprehensible. The road becomes more difficult when we allow past wounds to negatively impact our present journey. Our scars turn into treasures when we become fed up with living in emotional exile, take responsibility for our own happiness, rewrite our stories, name our fears, identify ourselves apart from our experiences, and become the example we yearn to experience in others. Don't let your scars just be scars; let them stand for something. Let them be a path for God's transforming work in your life. Oh, and remember to refill the water bottle so others may be refreshed by how you handled your own tribulations.

chapter two

Surprised by God

The older I get, the less interested I am in religion. Ever since the sixth grade when I was introduced to Him I have *always* been interested in God, but somehow along the journey religion got in the way. Religion is supposed to point to and reveal God, not become its own god. Hindsight is always 20/20, and now I see more clearly what was once obscure. Nowadays, I have little interest in anything else but Him.

It is hard for me to stomach much of what drives today's cultural Christianity with its penchant for things like safeguarding theological dogma, managing and maintaining religious power structures, self-righteously proclaiming extensive lists of "approved" behavior, and bickering over petty issues that consume our time and energy. I flatly reject any temptation to participate in the manufacturing of church drama that makes mountains out of molehills, or to be mired down in the muck of irrelevant and inconsequential religious concerns. Instead, I seek God and God alone. I yearn for the mystical over the mundane. I crave intimacy with my Creator rather than doing religious things for Him.

Crisis of Faith

Like many who are fed up with the shallow nature of cultural Christianity, I threw my hands in the air and cried, "That's it. I have had enough," and began to seek God afresh. I suppose, over the course of a lifetime, moments like these come to us and we are inspired to begin again. This time, however, was different. My crisis of faith came after nearly thirty years of ministry, either pastoring a church or serving Christian institutions of higher education. I was no longer a "rookie Christian" and the typical answers that once satisfied me couldn't keep pace with my developing faith. In many ways, I felt empty—like one of those edible Easter bunnies we initially think is made of solid chocolate, but is regrettably hollow on the inside.

I was tired of experiencing the many ways religion steps in as a substitute for God. At times, waves of self-doubt rolled over me and I questioned whether I ever really knew Him. Had I always been nothing more than a hollow Easter bunny, or had I been cleverly duped into a substitutional way of thinking? Deep down, I knew things couldn't go on as they were. Worn out from the confines of a tired faith, my previous journey prepared me for new understandings and deeper connections with God's life-giving Spirit. Something was changing in my heart, and I yearned for the match of God to light my soul on fire.

Here I was, a mature Christian man with years of faithful kingdom service under my belt seeking to commence a new journey of faith. How awkward is that? With firm command, I dismissed the dutiful soldier guarding my old way of "seeing," laid aside the armor that had for so long tainted my perspectives, and bore my naked soul before my Creator. In many ways I needed to unlearn what I thought I knew, so I laid aside my theology books, my degrees and education, and placed my assumptions, presuppositions, and spiritual arrogance on lockdown. I removed the biased spectacles that colored my outlook, and with childlike innocence, pleaded with God to speak to me. I knew *of* Him and I knew *about* Him, but my heart wondered whether I really *knew* Him.

Well-versed in all things religious and on friendly terms with the façade of cultural Christianity, I seemed to merely be surviving instead of thriving. I was fed up with such shallow living, and this was my way of casting aside the trappings of faith and getting back to my first love.

The burning desire for a fresh start changed my life. I doubt my new quest for God could have occurred at this second-half-of-life juncture without the collective experiences of years gone by. It would be a mistake to discard my previous journey altogether, for that would entail throwing the baby out with the bathwater. I rejoice in my valuable first-half-of-life faith, and at the same time, I fully recognize its insufficiency to carry me to the finish line. I now feel more closely connected to my Creator than ever before, and I better grasp the difference between a cheap substitute and the real deal. I much prefer the latter. No longer is there confusion between the instruments of faith and faith itself. I have little patience for a substitute God, no matter what form it takes—even religious.

When religion no longer moves us to genuine communion with the living God, it becomes nothing more than a moralistic and ritualistic substitute for God. When the symbols of our faith, which are designed to point toward something greater than themselves, become the very *substance* of our faith, a web of our own making ensnares our hearts and cheats us out of the real thing—experiencing our Maker. This kind of religion can be a hard taskmaster, cracking the whip against our sweaty backs and constantly reminding us of our many failures.

Intimacy That Transforms

My spirit yearns for deep intimacy with the Spirit of God—intimacy that transforms me from the inside out and moves me to higher levels of loving, serving, and being. This is a foreign concept to those who define God as a guiding principle, a cosmic energy, or a divine ideal. How can one fall in love with an impersonal force? Can you pray to a cosmic energy or commune with a divine ideal? From the Old Testament followers of Yahweh to the New

Testament disciples of Jesus, Scripture records story after story of faithful believers experiencing a personal God.

In one sense, as noted in Colossians 1:15, we actually beheld the face of God in the person of Jesus, for he "is the image of the invisible God." In his message to the exiled Jews living in Babylon, the prophet Jeremiah indicates that God can be sought, found, and experienced: "You will seek Me and find Me when you search for Me with all your heart. I will be found by you" (Jer. 29:13–14). Rather than seeking and finding an impersonal energy, principle, or ideal, they actually encountered the God of Abraham, Isaac, Jacob, Jesus, and Paul—a God who is present, real, genuine, and knowable.

The French Carmelite monk of the 1600s, known as Brother Lawrence, discovered the presence of God in his own life—a God who was living and present and could love and be loved. Much of Brother Lawrence's daily chores involved tending to kitchen duties on behalf of the monastery. Such a lowly task, and yet, he found God amongst the pots and pans. The Lord's presence was not only at the altar or within the sacraments but also in the tiny, menial tasks of daily living.

As a soldier in central Europe's Thirty Years War, Brother Lawrence was sent home after being wounded. It was during this time that he decided to become a monk. I can't help but wonder if the reflections of his heart thought, "That's it. I have had enough. War is hell, and I won't have any more of it. I want my life to count for something." I imagine Brother Lawrence earnestly seeking, finding, and experiencing God to such a degree that it transformed his entire view of the world, let alone his vocation. No longer would his interest be in the trappings of life, power, or self-promotion. Instead, his mind was centered on practicing the presence of God throughout the course of each day whether he was washing pots and pans, shining shoes, sharing a devotional talk, or kneeling at the altar.

Because many of us use religion to cleverly disguise the real issues of our heart, the sweet communion we long for with the Father is, unfortunately, never fully realized. Yet, it was this kind of intimacy that my heart was seeking—something deeper than what I knew in the first half of my journey. I desired what Brother Lawrence possessed and what so many others have experienced over the centuries. My mind, however, cornered me in the world of my own rational thought. Trying to figure everything out was exhausting, and I finally realized that God would never be constrained to the limits of my own feeble intellect. He was far too grand to be brought so low.

Though I desperately longed for conclusive answers and definitive boundaries, it was by letting go that I experienced new ways of knowing and experiencing Him. Newfound freedom overcame me as I learned to live with the profound mystery of God. I didn't have to know all the answers or arrive at absolute conclusions that boxed God into the many insufficient categories my brain constructed. Instead, I simply experienced Him in genuine ways that not only allowed the deep mystery to prevail, but also took me in, headfirst, and enveloped me like a mother hen gathers her chicks. There was no shaking of the earth, but rather, a shaking of my soul and a stirring of my heart that led to peace and presence. I began to live with the Great Mystery and simply started practicing the presence of God like Brother Lawrence. Though I value all of my experiences and understandings of the first half of my spiritual voyage, God, in His great wisdom, was moving me beyond them. He was recalibrating my heart, correcting my vision, and charting a new course for the second half of my spiritual journey.

It is the simple things that now bring me joy—the pots and pans of my own life. I sought God and found Him in unexpected places—simple, everyday places. I struggled to find Him in the halls of power or in the constraints of institutional religion. I didn't find Him in "right" theological beliefs or exhaustive performance of religious ritual. With joyous surprise, I found Him in suffering and among the downtrodden. I found His presence in creation. I found His reflection in others. I found Him within myself. I found Him at the edges and the bottom of life. I rediscovered Him by letting go of my biased perspectives and opening my heart to His expansive love.

Bumper-Sticker Religion

With a smug, overinflated ego, we somehow believe that God can be manipulated or bargained with—a genie at our command. We think that His world revolves around ours, just like our egocentric world. By dropping the appropriate coins in the religious vending machine, out pops a God who is supposed to behave according to our assumptions, presuppositions, theological bent, and expectations. Over time, however, we realize how limiting and infantile this perspective really is.

It is when life knocks us off our feet that the superficial answers we previously relied upon no longer suffice. During crises of faith we become non-swimmers in deep water, gasping for air and wildly thrashing about for something to hang on to. We stop spouting all those slick bumper-sticker slogans that do nothing but expose our thin veneer of faith. These crises can actually be healthy as they shake us to the core, breathe life into our dead bones, and jolt us into seeing new perspectives. Once we get to shore, we realize that He was with us the entire time. Much to our surprise, we begin seeing God in the most unlikely places—places we would never think to look, and places where His presence was thought to be absent. As the old saying goes, "When the student is ready, the teacher appears."

My friend Abigail understands what it feels like to be knocked off of her feet. She and her husband struggled for years to conceive a child and were considering adoption when she unexpectedly became pregnant. Overjoyed to be carrying the child they had always longed for, their elation was short-lived when their daughter was stillborn. This wasn't Abigail's only brush with trauma. Her husband developed severe heart problems at the age of thirty-one and underwent multiple surgeries, a pacemaker, defibrillator, an artificial heart pump, and finally a heart transplant. Had it not been for a fatal infection acquired during a stay at the hospital, they might have experienced many more sunrises together.

Abigail was emotionally, spiritually, and physically exhausted, not to mention stuck with mounting medical bills. Surrounded by loneliness, she sat on the sofa staring out the window and questioned where God was in all of this. She attempted to bargain with Him and lost. Her world fell apart, the pain was unbearable, and she struggled to even breathe. She now understood why many consider suicide as a way to end the pain.

For Abigail, the easy answers no longer worked for her reality, and she endured the empty slogans offered by bumper-sticker Christians. She was made to feel guilty, as though she had done something wrong to offend God. Maybe she didn't have enough faith, as some claimed, for they believed that all sickness was a shortcoming of belief. Her pain has since subsided, but she continues to wrestle with God. More importantly, she is learning to look at life a little differently. While answers to her questions remain out of arms reach, she has experienced God in deeper ways and views Him in a new light. She has moved from the kiddie pool of faith to deeper waters without her arm floaties. There was a time when she wondered how to continue without the safety net of shallow Christian slogans, but she now stands, surveys the horizon, and sees God's presence during those dark days.

Restricting God

With emotional frenzy, some believers act like spiritual junkies on a desperate search for one more spiritual high that affirms, sustains, and propels their commitment until the next exhilarating mountaintop experience. They are forever on the lookout for one more uplifting worship service to attend, one more rousing television preacher to watch, one more expensive conference to stoke their passion, another inspirational book to pump them up, and one more spiritual retreat to make them feel, well, spiritual. For these folks, intimacy with God is a series of mountaintop experiences that thrill the heart. The climb is meaningless and boring, and rather than being an integral part of the spiritual journey, it is viewed as an obstacle inhibiting breathtaking views from the summit.

Like the rest of us, these individuals simply want to be stirred within their deepest self. There is nothing wrong with worship services, television preachers, conferences, books, spiritual retreats, and the like. The danger, as with anything, lies in their subtle substitutional nature where the focus is upon the emotional moving rather than the Mover of emotions. There is a difference, and this is exactly how the trappings of religion negatively influence our spiritual life.

Even our beloved Scripture can be elevated to a God-like status, and anything that becomes a substitute for God, whether sacred writings or mountaintop experiences, is nothing more than a cheap substitute for the Holy One. The difference is between the instrument of faith and faith itself—a subtle, yet significant, distinction. The moving of God travels many pathways, and it is essential that we distinguish between the path and the Path-maker, otherwise, we fall victim to the subtle deception of substitution—a classic bait and switch scenario.

Another pitfall is restricting God's movement to a limited number of "approved" pathways, as though He needs our consent to function. For mountain-toppers who emphasize the summit, what occurs in the valley or during the climb is of no great consequence since it is merely thought to be annoying underbrush that impedes our pursuit of the coveted spiritual high. It fails to recognize that God is there as well, and that He uses both the valley and the climb to transform us. After all, if you are like me, you find yourself engaged in a whole lot more thicket-filled climbing than resting your laurels at the summit.

God is Present

This frantic search for the continual spiritual high is problematic in many respects, but the point I want to make is that it falsely sees God as being elsewhere—always some place other than where we are. In other words, God is forever "out there" while we never stop to consider that He may actually be "right here." We believe He is only experienced at the summit and strive hard to get there, when all along His presence is most felt in the valley and in the climb itself. We are surprised to learn that God is right here, right now, around us, beside us, and within us. He is everywhere, if we will just open our spiritual eyes and see.

This "out there" perspective creates a false sense of distance as to God's whereabouts. We have it in our minds that God is a large, physical being sitting behind a marble throne in a far-away place, ready to dispense harsh judgment upon those who disappoint Him. Even Isaiah has Him enthroned high above the earth (Is. 40:22), and yet, after the cherished ark of the covenant is brought into the magnificent temple, the center of sacrificial worship for the Jewish nation and a place where God's presence was expected to dwell, Solomon reminds the people in I Kings 8:27 that God cannot be contained in a building: "But will God indeed dwell on the earth? Behold, heaven and the highest heaven cannot contain You, how much less this house which I have built!"

When we realize they lived in a world that knew nothing of germs, viruses, technology, atoms, space travel, or the larger universe, we understand their use of metaphorical language to describe a God whom they knew to be far greater than themselves. It is not surprising that in their minds something greater had to be something "out there," far beyond the knowledge and imagination of their own world. Other metaphorical language is used to describe God in Scripture, for He is also said to be like a shepherd, a father, a rock, a light, a fortress, a husband, and so on. The throne metaphor helps us understand God's majestic nature, but it does little to help us understand His closeness. The idea that He is both greater than us and also near to us is what theologians call the transcendence and imminence of God. In other words, He is beyond us in so many ways, and yet, is also right here in our midst. Like forgetful people searching for lost eyeglasses sitting atop their own head, we seek an "out there" God when He has always been "right here" under our nose.

In John 4:24, Jesus states that "God is spirit," and by definition, a spirit has no physical body. God is not a great big one of us sitting behind a great big throne in an "out there" heaven, for He is spirit. When the Old Testament Jews thought they had contained God's presence within their precious temple, Solomon reminded them otherwise.

As a spirit, God is not sitting, standing, squatting, or jogging. Spirits don't do that. Instead, Scripture portrays Him as being everywhere, as noted by the prophet Jeremiah (23:23–24): "'Am I a God who is near,' declares the Lord, 'and not a God far off? Can a man hide himself in hiding places so I do not see him?' declares the Lord. 'Do I not fill the heavens and the earth?'" declares the Lord." The psalmist declares the same thing in Psalm 139:7–10:

> Where can I go from Your Spirit?
> Or where can I flee from Your presence?
> If I ascend to heaven, You are there;
> If I make my bed in Sheol, behold, You are there.
> If I take the wings of the dawn,
> If I dwell in the remotest part of the sea,
> Even there Your hand will lead me,
> And Your right hand will lay hold of me.

God's decision to create something out of nothing was also a decision to reveal Himself. Though all of creation is a reflection of its creator, only humans are purportedly crafted in the very image of God. In relating to other human beings we are interacting with fellow image-bearers, and if we are not careful, we could miss out on God's presence simply because we view them as roadblocks to the summit instead of channels of His presence. In one church I pastored, it was the church janitor who revealed the presence of God to my heart, and in another, it was a frail, retired lady who mirrored God to me—unexpected people bringing the unexpected presence of God to my surprised soul.

We always seem to look elsewhere for God when His presence dwells in every aspect of life itself. One place we fail to look for God is within ourselves. If we are indeed molded by His hand, created in His image, temples of His Holy Spirit, and partakers of His divine nature as 2 Peter 1:4 notes, then God's presence is found within each of us. It is what the Quakers refer to as the inner light—that of God in each of us. This isn't some funky New Age philosophy, but a scriptural teaching. While we are not God, He is certainly within us, around us, and beside us. We trace our DNA back to our Creator, for He is the very ground of our existence, as Acts 17:28 notes, "for in Him we live and move and exist." He is unexpectedly close—so close that He is within us, one place we often fail to look for Him.

Drawing Close to God

There are two main ways we draw close to God—two paths for opening our hearts wide enough to treasure His presence in unexpected places. One is the path of suffering, and the other comes through solemn seeking. Both paths can surprise our hearts and lead to greater awareness of, and appreciation for, the paradoxical tensions of the Christian life—the way up is down, we gain life by losing it, greatness comes through humility, and the like.

Suffering

Suffering may be the more difficult of the two, for who enjoys pain? We prefer the path of ease, and though it is far less painful, it produces very little in the way of spiritual growth and closeness with God. Today's cultural Christianity promotes easy answers and the spewing forth of Christian jargon rather than actually wrestling with the difficult questions of life. It is in the wrestling that we come face to face with a God who is real. How can you have all the answers without ever knowing the questions? Without some sort of internal wrestling match with life itself, we merely recite the pat answers of shallow thinking. Suffering is a path of hardship, questioning, and pain, and yet, it is the path of surprise where we draw near to God and unexpectedly discover His presence in the broken road.

Our perception of God is always clouded by our circumstances. When life is good, food is plentiful, and we are satisfied, Scripture is interpreted one way, but when life is falling apart and our heart is breaking, we read Scripture through a different set of lenses. Suffering has a way of softening up and breaking down a calloused heart. Suffering exposes our insecurities and the temporal, unstable moorings to which our life is anchored. But as 1 Peter 1: 6–7 notes, even precious gold is purified by fire: "In this you greatly rejoice, even though now for a little while, if necessary, you have been distressed by various trials, so that the proof of your faith, being more precious than gold which is perishable, even though tested by fire, may be found to result in praise and glory and honor at the revelation of Jesus Christ."

Suffering strips away the fluff and leaves us lying naked before our Creator. What remains after the refiner's fire is nothing less than pure desire for God and God alone. The tenuous moorings we were once anchored to have faded away, and the many ways we marginalized God by accepting cheap substitutes no longer satisfy the heart. In essence, suffering purifies and simplifies our desires so we become sensitive to God's presence. Even Old Testament Job wrestled with God and struggled to figure out why so many bad things were happening to him. At the end of the day, after being stripped of everything, it was just Job and God, and that was enough.

We rarely arrive at this level of motivational purity without experiencing the bumps and bruises of a faith-tested journey. In many ways, we must come to a crossroad where the rehearsed answers of old no longer suffice. Activated by pain, the systems and beliefs we once held onto so faithfully begin to collapse, unable to support our reality. All systems eventually crumble, because God is separate from—and bigger than—any system, no matter what it is. Letting go and coming to the end of ourselves is often traumatic, but necessary. Prying the fluff from our clenched fingers, even sophisticated, religious fluff, strips away everything but a pure desire for God Himself.

The son of an English doctor in the 1800s, Francis Thompson moved to the big city in pursuit of his writing passion. For three years he lived on the dirty streets of London, became addicted to opium, and slept with the homeless by the River Thames. His poetry was sent to a magazine publisher, and that was the beginning of his notoriety. His most famous poem, "The Hound of Heaven" depicts God as a heavenly hound who sniffs him down, finds Him, and refuses to give up on him. For solemn seekers, the roles are reversed as they become the hound pursuing God, sniffing Him down, and refusing to let Him go.

Solemn Seeking

Solemn seeking through prayer is the second path for moving closer to God. The ability of some to fervently pursue God is driven by their all-consuming passion to know Him. Throughout the centuries, there have always been those who pull back the curtain of unseen things in a way that others can't. The prophets of old did this, as did Jesus himself. They had the ability to see, know, and experience the spiritual realm to a greater depth than the rest of us. They caught a glimpse of another dimension in ways that profoundly altered their understanding and experience of God. Suffering and solemn seeking are key paths for discovering God in unexpected places.

Keep in mind that most of us don't strategically plan out our walk of faith. If we did, I doubt it would look anything like what God intends for us. Who of us would ensure that tragedy and suffering become a road well-traveled? Who of us would purposely invest the necessary time and energy in purifying our desire when cultural Christianity offers a more comfortable option? In reality, a closer union with God is most often stumbled upon.

Frequently, I am asked how I planned my route to earning several doctoral degrees. The answer is that I didn't plan it at all. I fell into it. I never took a book home during high school, was raised in a blue-collar town by blue-collar parents, and became a first-generation college student. My route to higher learning wasn't cleverly mapped out ahead of time; rather, I stumbled into it and discovered how much I enjoyed learning.

Our Christian journey is a bit like that. Life happens, circumstances occur, opportunities rise and fall, and people move in and out of our life. The deeper life of God isn't so much planned as it is stumbled into. Our spiritual eyes are opened through a chance meeting, an unlikely event, or another one of the various ways God nudges us forward. We don't plan to come to the end of ourselves as a necessary gateway for deep communion with our Creator. Instead, we fall into it.

By coming to the end of ourselves, I am referring to those times when we are out of options and there is no place left to turn—no more relying on our own intellect and no more trusting in fluff. The end of ourselves is near when we move beyond the limits of what cultural Christianity can offer, and the systems and beliefs we trusted in for years no longer possess satisfying answers for our reality. By wrestling with life's difficult questions, even though we may never arrive at the definitive answers we hoped for, we discover something far more precious. We meet God afresh—a God we weren't expecting, hadn't planned for, and much to our surprise, simply fell into. By coming to the end of ourselves, we experience a deeper level of communion with God.

Finding God in Imperfection

One of the significant outcomes of our wrestling endeavors is the realization that God can be found in the imperfections of life. This perfect, majestic, and powerful God is present within the imperfect, the less majestic, and the powerless. Breathtaking! For too long we have lived with an unrealistic worldview that sees most of life as sinful and profane. We can't imagine that God could be found in the ordinary; instead, we search for Him in our nice, clean categories of religion that place Him "out there."

The problem with this perspective is that it restricts where God can be found and limits how and when He can surprise us. Exclusion is the starting point for most religions. Life is put into clear categories of good and bad, profane and holy, when God is allowed to move and when He isn't, and so forth. By separating life into compartments like these, we automatically exclude His presence from most of the categories. When we come to the end of ourselves, however, we refuse to rule out anything, and we dare not eliminate the negative and imperfect. Religion is about excluding, but God is about including. Cultural Christianity attempts to eliminate the negative, but we can rejoice in imperfection, for God is found even there. This means that I can rejoice in God's presence within me, a man flawed in a thousand ways—imperfect.

Far be it from me to tell the Lord where and when He can reveal Himself in unexpected places. By not eliminating the negative, we begin seeing God in suffering, in pain, in the downtrodden, in the poor, and in the familiar mess of life. Brokenness and imperfection are not hurdles for God to overcome, but opportunities to experience His presence in the "here and now." Our gaze now scans the horizon for His handiwork—the bottom, the top, the edges, in, out, about, and around. St. Francis of Assisi embraced this perspective and was transformed by it. A dedicated follower of God, it was at the moment he embraced and kissed the untouchable leper that he experienced deep change. He was no longer simply ministering to lepers, but actually seeing God's presence in them. Unexpectedly surprised, St. Francis of Assisi discovered the presence of God in the imperfect.

Wisdom for the Journey

By affirming that God is everywhere, we allow for His presence to surprise us in unexpected ways, for no place or person is "off limits" since there are no categories of exclusion as to His whereabouts. The religious experience that initiated your entrance into the faith may not be enough to sustain it over time as the road miles pile up. Wrestling with life's difficult questions is not to be avoided, but encouraged, for it is through the wrestling that we come to the end of ourselves and enter into a deeper spirituality—a place where we recognize the difference between the moving and the Mover. God is with us on this journey and can be found in the here and now. Look for Him in unlikely places, and you will be pleasantly surprised by His wondrous presence.

— chapter three —

The Whole Enchilada

*S*hortly after accepting a new job and moving out of state, I received the devastating news. My sister-in-law, Linda, was diagnosed with breast cancer and did not have long to live. This information shocked us all. Since Linda and my brother were nearing retirement, and I sought a less stressful work environment, we all decided to move to Northeast Missouri where soil was black and land prices were reasonable. It was close to our hometown, and all three of us were looking forward to planting a garden and putzing around on a small acreage, so we put forth a plan of action. I moved first and was tasked with finding the right property to fulfill our dreams. That's when the sad news upended our lives. Within six months, one had passed away, one was reeling from unbearable grief, and I was left wondering what had just happened.

When Linda called asking that I conduct her celebration of life service, I wept uncontrollably, while mumbling, "I don't want you to go." She was stronger than me, stronger than all of us put together. For the next several months, I served as the family pastor, and though I lived out of town, I sent regular poems, prayers, encouragements, Scripture, and jokes. Each day I sought to uplift her spirit while her body weakened and her health failed. The way she handled herself during this dreadful ordeal was inspirational, and it reminded me of Paul's words in I Corinthians 4:16: "though our outer man is decaying, yet our inner man is being renewed day by day."

Death is real, and though it is inevitable, it need not be feared. We often think of death as an unfortunate event to avoid at all cost, but in reality, life and death are not two, but one, for though we are living, we are also in the process of dying. We age, our bodies steadily decline, and we have a final rendezvous with our own demise. By accepting death as a part of life—a simultaneous living and dying at the same time, we answer the door without surprise or resistance when death comes knocking. Linda understood this, and I have never seen anyone embrace death with such grace and dignity.

Linda was a practical person, a kind of rubber-meets-the-road individual. Abstract ideas, fancy concepts, and theoretical thinking were far removed from what she cared about—others. She was a lover of people. I often try to *think* my way into loving, but Linda knew that wouldn't work. Instead, by *acting* in love, our thinking is changed. In one of her communications to me, she shared how the Scriptural theme of love was also the central theme of her life. For Linda, love epitomized what it means to follow God. It is impossible to love Him well if we are unwilling to love others, for the two are intertwined. Realizing this, Linda would often say that love is "the whole enchilada." As she descended into the valley of death, she experienced both the love of God and the love of others, and through her, we experienced that love radiated right back to us.

Her catchy phrase and simple way of wrapping it all up caught my attention, and I couldn't agree with her more. Love is often discussed, sought after, and the topic of many good sermons. But, it is one thing to talk about it, or preach on it, and quite another thing to actually live it. Sadly, love can be watered down to a benign abstraction *discussed* in religious circles rather than something we actually do and something that actually guides our interactions with others. Paul says the same thing in 1 Corinthians 13:1–3, 13:

> If I speak with the tongues of men and of angels, but do not have love, I have become a noisy gong or a clanging cymbal. If I have the gift of prophecy, and know all mysteries and all knowledge; and if I have all faith, so as to remove mountains, but do not have love, I am nothing. And if I give all my possessions to feed the poor, and if I surrender my body to be burned, but do not have love, it profits me nothing…But now faith, hope, love abide these three; but the greatest of these is love.

The Apostle Paul was merely saying in his day what Linda was saying in hers: love is "the whole enchilada!" Without it, nothing else matters. Think about the impact of that powerful statement. No matter what you accomplish, what you claim to know, what your socio-economic status happens to be, or what size of investment portfolio you possess, it is all for naught if it wasn't done in, for, and because of love.

The Heart of Scripture

Love is at the very heart of Scripture. For instance, the first of the 10 Commandments, "You shall have no other gods before Me" (Ex. 20:3), is really a love commandment. To love anything or anyone ahead of our Creator is simply replacing one god with another, or, for our purposes, replacing one love with another. Referencing Deuteronomy 6, Jesus contemporizes the love principle for his own generation: "Love the Lord your God with all your heart, and with all your soul, and with all your mind" (Mt. 22:37). Basically, this is the first commandment, expressed a bit differently.

Even the crucifixion of Jesus is seen by Paul as a sacrificial act of love, as noted in Romans 5:6–8:

> For while we were still helpless, at the right time Christ died for the ungodly. For one will hardly die for a righteous man; though perhaps for the good man someone would dare even to die. But God demonstrates His own love toward us, in that while we were yet sinners, Christ died for us.

The writer of I John has this to say about love (I Jn. 4:7–11):

> Beloved, let us love one another, for love is from God; and everyone who loves is born of God and knows God. The one who does not love does not know God, for God is love. By this the love of God was manifested in us, that God has sent His only begotten Son into the world so that we might live through Him. In this is love, not that we loved God, but that He loved us and sent His Son to be the propitiation for our sins. Beloved, if God so loved us, we also ought to love one another.

Many of Jesus' teachings demonstrate the importance of love, such as the parable of the Good Samaritan (Lk. 10), the woman caught in adultery (Jn. 8), the story of Zacchaeus (Lk. 19), the woman at the well (Jn. 4), finding the lost sheep (Lk. 15), searching for the lost coin (Lk. 15), and the prodigal son (Lk. 15). We have heard these stories since we were old enough to attend Sunday School, and we have also listened to a good many sermons on the topic throughout the years, as well. It is a notable theme in Scripture for which our hearts rejoice. It feels good to be loved by God, and it feels good to love. Love transcends cultural barriers; anyone from anywhere can readily embrace it.

Though we are likely familiar with the many Bible passages on love, we may not fully grasp their implication for daily living. If love is the main thing, then the main thing is to keep the main thing, the main thing. To that end, let me share some perspectives that may help us better love God and others.

It is impossible, given the limitation of human language, to describe God with the full expression He deserves. With such limited vocabulary, how do we fully describe something that is beyond words, by mere words themselves? Yet, human language is the only tool we possess for expressing our encounters with the divine. Though language can be woefully inadequate, the power of metaphors helps us verbalize our sliver of understanding. We compare God to what we know and what is familiar to us, so we say that He is like a father, a shepherd, a potter, a groom, bread, light, vineyard, rock, fortress, shield, stronghold, the way, truth, etc. According to Scripture, He is also love.

The author of the epistles of John wrote more about love than any other New Testament writer, and it was unfathomable to him that anyone could claim to love God, who is love, and still be unloving: "The one who does not love does not know God, for God is love" (1 Jn. 4:8). Love is actionable and demonstrable, with real-world application. When we see love in action, no matter who is doing the loving, Christian or otherwise, we say to ourselves, "God is like that!"

Though we readily grasp Scripture's emphasis on love, it is the actual loving that is difficult; and yet, when we experience the type of love Paul describes in 1 Corinthians 13:4–8, we know it is of God, for this kind of love represents the God of love:

> Love is patient, love is kind and is not jealous; love does not brag and is not arrogant, does not act unbecomingly; it does not seek its own, is not provoked, does not take into account a wrong suffered, does not rejoice in unrighteousness, but rejoices with the truth; bears all things, believes all things, hopes all things, endures all things. Love never fails.

In response to a Pharisee's question regarding how to inherit eternal life, Jesus shares two great commandments. The first great commandment is to love God with our whole heart, soul, and mind. He then relays a second great commandment which is similar to the first: "Love your neighbor as yourself. On these two commandments depend the whole Law and the Prophets" (Mt. 22: 39–40). These weighty words help us fathom the significance of love—that loving God and loving others go hand-in-hand. In fact, to be aligned with God is to remain in love. When we commune in love with God, and are communally connected in love with others, God's Spirit flows freely through us, and out from us, to touch the hearts of others. There is nothing more gratifying than being in love with our Creator and dancing in love with fellow image-bearers.

Dualistic Thinking

Unfortunately, in an effort to justify himself, the Pharisee seeks an exclusionary loophole regarding the definition of "neighbor" by asking, "and who is my neighbor" (Lk. 10:29). That's what people do to justify their behavior; they resort to loophole thinking. The dualistic mindset permeating our culture creates a world of categories where some are in and some are out, some are invited to live in the neighborhood, while some are prevented from entering. To justify this conduct of categorization that accepts neighbors who are just like us and excludes those who are different, we seek to redefine "neighbor," just like the Pharisee who questioned Jesus.

By dualistic thinking, I mean our habit of dividing life into exclusionary categories such as the have and have-nots, the sacred and profane, and those worthy of our love and those deemed unworthy. There are a million ways we divide up life with a separatist mindset, and it is the reason that more than 30,000 different denominations exist throughout the world today, each one engaging in some kind of exclusionary thinking. One denomination, for example, accepts those who speak in tongues, while another rejects the practice as nonbiblical. One is in, and the other is out. Abstention from alcohol is a mark of true holiness for some, while imbibers are labeled weak believers, if not sinners. For some, baptism is essential for salvation, while it is a mere symbolic act for others. One group is in, while the other attains outsider status.

Dualistic thinking is useful in this life, but it doesn't get us very far when it comes to spiritual realities. If a doctor is needed, you certainly want an educated one that can discern whether a tumor is benign or malignant. If you need an attorney, you seek an intelligent representative who can differentiate substantive evidence from irrelevant rabbit trails. If your car breaks down, a mechanic who knows whether the problem is minor or major is appreciated. While dualistic, either/or thinking is extremely valuable, it is simply inadequate when it comes to experiencing deeper spiritual realities.

From a spiritual point of view, dualistic thinking is a defeatist perspective since it thwarts the very purpose of love, which is to be vast, accepting, and expansive enough for all. If we loved only those we considered "in" and rejected those we assessed as "outsiders" (dualistic thinking), we wouldn't be practicing the gracious love of God. Instead, we would simply be participating in a conditional, dualistic kind of exclusion mentioned in Luke 6:32: "If you love those who love you, what credit is that to you? For even sinners love those who love them."

Jesus kicked against this mindset by loving expansively, without restriction, and without conditions. He loved at the edges, at the bottom, at the top, and to the depths and heights. He loved sinners. He loved lepers. He loved the sick. He loved the spiritually weary. He loved the hungry. He loved the homeless. He loved both Jews and Gentiles. He loved across ethnic and social boundaries. He loved with his arms wide open and never withheld love on the basis of who was in and who was out. For Jesus, no one was an outcast because he saw the sacred image of God in all persons. When it comes to love, an either/or exclusionary mindset simply doesn't cut it.

While traveling from Judea to Galilee, Jesus passes through Samaria and stops at Jacob's well where a Samaritan woman comes to draw water. Given her status as the consummate outsider, the initiation of conversation by Jesus is astounding. In fact, even his disciples "were amazed that He had been speaking with a woman" (Jn. 4:27). Her "outsider" status was obvious even to his disciples, and yet, Jesus didn't see her that way.

The prevailing cultural norm of separating males and females into different worlds was discarded by Jesus, for it was taboo in his day for a solitary woman and a man to speak in public, and yet, Jesus intentionally does just that. Village women typically drew water at dawn and dusk, and by showing up at noon, as this woman did, her actions may have been perceived as improper. Not only was she a solitary woman speaking to a man in public, and not only was she drawing water at the wrong time of day, she was also a despised Samaritan, possibly the greater of the insults.

Samaritans were long despised by Jews as half-breeds for intermarrying with surrounding cultures that diluted Judaism with elements of idolatry. They built their own temple on Mt. Gerizim to worship God, while the Jewish temple stood proudly in Jerusalem. They rejected the prophets, abandoned many of the Jewish traditions, and believed only in the five books of Moses.

Samaritans were considered filthy outsiders, far removed from the "pure" Jewish traditions, beliefs, and lineage of the "in" group. These theological, moral, and cultural deserters were the "have-nots" in an exclusivistic world, and yet, Jesus demonstrates that his love is expansive enough for them. The fact that this Samaritan woman had five previous husbands and was currently living with a man was yet another unsightly stain upon her life. Yet, it is this despised half-breed, this "less-than" female, this dirty divorcee, this defiled "shacked-up" woman, this impure religious outsider that Jesus loves, seeks, pursues, invites, and embraces. She becomes the first person to whom Jesus publicly reveals his Messiahship!

When it comes to matters of the heart, dualistic thinking has been the prevailing mindset for centuries, and escaping its grasp in pursuit of spiritual realities is challenging. We believe in loving everyone, for instance, but happily exclude those who have wronged us, and we feel justified in doing so. We desire an enlarged neighborhood just like Jesus said, and yet, erect fences made out of privileged loopholes of justification that keeps out those with diverse convictions. We are open to dialogue with others, except those who disagree with us, all the while claiming Scriptural exemption for our actions.

I have witnessed the exclusion of people over such nit-picky matters as the version of Bible they read, whether women can wear makeup and jeans, and whether a specific passage of Scripture is interpreted in the same manner as another's beloved televangelist, who can do no wrong in their view. I have witnessed far more serious exclusion based on skin color, education, geography, age, gender, sexual orientation, religious belief, and the like. Exclusion is the natural result of dualistic thinking. One group is always in, while everyone else is always out.

It is this narrow, conditional kind of love that Jesus utterly destroys by talking with the Samaritan woman. By stopping to speak with her, he demonstrates that love is inclusive, expansive, accepting, and vast. His life's message was about bringing people *into* the neighborhood, not keeping them out. When our neighborhood becomes smaller and smaller and all of our neighbors look just like us, we have surely missed what love is—and who God is. Jesus saw others, no matter what side of the tracks they came from, as image-bearers of a God who wants us to love at the edges, at the bottom, at the top, and to the depths and heights. After all, "God so loved the world . . ."

If we want to know what God is like, we look to the life of Jesus. According to Colossians 1:15, Jesus was "the image of the invisible God," that is, he was the human form who flawlessly reflected the formless one, the "the invisible God." We dare not forget the formless one by focusing solely on the form itself. God reveals Himself in Jesus, but I am also reminded how rarely I consider other ways God has been revealing Himself since creation.

Before there was any created thing, there was God. By creating the stars, the moon, the grass, the land, the water, the animals, etc., God revealed Himself. The very act of creation is an act of self-disclosure—in much the same way an artist discloses herself on canvas, or an author reveals herself through the pages of a book. Creation is the incarnation of God in the sense that it pulls back the curtain for a brief glimpse of the eternal, and since all humans are created in His image, we, along with all creation, become both the revelation and reflection of the Creator.

In other words, all of life, all that we see and breathe, is of God. Love, then, refuses to exclude because everyone and everything not only *originates* from God but also *reveals* and *reflects* God. Unfortunately, we live in a world of exclusions, and by participating in an outsider/insider mentality, we wind up excluding what God includes. Dualistic thinking limits our understanding and experience of God, for we miss the depth and expanse of His love, all because we withhold our love from the things that He loves.

The key to loving well is to love expansively, without limits, without conditions, and without exclusions. When we love those who come to our wells to draw water, we see and experience God in a new light. By dancing in love, we begin to see this world—all of it—bathed in the light of His affection, which illuminates new perspectives and affords greater clarity. As divine image-bearers, we are loved organically for who we are, because the one who loves us is also the one who created us. We love others for the same reason. They, too, are divine image-bearers and organically loved by the Creator. Because of this, we love without exclusion by loving at the edges, at the bottom, at the top, and to the depths and heights.

Dualistic thinking can be harsh, causing us to be unkind, impatient, unloving, and compassion-less. It can make us harder to love, as well. Love, however, is a precious gift that everyone is capable of sharing. In fact, it is meant to be lavishly dispensed, rather than hoarded and rationed only for those deemed worthy. Our capacity to love seems to grow the more we give it away, and when we do, we share with the rest of the world God's reflection and revelation in, and through, us.

Loving God and others is not about limiting and narrowing, but about opening and expanding. It is easy to speak of love in lofty, impressive terms as some abstract ideal, but we must see through this smokescreen and bring the concept down onto the roadways of everyday living. Talking *about* something isn't the same as actually *doing* it. Asking, "Who is my neighbor," is a sure sign that we divide love into exclusionary categories.

By casting aside the constraints of dualistic thinking, we enlarge our neighborhood, and that is exactly what God wants us to do and what Jesus demonstrated for us. When we realize that the entire world is the revelation of God, we see His reflection in all things, for with God there are no outsider/insider categories, only His creation, His revealing—people who are created in His image. Since everything and everyone emanates from the Creator, there are no exclusions. Only when we love without boundaries are we able to live in larger circles and growing neighborhoods. What is the size of your neighborhood? Is it growing or shrinking? Is it inviting or fenced off?

Loving Well is Hard

It is hard to love—and even harder to love well. Loving only those who love us and forgetting the rest is a piece-of-cake, because it requires nothing of us—no thinking, no challenge, no growth, only self-centered ease. This path, in the end, is not a path of love, although it is often mislabeled as such. It is neither expansive, nor inclusive, and reminds me of a church that desired growth through outreach. They hired a new minister to lead them in their enthusiastic quest and expected him to grow their congregation, which he did. Their increase, however, wasn't the kind of new growth they envisioned or desired. The parking lot, once exclusively occupied with Mercedes, BMWs, Volvos, and other expensive gems, was now filled with rusted out Chevrolets and lowly pickup trucks. Gone were the days of shiny, well-to-do parishioners and expensive toys in the parking lot. Now their pews were filled with inferior "outsiders." The pastor didn't last. They fired him for enlarging the neighborhood with the wrong kind of neighbors.

I readily grasp that loving is difficult. There are people that I struggle to like, let alone love, and it is something I wrestle with every day. Loving the way God loves is something I know I should pursue, for I see it right in front of my nose. Though it seems so near, every time I reach for it, I realize it is farther away than it appears. I am forever grasping without ever fully attaining. That doesn't mean I can't love, or shouldn't love; rather, it simply means that love is ever-expanding, and although I get better and better at it over time, I can never wrap my arms completely around it. It is not meant to be captured, for it is always growing and always stretching me toward greater and deeper love.

If all we do is react to others based on what they do to us, how they treat us, or whether we like them or not, then love becomes situational. I will love you if, when, but, only. . . There has to be some perspective, some deeper thought, some grounding principle that allows us to rise above each incident or person we experience, despite the quality or nature of that interaction, and yet, still motivates us to see things from a larger, more expansive perspective. For me, that involves loving something in itself, by itself, and for itself.

We tend to love based on what a person or thing can do for us. I love you because you make me feel good. You laugh at my jokes. You think like I do, or by loving you I am more apt to advance my career, attain my goals, or profit from you. There are a thousand selfish reasons why loving something or someone can be in our best interest. Approaching things this way, however, places conditions on our love, while our actions are always prompted by some self-serving motive. Looking through this narrow lens keeps the neighborhood small and rejects the intrinsic and organic value of people and things as originating from, and reflecting, our Creator.

Love What God Loves

When we learn to love what God loves, that is, learn to love others in themselves, by themselves, and for themselves, rather than for what they can do for us, we have constructed the underlying foundation that allows us to love through all circumstances. If all of life, all of creation, reveals and reflects the Creator, and every single person is an image-bearer of God, then we can love every human being on that basis alone. It is in this manner that we can rise above any one person or circumstance and love from a larger reservoir of compassion.

It may be helpful to think of our lives as a large room filled with prejudice, hate, fear, anger, judgment, etc. Because of the tremendous clutter, there is no room for love, for it has nowhere to go. With such hoarding going on, we struggle to even open the door, and the only things we allow in are the same prejudices, the same fears, and the same judgments that validate our collection of trash already in the room. The only way to escape this closed mindset is to love others in themselves, by themselves, and for themselves.

When we begin to love people solely for who they are, the clutter holding our heart hostage is dethroned and taken to the curb for trash pickup. Love is allowed to expand and fill the space given to it. Specific people and incidents rise and fall, come and go, but now we are able to love others not for what they can do for us, but because they are the revelation and reflection of God and worthy of love in themselves, by themselves, and for themselves. It is freeing to love like this—absolutely freeing.

I realize that people frequently act in uncaring ways that makes loving them extremely difficult. In fact, much of the turmoil I have experienced in life has come at the hands of cold-hearted fellow believers. By stockpiling my hurts and disillusionments into a room already filled with fear, anger, resentment, and prejudice, there was little capacity to love. I realized that I couldn't live with this chaos of clutter and that it wasn't how I was supposed to live. I needed to experience love and be free to love, not build concrete walls around my heart that only served to protect worthless items. Until I understood that every person was both the revelation and reflection of God, including me, I was unable to place my junk on the curb.

The good news is that the seed for growing this kind of love is already within us, according to Romans 5:5: "the love of God has been poured out within our hearts through the Holy Spirit who was given to us." There is no need to search for this love, or pray to receive it, for it has already been poured into our hearts. Why pray for something we already possess?

It is the prejudices, the biting judgments, the me-first mindset, and all the other debris taking up residence in our heart that prevents us from experiencing God's thrilling and expansive love. Placing our clutter out on the curb opens the door to receiving God's love and sharing it freely with others. We could say that love was there all the time, hidden and stuffed in a corner, unable to fully function. Love doesn't expand when there is no inner freedom that allows it—freedom from the exclusionary prejudices that suppress it. However, loving people in themselves, for themselves, and by themselves causes us to live with greater compassion and empathy.

Our assortment of junk limits our perspective about what God can do, who He can love, and what He is like. It has been said that we become like the God we worship. In other words, if we view God as one who loves expansively, we begin to pursue that kind of love in our own life. Love allows us to swing the door wide open, leave base camp behind, and climb the mountain with God. Day by day, as we walk with Him farther and farther away from the safety of our tent, our prejudicial views and limited perspectives that kept us loitering around base camp, slowly loosen their grip. Hanging around the camp makes us feel like climbers, but we rarely ever climb. We just talk a great deal about climbing, think of ourselves as climbers, and wear climbing gear, but we can't bear to actually climb and have our assumptions challenged—assumptions that always keep us within safe distance of home. In reality, we may be nothing more than pretenders, projecting forth a desired image we want others to see, but living in the reality of a loveless, junk-filled heart.

God, however, leads us away from our loitering tendencies and away from the false security of erroneous thinking. Instead, He takes us on a journey and reveals new vistas and breathtaking beauty we never before dreamed possible. This was all available to us, but we never saw it because there was no room for love in a room littered with debris. Now, after seeing the exquisite flower on the mountainside that no human eye has gazed upon, we say to it, "You are beautiful, little flower, for you are the revelation and reflection of your Creator." We can look at others in a new light, and instead of seeing their faults and our own prejudices reflected back to us, we now say, "You are an image-bearer of God, a unique revealing and reflection of the Creator. I love you with God's love by yourself, in yourself, and for yourself."

Be fully warned—loving with God's love will lead you away from base camp. You will begin to feel less and less comfortable with previous perspectives that inhibited love. A new world will open as you sense both the freedom and desire to love like God loves. It is time to declutter your heart, let go of the prejudices that hold you back, open the door to love, and allow God to take you on the adventure of a lifetime. In doing so, you will experience an inner freedom to love what God loves.

An appropriate love of ourselves is also fundamental to loving others. Conventional wisdom declares that loving ourselves is negative, unbiblical, and always takes a back seat to loving others. But this isn't what Jesus said. He indicated that we should love others *as* we love ourselves, and he sees it as a necessary ingredient to loving others. Obviously, a narcissistic, me-first mentality that forever seeks its own interest is not in keeping with *any* of the teachings of Jesus. There is, however, an appropriate love of self that must exist if we are to remain healthy enough to love others.

Loving ourselves means seeing ourselves as image-bearers of God, just like others, and that we become comfortable in our own skin as the revelation and reflection of our Creator. In other words, we love our own self expansively in ourself, by ourself, and for ourself, simply because we reveal and reflect our Creator as image-bearers. This is the appropriate self-love that produces a positive, healthy basis for loving others. There is nothing in the world wrong with it, and Jesus commanded that we do it.

∽

Wisdom for the Journey

Love is a way of seeing and a way of being that causes us to act lovingly toward God and others. Without it, life's journey becomes a lonely excursion. Walking close to God is to walk in the way of love. Don't be a justifier who seeks loopholes of exclusion. Just love. Just do it. Always. Love with all you have and all you are. View others as the beautiful revelation and reflection of God they are, fellow image-bearers, worthy of love because they are His treasured creation. The time for cheap talk is over. Make your journey one of action. Love without limits, conditions, or exclusions, and love at the edges, at the bottom, at the top, and to the depths and heights. This keeps your heart soft as the Spirit of God flows to you, through you, and out of you. Instead of walking along the road of life, try dancing a jig and clicking your heels up in the air. Dance in love, and your journey becomes more loving.

chapter four

Different Shades of Blue

*T*wo plumbers. Two perspectives. Two justifications. Two Christians at odds with one another. Every Sunday, as I looked out over the congregation from my vantage point behind the pulpit, I couldn't help but notice the two men and their families. One plumber always sat on the left side of the church while the other plumber always sat on the right side. To avoid an awkward encounter in arriving at the same time to shake my hand, they strategically exited the sanctuary like chess pieces.

How could two fellow Christians, two brothers in the Lord, hold such disdain for one another that even the worship hour became a game of cat and mouse? The irony of two grown men with a history they couldn't let go of, both singing and praising the Lord as though nothing was wrong, didn't go unnoticed. If I preached on love, forgiveness, or any other pertinent topic, it was received by each as a message solely designed for the other. With such a conspicuous elephant in the room, how could this plumbing charade continue?

A Grand Illusion

Forgiveness without transformation is nothing more than a grand illusion. Claiming to follow the way of Christ without *actually* following the way of Christ is the epitome of self-deception. Though none of us are perfect, and we are often nothing more than great big bundles of contradiction, it seems to me that real faith *should* have an effect upon our life—our thoughts and behaviors. To know God is to participate in internal transformation. If a husband claims to love his wife and physically abuses her every night, does his claim ring true, and could it withstand the slightest scrutiny? Hardly. You don't need an Ivy League education to figure this one out.

When we are in relationship with others, endless opportunities for hurt and mistreatment exist on both sides. Intentional or not, it is simply the inevitable result of being human; we will get hurt. Though all of us carry excess baggage around that weighs us down, God desires our internal transformation—change from the inside out. Following the way of Christ is about *forward movement*, not merely *claiming* forgiveness without its ensuing effect. Any transformative declaration without a trace of evidentiary support is nothing more than a hollow and groundless claim. Like our two plumbers, we often allow little things to divide us, even when there is consensus on so much. I often share an Emo Phillips joke at speaking engagements to illustrate this point.

> Once I saw this guy on a bridge about to jump. I said, "Don't do it!"
>
> He said, "Nobody loves me."
>
> I said, "God loves you. Do you believe in God?"
>
> He said, "Yes."
>
> I said, "Are you a Christian or a Jew?"
>
> He said, "A Christian."
>
> I said, "Me, too! Protestant or Catholic?"
>
> He said, "Protestant."
>
> I said, "Me, too! What franchise?"

He said, "Baptist."

I said, "Me, too! Northern Baptist or Southern Baptist?"

He said, "Northern Baptist."

I said, "Me, too! Northern Conservative Baptist or Northern Liberal Baptist?"

He said, "Northern Conservative Baptist."

I said, "Me, too! Northern Conservative Baptist Great Lakes Region, or Northern Conservative Baptist Eastern Region?"

He said, "Northern Conservative Baptist Great Lakes Region."

I said, "Me, too! Northern Conservative Baptist Great Lakes Region Council of 1879, or Northern Conservative Baptist Great Lakes Region Council of 1912?"

He said, "Northern Conservative Baptist Great Lakes Region Council of 1912."

I said, "Die, heretic!" And I pushed him over.

With little effort, togetherness can fan the flames of conflict. Think about it: when people of different races, genders, cultures, values, goals, ethics, personalities, education levels, socio-economic statuses, upbringings, spiritual maturity levels, abilities, interests, and so forth, are thrown together in something called "togetherness" or "relationship," the requisite ingredients for a human Molotov cocktail converge, and an explosion is bound to occur.

Communication styles differ significantly between men and women. For instance, when he says, "I figured out a solution," she may hear, "You can't figure out your own solutions. Your emotions are irrelevant so let me figure this out for you." Yet, all he is trying to do is relieve her source of irritation. When she says, "Can we take some time to talk tonight?" he may hear, "You are in big trouble, buddy!" In reality, she simply wants to feel closer to him. It's as if men and women view the world through different lenses.

Not everything is black and white as some would have us believe; there are different shades of blue within the color spectrum, not just the shade of blue we perceive through our own lenses. While sitting on hard, metal bleachers that cause your backside to go numb, I watched my son pitch in a high school baseball game. Turning to my wife, I jubilantly exclaimed, "Wow! Did you see how Elliott's two-seam fastball cut?" Her attention was focused elsewhere and she whimsically replied, "Do you see all the different shades of green in the outfield?" We were physically in the same location but experiencing two different realities. Looking through our own set of lenses, we each saw different shades of blue.

In Here—Out There Syndrome

While serving as a senior executive in numerous Christian institutions, I noticed a peculiarity about the thinking of staff members. It is what I call the "in here, out there" syndrome that befalls even the best of us. It is the belief that our faith is to be lived "out there" in the big, bad world of nonbelievers. While this may be true, we often forget that the world of "in here"—the company of the committed—is also an important arena for demonstrating faith. Faith-filled living is not limited to "in here, out there" boundaries, for the dichotomy doesn't exist. Instead, there is simply living out our faith everywhere, all the time, wherever we are. As an integral part of our core being, faith is woven into the very fabric of our lives rather than conveniently separated into "in here, out there" compartments.

The church is no different as folks are challenged to "go forth" and be light to the world. There is nothing wrong with going forth and being light, but when we forget to demonstrate faith within the confines of the church, or within our immediate environment, we are blinded by the dichotomous "in here, out there" myth.

In discussing interpersonal relationships and behavioral expectations with staff, I challenged them to jettison "in here, out there" thinking and begin demonstrating their faith right here, right now, in the work environment. If we couldn't live out our faith among fellow believers, we surely didn't have a chance of success among those rejecting our shared foundational values. Instead of waiting for "out there" to arrive, I invited them to see that "right here, right now" is fertile soil for embodying what we say we believe, and that meant appreciating and valuing different shades of blue.

If everyone saw our shade of blue, life would be very pleasant—or so we tend to think. Instead, the world is filled with people who experience blue in various shades and tints. Even God's creative work differentiated the firmament from the earth, dry land from oceans, animals from fish, and male from female. By creating something one thing (a tree, for instance), means that it is not the other thing (a rock). God's creative work is an act of differentiation. Yet, our Creator declares the various shades of blue "very good" as noted in Genesis 1:31: "God saw all that He had made, and behold, it was very good."

A Brilliant Color Spectrum

Diversity is an essential element in God's design for our lives. He sees the color spectrum as positive, while we often view differences as nothing more than a headache to endure. The contemporary church, for example, is filled with various shades of blue. It is a ragtag collection of individuals, physically different in shape, size, color, and gender, whose situations at work and home vary, as does their contrasting views regarding methods, goals, vision, and values. How in the world are we expected to navigate these landmines when everyone sees blue in different shades?

Marriage is yet another setting where different perspectives rise to the surface. One is extroverted, while the other is introverted. One approaches problem-solving with logic, the other through values. One sees the bug on the bark of the tree, while the other takes in the panoramic view of the entire forest. One has a particular set of annoying mannerisms, while the other possesses annoyances of another kind. One is an early bird, while the other is a night owl. One is conservative, while the other is left of center. It takes hard work for two vastly different people to get along.

As we skip down the road of life, we constantly encounter fellow pilgrims who perceive things a little differently. We can't imagine how anyone could view life that way, especially when our own shade of blue seems so right and so obvious. We either experience constant frustration or latch on to a perspective that is healthy and beneficial. As challenging as it can be at times, we were not meant to traverse this earthly landscape alone, but in relationship with others.

Like a great big family, we experience individuals at different levels of growth and maturity. In the church, for example, we find spiritual newborns who lack experience and understanding. They need milk to survive, not a juicy porterhouse steak. Spiritual adolescents awkwardly transitioning into a more mature belief system are also part of the family. Various stages of adulthood also exist, such as our beloved elderly with years of experience under their belt of faith. One big family trying to get along.

In the Corinthian church, Paul experienced similar family dynamics that produced all sorts of problems. Some claimed to follow Paul or Peter, others Apollos, and still others Christ. As they gathered together for worship, differences surfaced in their expression of faith, and Paul addresses the ensuing chaos in his letters to them. The Christians in Rome may not have fared much better as sharp divisions arose between family members who set aside certain days as holy and refrained from eating specific foods (called the weak), and those who lived life without such cumbersome restrictions (called the strong). Though their particular struggles may be unfamiliar to us, they were no less problematic.

That's the thing about differences, they can either rip us apart or build us up. In Paul's day, it may have been easier to simply create two different churches, one for the weak and one for the strong. The weak folks could gather together in one spot, celebrate their holy days and eat the kind of food their conscience allowed, while the strong could huddle together in another location and celebrate their freedom from such self-imposed restraints. This perspective, however, is never given to us as a scriptural option. Instead, we are instructed to accept one another. It is easier to separate and cluster with likeminded individuals than to honor viewpoints that differ from our own.

To further complicate matters, opting to separate from one another is not a practical solution when we realize that we are all a mixture of weak and strong. Because we are never totally strong or 100 percent weak, sorting out the weak from the strong becomes extremely difficult. Which issue becomes the standard for determining strength and weakness, inclusion and exclusion? In essence, the issue of diversity never really goes away; we are stuck with each other. Besides, we were never meant to journey alone. God desires that we relate to others who are unlike us, for He sees different shades of blue as "very good." With the river of divergence so deep, how can we ever expect to cross over?

Embracing Differences

Our journey through life may be similar to a trip in the car, either a family vacation or a solo outing. As an introvert, I prefer to drive alone. I crank the music to my own comfort level, and I alone choose the genre. I set the temperature to perfectly match my climate preference. I stop when I need a break, choose the route I think is best, and open the moon roof if it suits my fancy. I am the king of my domain. No interruptions, no dull conversations, no drama, no conflict, and the only person I have to worry about is me—and I sure like pleasing me! It is easy. I am easy. I don't have to think about others— just the blessed triad of me, myself, and I.

By always driving through life alone, however, I miss out on relational elements that are good for me. We all need our alone time, but sojourning with only me, myself, and I resists the relational dynamics God wants us to experience. Through diversity, we learn and grow and are stretched to see new perspectives. Through community, we are both challenged and enriched at the same time. By appreciating the mosaic of God's creation, we learn patience, servanthood, loving, learning, working together, and valuing others. There is something about togetherness that God wants us to grasp. Relationships are so vital to our faith that God not only sees it as "very good," He establishes diversity as the necessary environment for testing, demonstrating, renewing, and enriching our faith.

In one sense, we are all in the "people business" fraught with differences, challenges, irritations, and annoyances. Rubbing shoulders with others can turn into a push-and-shove competition. The very thing God created to refine us (community) is often the very thing we seek to avoid. It is so much easier to journey alone in this life, blasting our car stereo to high heaven, but that merely isolates us from the community God insists is good for us.

Facing a recent relational roadblock, my initial reaction was to withdraw. Who needs the heartache, the headache, and the stomachache? I wanted to jump in my metaphorical car and start driving alone. The situation even caused me to question what I was writing in this chapter. Did I really believe the words I was putting on paper, or was all this talk about unity in the midst of diversity nothing but hot air? Yet, I realized that I needed to do the very opposite of what my initial reaction desired; I needed to turn *toward* my friend, not *away* from her. By turning toward her, our friendship was strengthened and we experienced new growth and understanding. It deepened us in ways that we would have never experienced had we taken the easy route of withdrawal.

We are most familiar with our own journey, our coming to the Lord, our expression of devotion, our view of Scripture, our perspective of how life ought to be lived, and so forth. This is the reality we know, and it is deeply meaningful to us. There is a tendency, however, to expect the experience of others to conform to our own. We believe their journey should mimic ours, and when it doesn't, suspicion and distrust prevail. Since our powerful faith experience is so personal to us, it is difficult to comprehend how other journeys could produce similar expressions of faith. This limited perspective essentially rejects God's freedom to work in the lives of others as He sees fit; it devalues the diverse ways God ministers to individuals from different walks of life, cultures, and faith traditions. Do you draw sharp lines of conformity, or are differences embraced as an avenue for nurturing the soul?

One positive way of embracing differences is respecting the spiritual journey of others, rather than insisting on rigid uniformity. I am convinced there is a God and that each of us experience Him in diverse ways. This means that no one journey is the same. God takes some around the mountain, while others climb it; some endure hardship, while others are spared. God speaks to some through music, others through the written word, and others through different means. It would be presumptuous of me to demand that your journey look exactly like mine. That's rigid uniformity and places me in the role of God, for which I am unqualified. Instead, God uses innumerable means, circumstances, people, and events to touch our deepest selves. Allowing room for the Spirit of God to move in each of us is not only an expression of love, but also reveals a deep understanding of the diversity He values.

In their book *If God is Love*, Philip Gulley and James Mulholland write of a caustic church business meeting where two well-respected leaders find themselves passionately advocating opposing viewpoints. In the heat of the moment, both men become ungracious to one another, and one of them storms out of the meeting.

He returns a few minutes later with a basin of water in his hands, a towel over his shoulder, and tears in his eyes. Kneeling down, he removes his adversary's socks and shoes and begins washing his feet. When the act of service is completed, he humbly states, "Please forgive me. I have treated you very poorly. I realized after I left that, if you were so passionate about this issue, there must be good reason. I need to listen to you because, even if we disagree, your opinion is important to me."

Two opinions, two journeys, two individuals placed together into one community—and when different shades of blue attempted to pull them apart, they decided to move toward one another rather than pulling away. Tolerance and cooler heads prevailed. It is these kinds of experiences that change us and enlighten us to deeper movements of God in our midst. Rather than making our own journey the only virtuous path, we embrace the various ways God ministers to our hearts by maintaining a soft and gracious spirit toward the divine color spectrum.

One Great Big Family

In one sense, we are one great big family. We live in the context of our immediate family, our extended family, our church family, our work family, our friend family, and so forth. We are also connected to others through our city, state, regional, and country family. In a larger sense, the entire global human family is interconnected. People are pretty much the same no matter where they live. We all put our pants on one leg at a time, have hopes and dreams, fears and anxiety, and possess the same basic needs. By valuing others, we honor different shades of blue within the family.

While shepherding a local congregation in the Southeast, our Wednesday evening service was revamped into an intergenerational family night. As we gathered together to begin the evening, I invited individuals from different generations to stand with me. There we were, teenagers, young mothers and fathers, little children, and elderly saints standing together in prayer with our arms around one another before partaking in a family meal. It became a treasured moment and physically symbolized our desire to value different shades of blue within the congregation. In a tangible, visible way, we boldly declared, "We are a family. Despite your shade of blue, you matter here." Upon my departure back into higher education, this church paid me the ultimate compliment: "You are the first pastor who has made us a family."

Recently, I visited my brother's small, country Quaker church, and a ninety-two year old woman with white hair and a beautiful smile introduced herself to me. She had difficulty walking, was noticeably hunched over, and the words of the Quaker poet Whittier were dear to her heart.

One day, this elder stateswomen happened to arrive in the parking lot at the same time as my brother. He reached out, took her hand, and together they walked into the church. As he relayed his story to me, my mind extended this picture to the entire church family, a place where different shades of blue gather together in love and acceptance. I imagined this ninety-two year-old woman with a crown of white upon her head, holding the hand of a fifty-eight year-old man with a peppered beard, walking beside his thirty year-old daughter with taut skin and beautiful flowing hair, holding the hand of her precious three year-old daughter full of life and innocence. That is a picture of a family—different ages, shapes, perspectives, needs, and blue shade glasses, coming together to show the world that diversity is "very good," as God declared so long ago.

When Quakers meet together on Sunday morning, you will often hear the words, "Are all hearts clear?" before departing from their Sunday morning gathering. One aspect of those meaningful words is the high value they place upon being in right relationship within a culture that values differences. Departing from each other's presence in love and harmony is something they pursue. To be a person who values differences is to be a person to whom others matter, despite their particular shade of blue.

Years ago, a wheelchair-bound friend of mine visited a local church and discovered the congregation only utilized the King James Version of the Bible. As he rolled himself into the foyer with a Living Bible on his lap, he was confronted and lectured to about his improper Bible choice. To be fully welcomed by this faith community meant adopting it's inflexible devotion to the King James Version of the Bible. His particular shade of blue wasn't welcome there.

One day, I found myself in need of a highly credentialed instructor to teach online business classes for me, and I asked a bright individual to do it. I had met Tommy while he was a seminary student of mine several years prior. As I traveled across the country conducting educational seminars, I often took cream-of-the-crop students out for a meal so I could mentor them, encourage them, and build into their lives. I did this with Tommy, and today, he is one of my best friends. As a savvy business owner, entrepreneur, educator, retired naval commander, and African-American, he lovingly jests, "Terry, you are my brother from another mother."

Realizing that I was serving at a Christian university with a sterling reputation, he sheepishly asked, "Are you sure you want someone like me teaching for you? I have just gone through a divorce." He was worried that my employer might place constraints upon my color perspective. I responded, "Tommy, you need to hear something from me. You are my friend, and there is not a thing you can do or say that will ever change my love for you." No matter what he was going through, no matter his shade of blue, I made it clear that he would forever find in me a loving and accepting friend.

On the other end of the telephone, unbeknownst to me, tears were streaming down his face. After being excoriated and ostracized by his church family for not measuring up, he was now experiencing selfless love. In the mind of church members, he was tainted, unworthy, unlovable, and unfit for kingdom service. Their words stung. They loved him when he was their kind of blue, but disowned him when the tint changed. On that day, my words of love, grace, and compassion became the healing hands of Christ to his hurting soul. No matter what shade of blue he was experiencing, he was loved, valued, and accepted.

God's Expansive Love

God's love is expansive and without limits. It reaches to all people regardless of where they are on the color spectrum. It is this kind of expansive love that is winsome and attractive. Why? Because it reflects the very heart of God who wants us to discover something about Him through community. He also wants us to learn something about ourselves. Unfortunately, we often seek to limit God's love, while He always seeks to expand it. We yearn to hold others to our own color of blue when God, the author of the color spectrum, sees different shades of blue as "very good." Love is expressed when we accept and value those who see the world differently than we do.

We think diversity is divisive and makes us weak. In reality, diversity can unite and strengthen us; it enriches our lives. Are we stronger when everyone sees the same shade of blue and uniformity exists, or are we stronger when differences abound and unity exists? Our knee-jerk reaction is to resist differences when God asks us to accept diversity.

An historical examination of any denomination, and there are over 30,000 of them worldwide, reveals a typical birthing process of splitting off from some other church group. Each cluster saw things differently and broke away, each claiming "their way" as the "right way." When we don't want to play nicely, we justify pulling away. When I was asked to leave a church I pastored for nearly five years, the rationale was, "Paul and Barnabas went their separate ways, so we have biblical precedent for asking you to leave." That's not a reason; that's a justification.

While teaching a pastoral ministry class to undergraduate students, one young lady shared of her recent departure from a local church because she wasn't "getting fed." After criticizing the church, its pastor, and its ministries, she justified her leaving as the only "spiritual" thing to do. As her rationale came under class scrutiny, she became openly hostile. How dare we question her beloved justification!

Unfortunately, the motto of the world we live in seems to be, "if you don't agree with me, you are my enemy." When fellowship within the church is based upon adherence to specific propositional statements about God, we are back to the Emo Phillips joke whereby one Baptist pushes another Baptist off the bridge.

The Guiding Principle of Love

What is our guiding principle in relating to others? Loving those who align with our perspective is easy; the real challenge arises in loving those who are dissimilar. For some, life is lived behind a "me-first" mindset, where every act and every decision is filtered through a narcissistic grid of how it propels self-interest. If it furthers my interest, I am for it, and if it doesn't, I am against it. But that is a far cry from the teaching of Jesus, who summarized the entirety of Scripture in Matthew 22:36–40:

> "Teacher, which is the great commandment in the Law?" And He said to him, "You shall love the Lord your God with all your heart, and with all your soul, and with all your mind." This is the great and foremost commandment. The second is like it, "You shall love your neighbor as yourself." On these two commandments depend the whole Law and the Prophets."

The guiding principle for relationship appears to be love. Yet, in all honesty, there are some folks who rub me the wrong way and annoy me for various reasons. Most irritations, from my experience, revolve around personality clashes. Differences of gender, race, size, domicile, accent, weight, and so forth, aren't too bothersome, but personality quirks can irritate the living daylights out of us. While personality differences can be annoying, it helps to remember that we are all perceived as annoying by someone. We are either doing the loving or becoming someone else's challenge of love.

Though I have explored the topic of personality to some depth, and despite my training in interpersonal communication and conflict management, I can become agitated with others. In many ways, I am a human version of my dog, Lottie, while out on a walk. Her tail swings happily back and forth at some dogs, and with other dogs she bristles and barks her disapproval. Personality differences do exist, for God designed things this way. To create an individual one way (extroverted, for instance) means that they are not another way (introverted), and it is in this world of differences that God asks us to love one another.

Paul elaborates on this human condition in his writings to the Corinthian church. Chastising them for being childish with regard to their differences, he notes that they are yet infants in Christ (1 Cor. 3). In 1 Corinthians 12, Paul illustrates unity amidst diversity by highlighting our diverse spiritual gifts, each arising from the same Spirit. The church, he notes, is like a body with various parts, each functioning according to its distinct role, and yet, moving together as one unit. Paul's unity amidst diversity theme is brought to a crescendo as he reveals a more excellent way—the way of love, of which 1 Corinthians 13 is wholly devoted.

In practical, rubber-meets-the-road ways, the guiding principle for relating to others is seen in 1 Corinthians 13:4–7:

> Love is patient, love is kind and is not jealous; love does not brag and is not arrogant, does not act unbecomingly; it does not seek its own, is not provoked, does not take into account a wrong suffered, does not rejoice in unrighteousness, but rejoices with the truth; bears all things, believes all things, hopes all things, endures all things.

Four Simple Rules

In my own spiritual journey, I try to implement the principle of love with those who are dissimilar to me. Four simple rules become my roadmap. First, I remind myself that experiencing dissimilarity is an opportunity for me to learn, grow, love, and implement my faith. It is this "opportunity mindset" that sets the tone for my demeanor and interaction with the color spectrum.

Secondly, I remind myself to pursue dialogue rather than judgment. I seek to listen and understand, not condemn or persuade. Thirdly, I remind myself to build upon common ground rather than erect walls of separation. I don't want to be pushing Baptists off the bridge. Fourthly, I remind myself to love others as God loves me. His love is expansive, and in seeking the good within others, I become the healing hands of Christ to their wounded souls.

When we view different shades of blue as part of God's intention, we stop resisting His design and allow diversity to enrich our lives. Love is the hallmark of our faith, and as we interact with each other in loving ways, we embrace the very thing a loving God desires for us. Our souls are deeply satisfied when we love and are loved. Wouldn't it be great if we committed to living our life with such acceptance that others are drawn to God? Wouldn't it be great if the brokenness of others was met with selfless love? Wouldn't it be great if we developed a culture of compassion and a habit of kindness in our life as the expression of true religion rather than frantically scurrying about doing religious things? Wouldn't it be great if we viewed unity amidst diversity as a good gift from the Creator's hand?

Wisdom for the Journey

Life is a kaleidoscope of differences, a brilliant rainbow of colors, all created by the hand of God to be embraced and treasured as "very good." Life's journey is easier when we grasp the larger picture of God's intention that diversity become the very environment for testing, demonstrating, renewing, and enriching our faith. Instead of withdrawing from others, or living a life of solidarity and rugged individualism, re-committing ourselves to relationship and community makes our journey more colorful and rewarding. While the road may get rocky at times, loving others expansively is a reflection of God's love for us. We are all a beautiful blue mosaic of God's creation.

– chapter five –

The Best of Me

There he goes again, sending me another one of his written "should do, ought to do, must do" sermons. I felt as though I was being pummeled with insufferable blows, over and over again. He perceived himself to be the anointed instrument of "should do, ought to do, and must do" religion, barking out directives for shaping up and earning God's approval by appeasing an angry deity.

Closing my eyes, I imagined what it would be like to sit in the audience Sunday after Sunday listening to this onslaught of verbal finger pointing. Many first-time visitors, I imagine, quietly scurried out after the service, hoping to go unnoticed. Others, I suppose, were just as eager to pounce, and appreciated a minister forcefully standing for their brand of truth. After all, someone has to crack the whip to keep wayward souls in line. Some, I bet, had listened to this kind of brow-beating for so long that it was all they knew of the church. In all likelihood, seeking a more positive worship experience or opting for sermons with loving content and thoughtful delivery didn't cross their minds. Like a broken marriage in which dysfunction becomes the operative norm, being whipped into shape every Sunday and feeling guilty about all their shortcomings helped them feel spiritual.

This older seminary student submitted sermons expecting to impress me and receive an A grade. I responded gently, asking him to present his thoughts in a more positive manner. As time went by, my comments became more direct, yet, none were incorporated into his messages. Finally, I had to lay it on the line since his train only traveled on one track. By continually ignoring my feedback, he was in danger of flunking the preaching course. From his perspective, he had been preaching this way for a long time and his congregation was used to it; changing now would be both unrealistic and undesirable. It is difficult to teach old dogs new tricks. The power of the bully pulpit is alluring.

How Do Others Experience Us?

I distinctly remember how unpleasant his sermons made me feel, and I was merely reading them, not receiving the barrage of verbal attacks in person. Somewhat stunned, I mumbled under my breath and shook my head in discontent. I wonder if he ever thought about how he was being perceived—how others experienced him. We readily grasp the effect others have upon us, but rarely do we consider our effect upon them. Has the thought ever crossed your mind? As I ponder how others experience me, I am not sure I like what I see.

While teaching an undergraduate class for adult learners, a young woman shared how her boyfriend had been stabbed during a raucous night out, how she responded to stressful situations, and how she could care less what anyone thought of her, or her actions. After shocking the class with these alarming revelations during class discussion, she closed her impromptu oration with an obstinate, "That's just the way I am."

In the awkward silence that followed, I slowly strolled to where she was sitting and quietly asked, "But, is that the way you ought to be?" The class wasn't expecting that kind of response, and neither was she. The point is that we do well to consider how others experience us. While we will never be able to control their feelings, we can conduct ourselves in a winsome manner. How do people experience you?

Without a shadow of doubt, I know that others can experience me in ways that I don't intend, or can't imagine. Though I try to maintain a motivation and intent that points true north, at times I can miss the subtle signals from those around me. Without intending to do so, my conduct and body language may be screaming "That's just the way I am," much like my bellicose student.

The Best of You = The Real You

When discussing this subject, two tricky items must be addressed straight away. First, the best you is the real you, and we are happiest and most fulfilled when we are being ourselves, not necessarily what others want us to be. Yet, "That's just the way I am" can become an excuse for not working on ourselves, a defense mechanism against hearing difficult words, or a smokescreen for bad behavior. It allows us to behave in any fashion we desire without having to deal with the consequences of our actions, their impact upon others, or their alignment with Christian values.

Rubber bands come in all sizes, thicknesses, and strengths. Increased tension is produced when rubber bands stretch, but they always return back to their original shape. People are the same way, and though we were created with distinctive design, we always strive to return to our original shape after stretching too far and for too long.

Introverts *can* engage in extroverted activities. Big-picture thinkers *can* bring themselves down from the clouds and walk among the weeds. Intellectuals *can* emote feelings. While we do stretch beyond our original rubber band shape, we cannot sustain this for extended periods of time without experiencing discomfort. People cannot consistently act in a manner inconsistent with their nature. After extroverted activities, introverts yearn to recharge their internal battery with precious alone time. Too much walking among the weeds of intricate detail can drive a big-picture individual crazy. We all long to return to our original rubber band shape—to just be ourselves. It is uncomfortable trying to be something or someone we were not meant to be.

As treasures crafted on the Potter's wheel, we begin to understand and appreciate God's design when we discover how He wired us. Armed with this knowledge, we can build strong foundations of self-identity so others have a "best of me" experience. Flippant "That's just the way I am" attitudes become flimsy defense mechanisms that mask our refusal to engage in the difficult work of smoothing out our rough edges. No one is perfect, and everyone has work to do. The tricky clarification is to acknowledge God's work of genius without resisting the refiner's fire. "That's just the way I am" is never a justification for bad behavior or an excuse to ignore our jagged edges.

The Opinion of Others

A proper perspective regarding the opinion of others is the second tricky element. Is pursuing "the best of me" placing too much emphasis on what others think of us? The last thing we want to do is jump on the people-pleasing bandwagon and return to the legendary encumbrances of peer pressure we faced in high school. We are beyond those childish distractions, aren't we? Our desire is to simply be the best we can be at being ourselves. When this occurs, others experience the very best of us. Yet, even at our best, we won't be able to please everyone. Our concern, however, isn't pleasing people, but understanding and refining our true selves. By pursuing "the best of me," we increase the likelihood of being welcomed and appreciated.

To merely do our "thing" without any thought of how our "thing" is experienced by others is the path of ease. I have mustered the courage to look in the mirror and honestly acknowledge my blind spots. Sanding down sharp edges has been one of my biggest challenges over the years, but it has also been one of the most rewarding. In fact, "the best of me" is not a destination so much as it is a continual state of pursuit and refinement. Over time, we see growth and the progress is gratifying. It is thrilling to be the kind of person others experience as positive and refreshing.

My propensity to slide into "attorney mode" is an ever-present danger. Tasked with making major decisions, I seek key pieces of information during staff meetings. From my perspective, I am merely asking pinpointed questions to identify essential information as quickly and accurately as possible. It is my role to analyze complex, and often contradictory, data while separating extraneous material from that which is truly significant. But that is *my* understanding of what is occurring. Staff experience, however, is much different. They feel like hostile witnesses being cross-examined by an aggressive courtroom lawyer. My behavior has appropriately been labeled "attorney mode."

The path of ease would have responded, "That's just the way I am" and left a trail of carnage in its wake. Instead, I pursued a "best of me" mindset and contemplated how I could obtain the required information without coming across like a grizzly bear awoken from its winter slumber. The troublesome issue wasn't *that* I was seeking information, but *how* I was acquiring it. Wanting my employees to experience the best of me, I worked to rid myself of one label and acquire a kinder one.

Across the hall from my office sat an extremely sensitive young woman who constantly worried that she had offended someone. It was comical, in one sense, to see the little things she fretted over. On the other hand, we had to be careful not to destroy her fragile nature. Whenever I left my office, I gave my office door a little pull to partially close it. Since it was large and heavy, I sometimes misjudged the amount of force needed, and on those occasions, the door would make a loud thud, causing my sensitive friend to think I was upset with her. When this was brought to my attention, I could have replied, "That's just the way I am. Get some thicker skin, young lady." Instead, I wanted her experience of me to be pleasant, so I slowed down and became more intentional in my approach to closing the door. It was a simple adjustment that made her life more comfortable. Now, she was experiencing a better me.

Most days, I have a great deal on my mind. My sister-in-law used to say, "You have a lot going on upstairs in that superhighway of yours." With a mind so engaged in its own world of thought, I am prone to missing details in my surroundings. On numerous occasions, I have backtracked to greet those I passed by but didn't really see. No ill intent is involved; I am merely trying to navigate the traffic jam on the superhighway upstairs. I could respond with, "That's just the way I am," and expect others to adjust to my mental preoccupation, but that is merely arrogance and immaturity working in tandem. Instead, I pursue "the best of me" so others can enjoy a pleasant encounter.

By making these simple adjustments, my essential nature isn't changing. I am not jumping on the people-pleasing hamster wheel, and I am not cow-towing to the opinion of others. I am merely becoming the best me I can be. My mind naturally analyzes large, complex issues, but it is not too much to ask that I would acknowledge a staff member as I pass by them. I naturally move with alacrity from one meeting to another in an effort to accomplish necessary tasks, but it is not too much to ask that I demonstrate greater care in shutting a large, heavy door so that it doesn't accidentally slam and irritate others. I need pertinent information to make significant decisions, but it is not too much to ask that I exemplify greater kindness in going about it.

My original rubber band shape is not morphing into an unrecognizable me, and I am not succumbing to the unrealistic pressure of opinions. Instead, I am simply smoothing out rough edges and pursuing "the best of me" so that others might find me to be a pleasant experience. I can do that. In fact, I like to do that. I believe God would want me to do that.

These are easy adjustments because they don't demand a change to my original rubber band shape—only that I refine the art of being me. If asked to alter my God-given hard wiring, I cannot comply. It is an unacceptable and unreasonable request, not to mention impossible. I can *refine* who I am, but I cannot fundamentally alter my rubber band shape. To do so would be a slap in the face of God, implying that He erred in His creative abilities by not meeting the unrealistic expectations of others. Unfortunately, the church furthers this uncomfortable dilemma by expecting us to become like all the biblical giants of faith.

Be Like Everyone Else?

Like you, I have listened to plenty of sermons extolling the virtues of Peter, Paul, John, Jesus, Barnabas, Mary, Joseph, Abraham, Noah, Isaiah, and the like, followed by an appeal to be just like them. Pointing to positive examples can certainly influence our own approach to living, but what I typically heard was a more insistent plea, "You *need* to be like …" that caused me to question my rubber band shape. One week I was told to be like Peter; the next week, Paul;

Joseph the following week, and so on. Over time, the message became clear: I needed to be like someone else when all I ever wanted to be was me. In all my years of ministry, I have never heard a minister speak about being yourself—being the person God created you to be, and turning that into the very best of you.

As I was observing a group of high school girls at the mall, I was amused by their "sameness." All teenagers seek their individuality, and yet, they all dressed alike. Peer pressure performed its faithful duty in bringing about conformity under the disguise of individuality. It would probably be years before they possessed a more mature attitude about the matter. Like many of us, they succumbed and joined the herd instead of truly understanding and accepting God's creative design.

After singing at special church meetings, I paused to process what had just happened. The minister of this rural, conservative congregation was not impressed with my singing abilities. He found it bothersome that I sometimes closed my eyes while singing a solo. He was annoyed by the clothes I wore, requested that I sing like someone else, decried the vocal runs in my songs, and was appalled that young church girls sought a front row seat. Barely out of college at the time, I apologized for my inability to please him and noted that I was unable to alter my singing style. Quite frankly, I didn't know how to sing like anyone else, and I doubt I could have pulled it off with much success even if I tried. How do you flip a switch and begin singing like Adam Levine, George Beverly Shea, Paul McCartney, or anyone else? Finally, I didn't think I *should* change, and I viewed his request as unreasonable and out of line. I kindly offered *not* to perform, but suddenly assuming the role of someone else simply wasn't going to happen.

This incident baffled me, for it was yet another "You *need* to be like…" episode. Realizing that my perspective might be off-kilter, I sought the insight of my hometown pastor. To my surprise, he agreed that I should have changed my singing style. What was the purpose of being me, I wondered, if I was expected to be like someone else? This implied a design flaw in God's creative process. He had fashioned me one way, while others pressed me to be another way. This just didn't add up in my mind. Either God made me incorrectly, or those expecting me to be something other than my original rubber band shape were crossing the line.

Knowing of his laid-back preaching style, I turned the tables on my hometown pastor and asked if he could prance about the stage waving his Bible high above his head, pointing his finger at the audience, and addressing the congregation in fevered pitch for fifty minutes. Would he be able to preach in a totally different manner? Should he be expected to? He got the point and confirmed his inability to suddenly transform into someone else behind the pulpit. Why couldn't I just be me? What was so wrong with that?

My hometown pastor referenced 1 Corinthians 9:19–23, where Paul indicates that he is a slave to all so that he can win some to God. To the Jew, he becomes a Jew. To one under the Law, he becomes Law-abiding. To those not under the law, as someone without law. To the weak, he becomes weak. Paul becomes "all things to all men, so that I may be all means save some" (vs. 22).

At first glance, it appears that I should meet everyone's expectation and bite the bullet in order to win others. This, however, is shallow and nonsensical thinking. It is literally impossible to be all things to all people. If there were a Jew under the Law in a room with a Gentile free from the law, along with a weak individual and a strong person, which one do we become in order to fulfill Scripture? Do we become drug addicts in order to save addicts? To the adulterer, would we become adulterers ourselves? We would forever be chameleons, always changing and never being our true self. This is absurd. There must be a more accurate understanding Paul's teaching.

As a missionary, Paul traveled from one region to the next, convincing those of different faiths in various cultures that following the way of Christ was reasonable. His tactic, as he moved into diverse regions, was to blend in as much as possible so that cultural differences didn't become a roadblock to the message itself. Hudson Taylor, the famous missionary to China in the late 1800s, pursued this same tactic as he lived among the Chinese. In fact, he was soundly criticized by religious folks back home for wearing his hair in a pony-tail and dressing like the Chinese. Being sensitive to, and aware of, cultural differences is a solid missionary strategy.

Burping after meals, in some cultures, is a sign of appreciation to the chef, while in others, it becomes a rude gesture. Shoes are left at the door and exchanged for indoor flip-flops in some cultures, while in others, they are left on. Food differences, language differences, non-verbal differences, and all sorts of differences exist between cultures. Valuing these differences in missionary endeavors is worthwhile, as Paul notes, but changing our fundamental rubber band shape to meet the petty expectations of another is the farthest thing from Paul's mind and a misappropriation of his teaching.

A congregational member once cornered me to say that she didn't appreciate my preaching. When I asked what she didn't like about it, she was unable to articulate her thoughts. Instead, she noted that I should preach just like Charles Stanley, the Baptist megachurch pastor on television. I responded that there was one major problem with her request—I was not Charles Stanley. What if others requested that I preach like their favorite television celebrity? I couldn't mimic Charles Stanley if I tried, let alone all of the other requests. In fact, I don't want to be like any of them. This was simply another disappointing "You *need* to be like…" moment.

Another time, a woman with health problems sought me out after the Sunday morning service to relay how I didn't measure up to her expectations. The main reason for her contempt was that I didn't hold her hand during home visits. Apparently, she and her husband thought it was the pastor's solemn obligation to hold hands during conversations, although this expectation was never verbalized to me. Here we go again, I thought, another unfortunate rendezvous with the pervasive "You *need* to be like…" attitude.

Near the end of our lengthy conversation, I held her hand and gently responded, "Barbara, I am sorry that I didn't meet your expectations. Please forgive me. God made you to be you, and He made me to be me. Why don't I let you be you and you let me be me. In that way we can each be who God made us to be and can celebrate one another as spiritual brothers and sisters in the Lord?" As anticipated, my response didn't meet her expectation, and the couple left the church because I didn't hold her hand.

Our original rubber band shape can, and should, stretch at times, but not so much as to break or lose our original shape. Learning, growing, and smoothing rough edges is expected, but when "You *need* to be like…" threatens our God-given "me-ness," it merely becomes another pressure tactic for conforming to someone else's unrealistic expectation. The good news is that God does not expect this of us and simply says, "You just be you. I made you; now go and be the best you can be so others can experience My magnificent design." What a breath of fresh air; what a simple truth! God wants you to be you.

Bringing Out Your Best

One day, I was fortunate to come across a personality profile tool for understanding ourselves and others. After completing the questionnaire, I wept while reading the results of my personality type. How did they know so much about me? God used this instrument to show me that I was not deficient in any way; I was just me. Like all people, I had specific preferences, strengths, and weaknesses, but to recognize how magnificently God had crafted me was an incredible moment in my life. I didn't need to be like anyone else; I just needed to be me, and being me was just fine. It was exactly what God desired, and celebration was in order.

All this "You *need* to be" talk ignored who I was. It disregarded my preferences, strengths, personality, weaknesses, calling, passion, dreams, and the total rubber band package of God's design. I realized there were no defects in God's handiwork, and I became comfortable in my own skin. Armed with self-assurance and a new perspective, I initiated the fine-tuning process so I could become the best me possible.

In contemplating how to become a better me, I took stock of factors that brought out the worst of me and the conditions that helped me to shine. There were no stark surprises. Conditions of stress, fear, worry, and uncertainty brought out my unseemly side. Sound familiar? I have to work extra hard at being my best when these elements are present. I don't always succeed.

Living in a perpetual state of transition has been my lot in life for the past several years. Nearly everything I own is packed away in boxes, including my precious library, the tools of my trade. Currently, I rent a tiny, cracker-box house that functions more like a mini-storage unit with a bed. The residence has no stove, and I cook on a handy George Foreman Lean Mean Fat Reducing Grilling Machine, my new best friend. Only two rooms are heated during the winter, and there happens to be a window in my shower, right above the old green bathtub. This kind of transitional uncertainty, along with a dash of fear and worry, can get me down, make me irritable, and produce stress. The path of ease is to function sub-optimally, always less than my best.

While my current circumstances produce plenty of humiliating moments, I look to the larger picture of what God is doing in my life and relentlessly pursue those things that bring forth the best of me. For instance, when I slow down and take time to remember what is important in life, I elevate my game. When reflection and prayer become my daily routine, peace overwhelms me. As I eat healthy and exercise, my mind is clearer, my energy is higher, and I seem to be in a better mood.

My best also rises to the surface when I pursue goals that are important to me. Each year I draft various personal and professional goals along with the necessary action steps that bring them to fruition. A time will come when transient living is replaced with more pleasant arrangements, but until that day arrives, I focus on bringing forth the best of me. Why? Because the way I live life isn't dependent upon my circumstances, but upon my values. I value being the best me possible so that I can bring blessing to others and walk in step with the Spirit of God.

If we are going to practice a "best of me" lifestyle, a paradigm shift may be in order, whereby one way of thinking is replaced with another way of thinking. In essence, we push the reset button in our mind. In reality, it isn't as easy as pushing a button, though I wish it were. Instead, we fight internal habits of the mind that have been there a long time. But changing our thinking can, and does, occur. Your mind is the most expensive piece of real estate on this planet. Don't allow just anything to take up residence there.

Like a garden, we can plant thoughts, water them, feed them, and nurture the kind of thinking we desire. If we approach every situation with "That's just the way I am" outbursts, we harvest the same debilitating results. By planting and nurturing a garden of "best of me" thoughts, we begin to think and behave differently over time.

Paradigm shifts are often initiated by a catalyst—a precipitating event that prompts a desire for change. It could be just about anything, but it causes us to stop in our tracks and reconsider our current approach to life. Rather than continuing in a paralysis of paradigms, a change is needed. Do you need to alter how you think about you?

Many attractive qualities abound in others that inspire us to be better in our own life. All too often, however, the cups in the cupboard want to be plates; the plates want to be bowls; the bowls want to be forks; the forks want to be knives, and so forth. Many never seem to be content with who they are. The young girls at the mall weren't comfortable in their own skin, so they tried to look like all the other girls. We seem to think the grass is always greener on the other side of the fence.

I wonder if Peter and Andrew ever felt this way, each wishing to be more like the other. Peter was outspoken, a leader, good in front of people, and always in the throng of things. He was bold and willing to take risks. His brother Andrew, on the other hand, was quiet, in the background, always supportive and reserved without pursuing high-risk situations. Andrew could have said, "I wish I was like Peter. He is so bold and brave and such a strong leader. I just sit back and watch." Peter may have been thinking, "I wish I was like my brother Andrew. He is wise, never gets in hot water, and just keeps bringing people to Jesus." Although these sorts of thoughts go through our mind, we must resist trying to be like someone else when it threatens our original rubber band shape. It is a fruitless endeavor and a useless battle. We can never be someone else, ever. We can only be ourselves.

During my first pastorate, two men played a brass duet for the morning service. The beauty of their sound was mesmerizing, and I immediately wanted to explore the trumpet. One of the horn players provided me with a used trumpet, and I began practicing. It wasn't as easy as these fellows made it look. Growing a bit impatient, I contacted my brother, a professional trombone player, and asked how long it would take me to play like Wynton Marsalis, a trumpet virtuoso. He began to chuckle, and with all the kindness he could muster, replied, "You will never be able to play like Wynton Marsalis." Thanks so much for the encouraging words!

I am not gifted in the music arts like my brother, and here I was, trying to be like someone else. While I accomplished my goal of playing in a brass trio for the morning service, it would take years of practice to play with any semblance of proficiency. My strengths and gifts lie elsewhere, but I gained a new appreciation for musicians.

There is nothing wrong with aspiring to play well and utilizing Wynton Marsalis as an inspiration. However, feeling like a sub-par, less-than, nobody because I can't perform like him crosses the line into discontent. Just be who God made you to be. Be happy with how He created you. Be content with your strengths, gifts, and abilities. Look in the mirror and boldly proclaim, "Thank you Father for making me just right." Be comfortable in your own skin. Love yourself. Once you quit trying to be like everyone else, you can then work on being the best you possible.

One constructive action I pursued in becoming "the best of me" was learning how God crafted me. This was foundational to how I perceived myself and filled my heart with thanksgiving. A new sense of awe at the handiwork of God was birthed. Learning about me was exciting. I read numerous books, took various personality inventories, and soaked up as much as I could about how God created me. Though we are much more complex than the results of personality tests, they become tools for opening our eyes to greater insight and self-understanding.

Once the foundation for self-understanding had been laid, I took time to assess every aspect of my life. I evaluated every job I held, what went well, what didn't, and what I liked and disliked about each one. I probed what excited me in life, as well as what drained me. Through this deep dive into self-examination, noticeable patterns emerged that helped me gain even greater insight into myself. Though I am still exploring the world of me, I now have a pretty good handle on how God shaped me. In fact, I can't imagine being any other way. While it has taken me years to get to this point, I actually like being me.

Once I understood myself, I connected my passion with my strengths and began practicing the art of being, living, and doing me. By painting my world in a way that was expressly me, I was released from the shackles of trying to be like someone else, and I could live with total abandon for my Creator. The road of life is rarely easy, and I get tripped up like the rest of us, but I pick myself up, dust myself off, and keep moving forward. I learn from my successes and my failures, but I never change the fundamental core of who I am. All this learning from life, the ups and the downs, simply make me a better me. In fact, there may be nothing more beautiful than human beings who are content and comfortable in their own skin, living life to the fullest and blessing God along the way.

Wisdom for the Journey

Stop trying to be like someone else. Discover how God made you, and then embrace, celebrate, and live you. Life's journey is so much more meaningful and pleasant when you become comfortable in your own skin. Become the best you that you can be. In this way, you will not only live life with authenticity and joy, but you will travel in accordance with your God-given rubber band shape.

#

quit thee, I quit thee, oh, let me count the ways I quit thee! Yep, that's me, a quitter to the nth degree. As a young person, I gave up on just about everything. A sampling of my quitting prowess ought to impress; I quit football, wrestling, baseball, guitar, drum, saxophone, singing, stamp collecting, fish aquarium hobby, and flying lessons, just to name a few. It was a well-rehearsed habit of mine. My "stick-to-itiveness" was non-existent; in fact, I don't think I even knew what that was.

Why did I quit so many things? I am unsure how to answer that question, largely because I do not know the answer. Though the topic has occupied my thoughts on numerous occasions, I don't have a ready explanation. It certainly wasn't the result of twisted parenting. My father and mother were loving individuals. My penchant for abandoning certain endeavors could be the result of fear, an inferiority complex, or maybe I was simply a young man who just thought, "I don't want to do this anymore; time to try something different." Who really knows? I certainly don't.

Then came that fateful day when I stumbled into Bible College totally unprepared for the rigors of higher education. While in high school, I happened to take the ACT college entrance exam. I had no idea what it was or why I was taking it, but many of my classmates sat for the test, so I participated. I certainly didn't study for it, for I never took a book home during high school.

Mr. Average

As it turned out, my test results confirmed that I was Mr. Average. Not the dullest light bulb in the room, but far from being the brightest. Off to Bible College I went, not for the purpose of study—a foreign concept to me—but to pursue what I sensed was the calling of God upon my life.

Arriving to campus, with its central building in the shape of a cross, I was in for a big surprise. The freshman class all seemed to be ahead of me, and I was blown away by the amount of work required for each class. *What is this thing called a syllabus?* I was in the dark and overwhelmed by my own shortcomings. While others enjoyed the greater joys of college life, I was in my room studying without a clue how to go about the task. With so much course work to complete and so little preparation, I realized that to be off socializing meant moving down from my esteemed status as Mr. Average. I studied a minimum of five hours each night just to keep up. My roommate understood the nature of learning and had actually studied during high school. He was well prepared; I wasn't. Often, I tried to best him on quizzes and tests, but I always came up short. For me, the learning curve was steep and the effort Herculean.

After that first year of Bible College, I wasn't sure what to do. To return meant depleting my savings with no way of paying for the remaining years. So, I took some time off (euphemism for quitting), and enrolled in a short-term welding program at the local community college—it was inexpensive and provided the necessary time for figuring out my next move. With good fortune, I discovered a private college close to home that graciously provided a 50 percent tuition scholarship, not for academic reasons, but simply because I was pursuing full-time ministry. Imagine that—one school charged for ministry training while another reduced tuition because of my desired profession. The decision was a no-brainer. I pursued my bachelor's degree while living at home and working full-time, and I graduated with my savings intact.

I Quit Quitting

This time around, however, my quitting abilities had to be dealt with. I could ill afford to continue the practice. With one year of college under my belt, I knew what I was up against in continuing my education, so I made a decision—one of the best ones I have ever made. I decided to quit quitting and see something all the way through. Hungry to prove that I could do it, I chose a major that I strongly disliked just to push the limits of my decision. I dedicated myself, diligently studied, and held myself to high standards. Quitting was no longer an option.

To my surprise, I discovered that I could learn, enjoyed learning, and even appreciated its role in my life. I was learning how to think and reason, ask pertinent questions, engage in analysis and evaluation, and earned cum laude honors at graduation while maintaining a 4.0 in my major field of study. That is quite an accomplishment for a first-generation college student—a quitter. I persevered, and since making that historic decision, my tenacity and perseverance is no longer questioned.

Over the years, this resolute perspective has served me well as a key component to my success and dogged dedication to causes worth pursuing. Now, after working so hard to overcome my quitting tendencies, imagine my dismay at the thought of reverting back to something I once worked so hard to overcome. Every fiber within me revolted against the thought of quitting.

Yet, in many respects, Scripture implores us to be quitters. We are to quit worrying, quit striving, quit conforming to the world, quit fighting amongst ourselves, and the like. In this sense, quitting is positive and expected. Yet, it seems so contrary to everything we have been taught. Jesus used paradox to show that following God not only *looks* different than our contemporary cultural values; it *actually is* different. When our culture says the correct way is up, that usually means the proper road is down. The way of God is the narrow path that few travel. Why do so few walk the narrow way of Christ? It may be that traveling in the company of the masses is the path of least resistance, while the narrow way demands inner transformation—actual change within our heart, the deepest core of our being.

Look at Life Differently

Jesus asks us to look at life differently and not be duped by meaningless cultural values and beliefs. Following God is about transformation. If our behavior and thinking is no different than the masses, what real effect has following God had upon us? God-followers are different from the inside out, born of the Spirit, and seek to live counter-culturally. Paradoxically, Jesus said the last shall be first, life is found by losing it, greatness arises from serving others, receiving comes from giving, and so forth. His words must have seemed backwards to his disciples. Who talks like that? Who sees the world that way? It is exactly the kind of inner transformation Jesus seeks among his followers, and it runs counter to the values our culture promotes. It is the narrow way of heart transformation. It is the way of quitting.

At times, I like being a *member* of The Way more than actually walking *according* to The Way. The broad path is easier and sometimes more attractive. I am comfortable clutching needless things like fear and worry so tightly that letting go doesn't seem right, and yet, it is precisely what the narrow path calls for. Is it time to quit worrying? Is it time to let go of fear? Is it time to actually begin walking the narrow path and practicing what we offhandedly preach to others? Is it time to jettison the cute Christian slogans we live by and unlock the shackles that restrain us from participating in the life of God?

In Mark 10:17–27, Jesus encounters a wealthy man unwilling to let go of his riches—something he clutches tightly and prevents him from experiencing the kingdom. The path of inner transformation, of change at the very core of our being, is different for each of us. For the rich young ruler, the path of transformation was letting go of his security blanket—his possessions. He loved and trusted in material items more than he desired God. Our Creator has an uncanny ability to pinpoint those things in our life that need to be addressed, and most often we know exactly what they are.

A Learned Comfort

In many respects, we experience a "learned comfort" with one foot in the boat and the other on the dock. We are okay with following Christ as long as we don't have to follow *all the way*—with 100 percent commitment. Like the rich young ruler, we may be too frightened to give up our security blanket that has provided comfort for such a long time in exchange for the "unproven" route of letting go. But it is in the letting go, the quitting, that we find freedom and new life. It is precisely what inner transformation is all about. If we are unwilling to quit worry, fear, religiosity, worldly values, and the like, we walk away sad like the rich young ruler.

What would it take for you to put both feet in the boat? What would it take for you to quit the things that hold you back and begin living the kind of life God intended? Are you tired of clutching useless items—grasping at the wind and trying to hold on to air? Do you desire more than merely trusting in a temporal security blanket? It may be time for you to quit—to let go and live.

When I started out as a young minister, I was unprepared for the amount of criticism within the church that would be directed my way. One segment of the congregation actually liked me, was deeply touched by my efforts to serve, and felt blessed by my presence. Another group was unhappy with everything about me. No matter what I did, they were unsatisfied. I didn't visit enough, used the wrong sermon illustration, wasn't in the office every time they stopped by, and wasn't the kind of minister they thought I should be. The third group was sometimes positive and sometimes negative, depending on which way the wind blew. I quickly learned that I could not please everyone regardless of how sincere my motivation or how dedicated my efforts.

On one occasion, an elder came to see me. He was a longtime resident of the town and his wife held a nasty reputation in the community. A regional group of ministers often met together on Mondays, but because this was the regular day I took off to be with my wife and two young children, I did not attend. I asked the group members if they were open to changing the meeting time, but they were unwilling to reschedule. Sundays were demanding days for me. Up early in the morning, and the first to arrive and the last to leave church, I always came home exhausted. I needed Monday to decompress, gather my wits about me, and spend dedicated time with my family.

Arriving at my office and pulling up a chair, the elder couldn't stop the nervous shaking of his legs. I knew he had something on his mind. "Pastor, you need to go to the Monday regional meetings," he stated. When I shared with him why I did not, he responded, "Your day off should be the day you don't have other commitments." To this I replied, "If I take off whichever day of the week holds the least commitments, and this week it is Thursday, next week it is Tuesday, and the following week it is Friday, what have I communicated to my family over the course of a year?"

He couldn't answer the question, so I answered it for him: "By taking off whichever day of the week doesn't have a demand on my time, I have communicated to my family that they take last place in my life. They get the leftovers, whatever day no one else wants. My family is important to me, and Monday is the day we have set aside to be together."

He quickly responded, "You are setting a bad example."

"No, I am setting a positive example," came my reply. Realizing he wasn't getting anywhere, he fired off a parting shot, "You are a bad pastor," and left my office.

Quit People-Pleasing

Whether I properly handled the situation or not is debatable. One thing is for certain; it was becoming clear to me that no matter how hard I tried, I was unable to please everyone. So, I did something for which I am eternally grateful—I quit trying to please people. It's not that I didn't want them to be happy with me, for we would all like that, but the significance attached to that kind of thinking was no longer valid in my mind. Of paramount importance was living my life in a manner worthy of my calling and serving my Creator with integrity and joy. I quit worrying about whether everyone else was pleased and let the chips fall where they may.

Determined to quit trying to please everyone may not seem like a major decision, but as a pastor, people become the entire context of your profession. They are not an ancillary element to ministry, but the very heart of it. As a young minister, the decision also had financial repercussions. Unhappy people create all kinds of justified excuses for withholding financial support. In many cases, to offend someone meant that their giving was earmarked for special projects, sent to another ministry, or suspended until their demands were met. This maintained their sense of spirituality without stooping so low as to put money into the general fund from which the pastor is paid.

Sometimes it is costly to displease people. In my case, after serving this church for nearly five years, I was let go, not for theological or moral reasons, but because I was unable to please the right people. With one fell swoop of the henchman's sharp axe, I lost my church family, my parsonage housing, my income, my benefits, my job, my community, and a good portion of my dignity. It was traumatic, but not insurmountable. It wasn't that I was being purposefully displeasing to folks; it was that I couldn't measure up to the unrealistic standard a select portion of the community set before me.

I quit being a people-pleaser and it cost me my job. I couldn't be happier. Although painful at the time, I became a better person because of it, and I have never gone back to the hamster wheel of trying to please people—an impossible task. Now, I just focus on pleasing God and being the best me I can be. Some folks like it, others don't, and still others swing from one side to the other depending on what direction the winds of self-interest are blowing. That's life.

I am reminded of Jesus' own ministry. As the reflection of God in human form, even he couldn't please everyone. The threatened Romans crucified him. The jealous Pharisees sought to discredit him and bring about his downfall. His fearful hometown asked him to minister elsewhere. The self-centered disciples were dull and unresponsive, while grieving Mary was upset that he didn't immediately save her brother from death. The fickle crowds often followed him, not for who he was, but because of what they could get from him. Jesus couldn't please everyone, and we can't either. That's just the way it is.

I was in a no-win situation, so I quit. It felt good to let go. People-pleasing is exasperating work, and a weight was lifted from my shoulders. I began to experience what Jesus was talking about in Matthew 11:28–30 when he said, "Come to Me, all who are weary and heavy-laden, and I will give you rest. Take My yoke upon you and learn from Me, for I am gentle and humble in heart, and you will find rest for your souls. For My yoke is easy and My burden is light."

Knowledge and Volition Align

There came a point when knowledge and volition aligned. I knew what was occurring in my life, and I was sick and tired of trying to measure up. So, I made a decision to quit. That decision wasn't the same as trying to choose between beige and dark brown carpeting for the bedroom; those kinds of decisions are inconsequential. But life-changing decisions are often made when we know what is going on around us and are sick and tired of it. Serious changes in direction occur when determination, intellect, and emotion converge to produce unwavering resolve.

First-century Palestine was in a disgraced state of affairs. The hallowed Promised Land had fallen from its zenith and was now occupied by Rome's expansive reach. It was Pontius Pilate, the Roman prefect for Judea, who sentenced Jesus to death. Spiritually, the Jews had turned a heartfelt religion into the burdensome task of maintaining extensive religious requirements. Jesus excoriated knit-picky Pharisees in Matthew 23 for demoting religion to nothing more than external rituals when it was the heart that mattered. Finally, in 70 CE, the enduring passion of Judaism crumbled as the Romans destroyed their sacred Temple. Oh, how far they had fallen!

Living in a culture taken hostage by well-meaning but erroneous legalistic teachers, Jesus' message was to stop it—to quit. He called for inner transformation of the heart. He encouraged followers to leave the broad path and begin traveling the narrow way. Quit thinking as the world thinks, he challenged. Quit valuing what the world values, he exhorted. Quit running on the hamster wheel of performance and bask in the love and acceptance of God.

Those who travel the narrow way experience God afresh and discover peace, joy, freedom, love, and acceptance. But it takes a change, a quitting, or as Jesus said to Nicodemus, a "born from above" experience (Jn. 3:3). An internal change is what moves us along the narrow path.

A Partial Christianity

The quitting I am referring to is a mental resolve leading us to alter our path and travel the narrow way of Christ. It is a point where we say, "I have had enough, and I quit. Let the chips fall where they may. I am going to follow the way of Jesus." For most of us, we already know what we need to stop doing. It isn't rocket science. Yet, we hold on to those things that destroy us mentally and physically. We know we shouldn't worry, but we do. We know we shouldn't be afraid, but we continue to embrace the fear. It's almost as if we enjoy living with a partial Christianity that is strong enough to believe in but too weak to catch us when we let go of the things that zap our strength. Are we vibrant human beings experiencing the abundant life of God, or are we spiritual zombies, unable to make up our minds whether to be alive or dead? Fully experiencing the life of Christ requires an intentional decision to quit—to let go and walk the narrow way.

Recently, while leading an educational institution toward increased growth and refined operational processes, it became evident that a new position was necessary to meet future goals. Advertising the opening didn't bring in the pool of candidates we were hoping for, so I began to think a bit more creatively. Could we divide up the duties among existing staff? Were we overlooking current employees capable of filling the role?

While seeking staff feedback, an outstanding employee with an MBA expressed interest in the position. Our initial conversation was cordial, but I noticed that instead of being excited about the new role and how her abilities could be maximized, she raised concerns about job security, possible failure, and what would happen to her if... The next day, she asked to speak with me again and raised additional issues of the worrying sort.

There is nothing wrong with an inquisitive spirit, but her worry-wart demeanor was disconcerting. I wished she would have shown greater interest in tackling challenges and moving the institution forward rather than elaborating on her fears. When she told me she was a worrier, I asked if she was a Christian woman (already knowing that she was) and received an affirmative response. Inquiring further, I asked what her faith had to say about the topic, and she recited several applicable Scriptures. I found the entire conversation revealing. Here was a solid Christian woman who intellectually understood the unproductive nature of worrying and could readily identify biblical passages on the topic, but was reluctant to actually stop worrying. She brought up the familiar passage in Luke 12:22–28:

> And He said to His disciples, "For this reason I say to you, do not worry about your life, as to what you will eat; nor for your body, as to what you will put on. For life is more than food, and the body more than clothing. Consider the ravens, for they neither sow nor reap; they have no storeroom nor barn, and yet God feeds them; how much more valuable you are than the birds! And which of you by worrying can add a single hour to his life's span? If then you cannot do even a very little thing, why do you worry about other matters? Consider the lilies, how they grow: they neither toil nor spin; but I tell you, not even Solomon in all his glory clothed himself like one of these. But if God so clothes the grass in the field, which is alive today and tomorrow is thrown into the furnace, how much more will He clothe you? You men of little faith!"

Do you see the problem? She knew worrying was a waste of time; yet, she continued wasting her time. She knew the Bible instructed her not to engage in this fruitless activity, and yet, she continued the debilitating behavior. Instead of actually quitting, she verbally disguised her troublesome habit as a sugar-coated quirk about herself by saying, "I am such a worrier" and laughing about it as though it were the same as saying, "I am such a softy for stray cats." This trivializes what Scripture values and attempts to justify our actions, mitigate the responsibility for change, and make us feel better about continuing on a path we know is not right.

No one is perfect, and we are all on a journey to wholeness, but what does it say about our faith if we trivialize the important and ignore the inner transformation God desires? What does it say about you? Does it not, to some degree, reveal a disconnect between what we profess to believe and how we actually live? Of course it does. What if your Christian teenage son laughingly said to you, "I know that Scripture says drunkenness is wrong and I know I shouldn't get drunk, but Mom, I am such a drunk." Isn't this the same as saying, "I am such a worrier?" Sure it is. Though obviously different issues, the same level of reasoning exists with both. We know what Scripture teaches, but…

Divorce

Quitting can be fairly easy, and at other times traumatic. Sometimes we enjoy talking about the need to quit rather than actually quitting. Letting go can be monumental in nature and mustering up the courage to move ourselves into a right frame of mind can take years. Divorce, for example, is an act of letting go, often accompanied by pain, shame, and all sorts of vitriol from well-meaning Christians. It can scar us in many ways, and yet, in some instances, as odd as it may seem, it may actually be a path that sets us free.

Divorce is a hot-button issue within Christian circles, and unfortunately, I am unable to give the topic its just deserve because my present interest is limited to the fact that divorce can sometimes be a path to wholeness. This kind of talk drives biblical literalists up the wall since many believe divorce is never allowed or is severely restricted in its exceptions. Think about how crazy things have become. Catholics annul marriages long after they have been consummated. How does it make sense to say no marriage existed when, in fact, it really did? On the opposite side of the fence are hyper-fundamentalists who believe a woman beaten every night by her husband is obligated to stay in the marriage. By divorcing, she is ostracized for sinful behavior, while the inhumane husband becomes the innocent party and is allowed to remarry and beat his next wife. Unfathomable! This is insanity at its best. As icing on the cake, the church often treats divorced individuals like they have the plague; "less-than" people, totally unfit for significant ministry roles and forever banished to the trash bin of life. It is a shame.

How the church treats divorced people, outcasts, down-and-outers, and the disenfranchised just befuddles me. The prevailing attitudes of judgment and condescension are antithetical to the compassion Christ exemplified. An evangelist once noted that he could find more honesty and transparency in a local bar than he could within the church. What an indictment. The church's holier-than-thou attitude is baffling in light of the giants of our faith we seek to emulate. Noah, the only righteous individual God could find prior to the flood, departed the Ark and quickly became naked and inebriated. Abraham, our great example of faith, couldn't believe God for protection as he lied about his wife to save his own skin. The venerable prophet Isaiah, upon defeating 450 prophets of Baal, retreated into the desert to hide from wicked Jezebel, afraid for his life. King David, the iconic warrior who defeated the arrogant Philistine giant and became the apple of God's eye, was a murderer and adulterer, fathering a child out of wedlock. Even Jesus didn't come from renowned stock, with a prostitute and murderer in his lineage.

You can be a murderer, prostitute, liar, and drunkard, and be elevated in the faith, but a terrible line is crossed if one is divorced. The absurdity of such thinking is beyond the realm of reason. Jesus' words in John 8:7 seem apropos: "He who is without sin among you, let him be the first to throw a stone at her." A lasting marriage is God's ideal. It is a good thing and should be entered into with all seriousness, but even the best of intentions don't always work out. Life happens. People change. Circumstances become unbearable. Marriages don't always last, and sometimes quitting is the right thing to do.

I know folks who remain in destructive relationships despite a serious decline in their mental, physical, and spiritual health. Marriage takes hard work on the part of both parties—no doubt about it, but there comes a time when quitting may be the best alternative. It takes unshakeable courage to move forward when you have been taught that divorce is always sinful. I am not encouraging divorce, only noting that it may be the right move in certain situations, and when those situations are ripe, resolute effort is required to follow the narrow way. I have watched individuals take that difficult step of faith, weather the church's scurrilous reprimands, and come out on the other side experiencing life, freedom, and renewed commitment to God. Yes, in the right circumstances, quitting may involve something so cherished as the bond of marriage.

Wisdom for the Journey

Walking the narrow way means turning from the world's conventional thinking and intentionally moving toward inner transformation of the heart. Decisions must be made in our journey whereby we gather our courage and boldly proclaim, "I have had enough. I will no longer continue down this fruitless road." Our path is intentionally altered in hope of altering our outcome. What must you quit in your life in order to really live, to thrive, and be true to your faith?

chapter seven

Release the Gift

*L*ove might be the topic most preached from American pulpits these days, while its first cousin, forgiveness, is not far behind. It is difficult for one to thrive without the other. Love is the gift we extend to others, while forgiveness is the gift we give to ourselves. Some of us aren't very good at giving ourselves gifts, and we would rather admire the box wrapped in shiny paper and big red bow than actually open the gift and put it to good use. Forgiveness triumphantly performs its healing craft upon our wounded souls when it is released and received. As the antidote for so many of our problems, keeping it under wraps is a colossal mistake.

Varying degrees of difficulty are experienced in my own attempts to forgive, and notice that I said "attempts," for I struggle just like everyone else. This increasing difficulty might be analogous to the difference between jaywalking, driving under the influence of alcohol, and first degree murder. As the severity of the crime increases, so does its consequences. Similarly, forgiving a friend for cheating you out of five dollars is much different than forgiving a father who beat you every time he came home from the local bar. My point is this:

when it comes to forgiveness, the greater the perceived offense, the greater effort it takes to forgive.

I Am Offended

Our politically correct culture comes with plenty of individuals who annoyingly shout, "I am offended" whenever they see or hear something that doesn't tickle their fancy. It isn't a crime or an act of moral turpitude that stirs their ire; we just happened to step into their stinky pile of personal preferences which no one is allowed to question. To safeguard their fragile viewpoint as "the" perspective to which all others must adhere, they scream, "I am offended" at whatever doesn't align with their version of reality. It is an infantile response—akin to a child's temper tantrum when told "no."

Totalitarian regimes have tried this very approach—that is, curtailing the rights of others and suppressing disagreement, with disastrous outcomes. I actually possess a sad reminder of totalitarianism's failure—a small piece of the once proud Berlin Wall that separated West German freedom of thought from East German thought control. This kind of fascist endeavor never works, for we are not programmable robots, but complex beings with various perspectives on any given topic. Our esteemed American constitution preserves our right of free speech—a right whereby one's belief, speech, and conduct may, in fact, be contrary to another. This is the very heart of what the First Amendment protects—the freedom to say, think, and do things that others may find disagreeable.

There are reasonable limits to this freedom (you can't falsely yell "fire" in a crowded movie theater), but hiding behind the smokescreen of political correctness or childishly pouting, "You didn't do or say what I think you should do or say" is beneath us. Why must I do or say what you think I should? The freedom of disagreement allows us to do our own thinking and arrive at our own conclusions about things.

We all know hypersensitive individuals who wind up with hurt feelings over trivial issues. Once, I asked an employee to provide information for a report I was producing, and upon learning that I made a minor adjustment to her work, she hit the roof, perceiving it as a total rejection of her as a person. How dare anyone mess with her "perfect" work of art! Emotions hijacked reason, and her sensitivity meter was in need of a dial-down. Living on the knife's edge put everyone else on the brink of madness as we tiptoed around her emotional instability. Being mindful of those around us and implementing kinder and gentler approaches to interpersonal relationships is wise, but, in my mind, forgiveness is connected to more substantive matters than issues of hypersensitivity and free speech.

Degrees of Difficulty

I seek to differentiate between immaturity, hypersensitivity, matters of free speech, and the challenging work of forgiveness. In other words, I see degrees of difficulty between the lesser items of forgiveness and the bigger incidents that require us to dig down deep in order to let go. For instance, some offenses, as 2 Peter 4:8 notes, can simply be placed under the cover of love: "Above all, keep fervent in your love for one another, because love covers a multitude of sins." At various times and in diverse ways, we all become wounded in one way or another. With small cuts and bruises we simply clean the laceration, affix a Band-Aid, and apply a generous portion of love to the wound. A trip to the doctor's office or emergency room is unnecessary, for we realize the minor injury will quickly heal. In these situations, our capacity to love rises above the altercation, refuses to create a scene, and chooses to forgive and move on. We do this frequently in our journey through life. It is big of us, and the right thing to do. By refusing to allow small matters to fester, we live according to the scriptural standard of love.

Placing a Band-Aid on small owies is simple enough, but some situations are approached more directly, especially when communication, clarity, awareness, and the processing of feelings becomes indispensable to maintaining right relationships. The following verses remind us that standards of interaction exist for the community of faith: "So, as those who have been chosen of God, holy and beloved, put on a heart of compassion, kindness, humility, gentleness and patience; bearing with one another, and forgiving each other, whoever has a complaint against anyone; just as the Lord forgave you, so also should you. Beyond all these things put on love, which is the perfect bond of unity" (Col. 3:12–14); "Let all bitterness and wrath and anger and clamor and slander be put away from you, along with all malice. Be kind to one another, tender-hearted, forgiving each other, just as God in Christ also has forgiven you" (Eph. 4:31–32).

This notion of forgiveness was so significant in the early church that, according to the Gospels of Matthew and Luke, God's forgiveness of us is conditioned upon our forgiveness of others (Mt. 6:15; Mk. 11:25). This is striking, and thorny verses like these make us uncomfortable, for they emphasize the call upon our life to be forgiving. We can all agree on the fact that forgiveness is a critical element to following God. In teaching us to pray, Jesus asked that we forgive those who trespass against us (Mt. 6:12). Even the disciples marveled at Jesus' teaching of expansive forgiveness: "Then Peter came and said to Him, 'Lord, how often shall my brother sin against me and I forgive him? Up to seven times?' Jesus said to him, 'I do not say to you, up to seven times, but up to seventy times seven'" (Mt. 18:21–22). The point isn't to limit forgiveness to 490 times (70 x 7), but that forgiveness become a way of life— an integral aspect of character that flows from a heart graciously touched by the hand of God. Even during his excruciating crucifixion, Jesus modeled forgiveness: "Father, forgive them; for they do not know what they are doing" (Lk. 23:34). Being a forgiving person is an important element in pursuing the ways of God.

When we realize that minor offenses don't matter in the larger scheme of things, we are able to quickly cover them in love and prevent their noxious influence from spreading. Other offenses require a more direct approach as we pursue the unity and forgiveness Scripture endorses. Finally, there are the momentous, traumatic events that rock our world to the core, and yet, we are still asked to forgive. As the pain increases, so does the difficulty of forgiving. Many offenses are Band-Aid issues, some entail direct interaction, and others are so severe that forgiveness becomes a lifelong struggle to let go. Moving from fury to forgiveness is sometimes more of a process than an event.

I counseled a woman whose secret scar occupied a hidden, but prominent place in her life. She was molested as a child by her father. Her private pain wasn't of the Band-Aid sort. Her father was long gone, couldn't have cared less about his role in wounding her, and would never have availed himself to any sort of direct communication about the matter. With the help of her pastor (me), she was forced to dig deep within herself. During our time together she wailed in emotional pain, and as deeper levels of agony were exposed and released, the greater her wailing. At the conclusion of our sessions, she experienced the freedom of forgiveness and no longer carried the weight of such a burden.

In situations of deep wounding, true forgiveness rarely occurs without profoundly touching the emotions. To think that trauma can be readily dismissed without some sort of inner wailing only serves to cheapen the pain, and it doesn't bring about the full release we seek. Generalizing how others have wounded us fails to capture the depth of the pain we experience. Saying an all-inclusive "I forgive you" doesn't deal directly and specifically with the deeds in question. In counseling situations, I ask individuals to name each behavior that was hurtful. They list their grievances individually so that they can forgive with specificity. Forgiveness seems to reach deeper into our hearts when each item of pain is identified and dealt with rather than offering up some blanket statement of generalized forgiveness.

The Meaning of Forgiveness

If forgiveness is a principal teaching of Jesus and an expectation within the community of faith, what does it actually mean to forgive? We should understand exactly what it is we are being asked to do. Forgiveness is a gift we give to ourselves that often requires tremendous strength and courage. The people who hurt us may or may not be aware of our effort to forgive, and they may not even care. In all honesty, it doesn't really matter because forgiveness is about us, not them. That may surprise you, but it is absolutely true.

If left unchecked, our wounds can build up pressure and explode in unpleasant episodes of hostility. This means that the original wound multiplies its effect and turns into a perpetual hurt that wallops us over and over again long after the initial blow. Forgiveness is a method for releasing that pressure and loving ourselves well, which in turn, helps us better love God and others. Freedom from the past, of course, takes deep courage, and I am constantly amazed and inspired by those who choose the path of forgiveness after enduring so much pain. By choosing to release the gift of forgiveness, they embrace and experience healing, empathy, patience, relief, happiness, freedom, and a return to their true self.

The parable of the two debtors in Luke 7:40–47 becomes a teaching moment for Simon and a powerful lesson to us that "he who is forgiven little, loves little."

> And Jesus answered him, "Simon, I have something to say to you." And he replied, "Say it, Teacher." "A moneylender had two debtors: one owed five hundred denarii, and the other fifty. When they were unable to repay, he graciously forgave them both. So which of them will love him more?" Simon answered and said, "I suppose the one whom he forgave more." And He said to him, "You have judged correctly." Turning toward the woman, He said to Simon, "Do you see this woman? I entered your house; you gave Me no water for My feet, but she has wet My feet with her tears and wiped them with her hair. You gave Me no kiss; but she, since the time I came in, has not ceased to kiss My feet. You did not anoint My head with oil, but she anointed My feet with perfume. For this reason I say to you, her sins, which are many, have been forgiven, for she loved much; but he who is forgiven little, loves little."

Forgiveness isn't about forgetting the circumstances that caused our pain. It is impossible to forget, and thinking that we could ever do this is pure folly. Forgiveness isn't declaring that what happened to us is okay, for it isn't and it wasn't. We are not denying its negative effect or justifying the damaging actions of others; instead, we are releasing its negative hold upon us. Forgiveness isn't about reconciliation, either. This would certainly be a pleasant outcome, but it doesn't always happen, and our ability to forgive isn't dependent upon reconciling with those who harmed us. We don't control the emotions, decisions, and conduct of others any more than we can harness the universe. In fact, about the only thing we can control is ourselves—a herculean task in its own right that is often swing-and-miss. Many feel that forgiveness is incomplete if reconciliation doesn't occur, but forgiveness is all about what *we* do, not controlling what others do or don't do.

The purpose of forgiveness is to bring healing to our lives—a restored sense of well-being. It is a way of making us whole again and releasing the incredible burden we carry around in our heart. Forgiveness isn't contingent upon those who wronged us making the first move, for if that were the case, we could forever be locked into a prison of pain, waiting for others to fetch the key. Fortunately, forgiveness is something *we* do—a gift *we* give to ourselves whereby *we* release the hurts and grievances that cling to us like barnacles. We are the ones who hold the key to unlocking our own shackles.

In reality, it is far easier to latch onto our grudges with determined resolve as a way of making us feel less like a victim. Since we can't control others, nursing our grievances provides a sense of empowerment and defiance. Unfortunately, it is undeniably the worst response we could engender. It reminds me of the old home remedy of putting egg whites on burns—the exact wrong thing to do back in the day. Egg whites increase the risk of introducing dangerous bacteria into the wound, such as salmonella, that can create additional health concerns. Harboring painful hurts isn't the answer because it creates far more trouble for us. Our focus is diverted away from the present and back to the past. Sheltering our pain isn't the path Scripture encourages.

By letting go, I mean that we no longer allow our hurt to control us, rule us, or maintain its power over us. Forgiveness strips away its power so we can move from bondage to freedom. We make peace with our pain by consciously and constantly denying its power over us. Since it is a conscious decision, and one that flies in the face of revenge mentalities, it takes inner courage and strength. If we are unwilling to stand up to its quest for power, we are simply putting egg whites on burns in an attempt to feel less like a victim. This response, unfortunately, only tightens the noose and accomplishes the exact opposite of the freedom we so desperately desire and need. Freedom comes by releasing pain rather than holding on to it. To forgive means that we have reached a point where the offense no longer rules us—its power over us has been released, let go, and kicked out. Without its controlling influence, we are free to experience life in the Spirit.

Forgiveness falls into three main categories: forgiving God, forgiving ourselves, and forgiving others. We forgive God not because He has done anything wrong, but because we hold Him accountable for the bad things that happen to us. If He is all-powerful and all-knowing, then He is ultimately responsible for bad things happening to good people, or so the argument goes. When Martha's brother, Lazarus, died and lay in the tomb for four days, we sense a twinge of resentment in her response to the slow arrival of Jesus upon the scene: "Lord, if You had been here, my brother would not have died" (Jn. 11:21).

Forgiving God

Many carry deep resentment toward God for the unexplained tragedies in their life. "Why did God let my spouse die from cancer at such a young age? Why did God permit my child to be brutally murdered? Why did God allow my marriage to fall apart and end in divorce? Why did God sanction a natural disaster that caused so much damage and so many deaths?" We have all carried our wounds to the foot of His throne and questioned why we experience so much pain in this life. I know I did.

Raising questions like these is healthy, and any serious pursuit of God must deal with them. Though we may never obtain full answers to our questions in this mortal life, we know deep down that God is not guilty of anything, although He often takes the brunt of the blame. In this life, as Paul notes, "we see in a mirror dimly, but then face to face; now I know in part, but then I will know fully just as I also have been fully known" (1 Cor. 13:12). God is big enough, however, to allow us to crawl onto His lap, pound fists of rage upon His breast, and "be forgiven" by those with such limited understanding. By "forgiving Him," the hurt we so readily attribute to the all-powerful one is released. We free ourselves to live with the tension between our own finite understanding and His great mystery until the day we "know fully."

Disillusionment with God can be a genuine obstacle to the Spirit's work in our lives, and by crawling out from under its stubborn domination, we remove a very real barrier between ourselves and our Creator. In my own life, I wondered how God could take a dedicated young man whose sole desire was kingdom service and place such an arduous journey before him that it nearly snuffed out the flame altogether. My painful experiences simply didn't make sense to me. It would be five years before I could partake of communion again with any sense of spiritual integrity. My heart still struggles to sing like it once did, and yet, by forgiving God, I became deeper and more reflective. There is now depth and substance to my faith. My commitment is stronger than ever before. Though the process took its toll on me, I wouldn't change the ensuing result. He graciously allowed me to "forgive Him" because He knew I needed it, and it has made all the difference to me. I would not have been able to receive the Spirit's good work in my life without releasing the pain for which I held Him accountable.

Forgiving Ourselves

Forgiving ourselves is the second arena worth exploring. We are often harder on ourselves than we are on others, and this makes self-forgiveness much more difficult. With God, there is a mystery we cannot fully piece together, but when it comes to ourselves, we know what we did, why we did it, how we did it, its wrongful nature, its negative impact upon others, and we intentionally did it anyway. "How is that forgivable," we ask ourselves?

Some folks unfairly blame themselves and become overly critical of everything they do. They live in a prison of unrealistic expectations, constantly unable to forgive themselves for not measuring up. The opposite extreme exploits the "I am just human" excuse in order to avoid any inkling of responsibility. One is too hard on oneself, and the other is too easy. Balance is the key. In order to forgive ourselves, it is necessary that we recognize the harm we have perpetrated. After all, why would we need to forgive ourselves for something we don't recognize as wrong? Furthermore, it is essential that we love ourselves enough to extend forgiveness for our hurtful ways. Loving ourselves and forgiving ourselves are two sides of the same coin.

Because we see others as outside of ourselves, extending forgiveness seems easier. When it comes to self-forgiveness, however, we feel as though we are erasing a piece of ourselves. Outsiders act upon us, but our own actions arise from within us. We can more readily let go of what someone else has done to us because it is a part of the past—something out there, something beyond us. It is them, not me. Forgiving ourselves, on the other hand, feels like letting go of an essential aspect of our identity—losing something that we experienced so deeply. This time it is me, not them.

We tend to forgive to the degree that we love—a kind of proportionality factor. An unwillingness to forgive ourselves is essentially an unwillingness to love ourselves. We more easily forgive those with whom we have a loving, trusting relationship, but we rarely consider our need for a healthy, loving, and trusting relationship with our own self. We are also more willing to forgive those we will never see again or be in contact with, but we are stuck with ourselves—all the time. In a sense, we give ourselves permission to love God and others, but we withhold permission to love ourselves. This must change before forgiveness can take root.

Do you love you? Do you take care of the "me" relationship—not in a narcissistic manner, but in a wholesome way? We easily see the goodness in others; why not discover the goodness within ourselves? When others fail, we readily extend forgiveness. Why not love ourselves by forgiving our own failures? When we love everyone else but ourselves, the pain we experience is self-inflicted. We become slaves to the tyranny of our own unwillingness, which prevents us from becoming whole. Love yourself enough to forgive yourself. It is a precious gift waiting to be unwrapped.

Forgiving Others

Forgiving others is the final area of consideration. I have been a devout God-follower for many years, and you would think that I could extend forgiveness at the drop of a dime. Sometimes I can, and do, but most days, I don't. The struggle continues. I seem to be on a first-name basis with the ill-effects of unforgiveness from a physiological, emotional, and spiritual perspective. Yet, I have also experienced the positive results of letting go, including peace of mind, less stress, better relationships, greater compassion, more empathy, and the like. But with the distance I have journeyed over the years, I hoped I might be farther along.

This tells me two things. First, that true forgiveness is not so easy. Portraying forgiveness to be as simple as breathing is a tremendous disservice to those who truly desire to let go but struggle to do so. Forgiving deeply and wholly is often not a one-and-done phenomenon, but a lifetime of little choosings on our part. It's a way of living rather than a rush of hurried moments. It is like trying to lose weight by bouncing from one diet to the next in a constant up-and-down battle. The best way to lose weight, however, is to consider healthy eating as a new lifestyle—the new norm. When healthy eating and exercise become an essential part of our daily routine, greater success ensues over the long haul.

Secondly, releasing the hurt inflicted by others can sometimes be so difficult that I am not sure it can be accomplished apart from the Spirit's help. The kind of pain, hardship, and wrongdoing some people suffer is unimaginable. Humans can treat one another so poorly. Many maintain a private pain in their innermost being—a pain buried so deep that no one else knows but God. It is real, but it is hidden, and it bleeds internally. If we do not surface the pain and seek release, life becomes a façade built around our heart as a protective measure. Though I understand this unseen private pain, it makes me sad that so many fail to experience the full freedom forgiveness brings. Forgiving others, even those who have severely wounded us, is possible, but just as the Lord spoke to Zerubbabel in the Old Testament, it will come about "Not by might nor by power, but by My Spirit" (Zech. 4:6). To sustain a life of forgiveness, we need the Spirit's help.

Unfortunately, we mistakenly believe the process of forgiveness is designed entirely for someone else when it is really all about us. Maybe that is what trips us up—wanting others to pay for their crime of hurting us and feeling as though forgiveness provides a free pass. I have long ago stopped trying to be judge, jury, and executioner. That isn't my role—and even if it was, I don't possess the needed attributes to be fair in my application of justice. My role is to forgive as God desires, for He knows what is best for me. When I say that forgiveness is all about us, I mean that it releases the oppressive burden we carry.

Grudges, bitterness, unforgiveness, and revenge mentalities become a heavy load upon our shoulders. With such weight holding us down, it becomes difficult to move, walk, live, and breathe. Forgiveness allows us to lay the burden aside. Another metaphor is being caught in a sticky spider web that restricts our movement. Forgiveness allows us to cut the web away. A final illustration might be a toxin in our body that wreaks havoc on a cellular level. Specific drugs or eating in a healthy manner removes the toxin from our body so that we become healthy again. All of these images help us understand the freeing nature of forgiveness upon our lives.

How we respond to those who harm us is a choice left up to us. By forgiving others, we break free from past wounds that strap us down in the present. It is okay to feel the full range of emotions associated with wounding, for we are merely being human. By releasing its stranglehold over us, however, we are able to write the ending to our own story. Though forgiveness may be helpful to others, we are the primary benefactor, and in this way, it is all about us.

Our willingness to overlook a wrong against us is seen by some as a sign of weakness, but as Gandhi once said, "The weak can never forgive. Forgiveness is the attribute of the strong." Since forgiveness is one of the greatest forms of love, and since the love of God has already been poured into our hearts, it stands to reason that we already possess the capacity to forgive. Sometimes forgiveness can be extended quickly and fully, and at other times it takes years to realize the inner peace of letting go. Whether the path takes minutes or a lifetime, the journey itself is a sign of strength and courage.

Forgiveness is life-transforming and contains healing properties for ourselves and others. It has a way of opening up our hearts like a great big hug, whereby we embrace others and become more accepting, more understanding, and more empathetic. We identify with their struggles and recognize that their ups and downs are similar to our own. Forgiveness changes us and strengthens our compassion. It becomes a part of life—an integral part of our journey.

What follows Jesus' instruction to forgive seventy times seven is a parable about an unmerciful servant who reaps what he sows. He was forgiven much but was unwilling to forgive others, and he ultimately paid a heavy price for his harsh actions (Mt. 18:23–35):

> For this reason the kingdom of heaven may be compared to a king who wished to settle accounts with his slaves. When he had begun to settle them, one who owed him ten thousand talents was brought to him. But since he did not have the means to repay, his lord commanded him to be sold, along with his wife and children and all that he had, and repayment to be made. So the slave fell to the ground and prostrated himself before him, saying, "Have patience with me and I will repay you everything." And the lord of that slave felt compassion and released him and forgave him the debt. But that slave went out and found one of his fellow slaves who owed him a hundred denarii; and he seized him and began to choke him, saying, "Pay back what you owe." So his fellow slave fell to the ground and began to plead with him, saying, "Have patience with me and I will repay you." But he was unwilling and went and threw him in prison until he should pay back what was owed. So when his fellow slaves saw what had happened, they were deeply grieved and came and reported to their lord all that had happened. Then summoning him, his lord said to him, "You wicked slave, I forgave you all that debt because you pleaded with me. Should you not also have had mercy on your fellow slave, in the same way that I had mercy on you?" And his lord, moved with anger, handed him over to the torturers until he should repay all that was owed him. My heavenly Father will also do the same to you, if each of you does not forgive his brother from your heart."

Being a forgiving person is not only beneficial for us from a physiological, spiritual, and emotional perspective, it is what God-followers do and what God desires of us. The byproduct of a life profoundly touched by God is an overflow of love and forgiveness that spills into the hearts of others.

Give forgiveness a try, for as difficult as it may seem, its results make the process worthwhile.

Wisdom for the Journey

It is impossible to journey through life unscathed by the wrongdoing of others. Hurt is the inevitable result of being human and interacting with others. As injuries slither into your heart, be quick to forgive so the offense doesn't hold you hostage. Your first reaction may be to embrace revenge mentalities, but true healing comes through releasing the pain—through forgiveness. When we no longer carry the weight of unforgiveness in our heart, we journey with joy and contentment. Be a forgiving person by forgiving God, forgiving yourself, and forgiving others.

chapter eight

Forgotten Virtues

Sometimes I wonder if I am seeing things correctly, or if culture has shifted so dramatically that a simple surprise is turned into shock. I can't remember a time when civility and virtue were locked into such a neglected predicament. It may be that this sorry state of affairs has been with every generation and I am just now noticing, or it could be that forgotten virtues is becoming the new norm. It may be a little bit of both.

Treating Others Well

I am always taken back, for instance, when I enter a store, stroll up and down the aisles, and walk out without one employee ever saying hello, or in any way acknowledging my presence. I am just darn lucky, I suppose, to have been allowed to enter, and should be ever-grateful for the privilege of beholding their cherished goods. I rarely purchase anything at these kinds of shops, and I wonder how they stay in business. Many of them don't. Is it too much to ask for a simple smile, a greeting, or a friendly offer to help? I hardly think so.

Values, character, virtue, civility, and the like become a part of our lives when they are taught to us—or when they are modeled for us and expected of us. How can employees be counted upon to kindly greet a customer if they are never required to do so? How can children implement virtue if it is never modeled for them or expected of them by their parents? It is difficult to give what one does not possess. And yet, basic human decency is hoped for by all. Virtue can be learned, and it is something that makes our journey much more pleasant for ourselves and others.

Though we tolerate disinterested store employees who ignore us, we realize they are merely symptoms of a much larger issue. While nations, in the course of their history, endure periods of rest and unrest, the incivility in our national discourse has become untenable. Often, the way we interact with one another is downright shameful. There exists, in our modern world, an unprecedented hostility and desire to squash all dissent while branding opponents as unworthy of life itself.

In treating others so poorly, we end up discarding the very values we supposedly promote. Instead of healthy dialogue, we choose to demonize the other side. Basic respect seems nonexistent, as is the ability to engage in civil dialogue. Irony exists in the fact that, while our patience with one another may be at an all-time low, God continues to display enduring patience with the human race. The current level of vitriolic discourse is sad and unbecoming to our national unity and has surely affected our own efforts at civility. Realizing that difference and discourse are two sides of the same coin, Thomas Aquinas rightfully notes, "We must love them both: those whose opinions we share and those whose opinions we reject. For both have labored in search for their truth and both have helped us in the finding of our own."

By forgotten virtues, I am referring to such things as kindness, honesty, integrity, character, decency, civility, respect, saying "thank you," and "I am sorry." Life is a journey, but it is often *how* we journey that makes the difference. It isn't as though virtues don't exist, for they do, and many folks live by, and uphold, them. The problem is that we don't consistently see enough of them, and their significance may be waning as the politics of demonizing others takes center stage. It seems to me that if we restored forgotten virtues, our disagreements could be handled much more effectively.

I enjoy watching vintage television shows, such as *The Andy Griffith Show*, where the idyllic world of Mayberry seemed like a simpler place and family life was highly prized. Something strange happens to me as I watch the various episodes—I get teary-eyed when virtuous acts of human kindness come across the screen.

Episode one, season three of *The Andy Griffith Show* aired on October 1, 1962. Andy, the town sheriff, taught his son Opie to never tell a lie. When little Opie announces that he met a man while out in the woods who walks in the trees, jingles as if wearing bells, dons a shiny, silver hat, and blows smoke from his ears, he is accused of confusing a wild imagination with reality, and he is threatened with corporal punishment for not telling the truth. Though dejected, Opie is unwilling to denounce his story, and with pleading eyes asks, "Don't you believe me, Pa?" Andy gives Opie his assurance, and when Barney and Aunt Bee ask how he can believe such an obvious fabrication, Andy replies, "I do believe in Opie."

Still trying to make sense of it all, Andy goes for a walk in the woods where Opie claims to have seen his "imaginary" friend, and much to Andy's surprise, a telephone repair man comes down from the treetops, wearing a shiny, silver hat, jingling like bells, and introducing himself as Mr. McBeevee, the tangible confirmation of Opie's truth-telling. The scene touches my heart because Opie did the right thing by sticking with the truth, and Andy did the right thing by believing in the character of his son. That is virtue. That is decency. That is right, and it gets me all misty-eyed.

Why You Gotta Be So Mean?

On my bookshelf sits a small wooden block emblazoned with the words "Kindness Matters." Given to me by an individual who didn't experience kindness from me, I display the gift in a prominent place to remind me that every interaction of mine should be one of kindness. Taylor Swift, on her 2010 *Speak*

Now album, recorded the song "Mean" with the following lyrics: "And all you're ever gonna be is mean. Why you gotta be so mean?" Kindness really does matter, and we can disagree without being disagreeable. Kindness goes a long way toward healing relationships, getting our point across, and understanding the perspectives of others. This is virtue. This is decency. This is right. Even the Bible depicts kindness as worthy of pursuit, "Be kind to one another, tender-hearted, forgiving each other, just as God in Christ also has forgiven you" (Eph. 4:32), and I Corinthians 13:4, "Love is patient, love is kind. . ." If kindness is a scriptural virtue, we have to ask, "Why you gotta be so mean?"

Modeling Virtue

While teaching students in the classroom, I often share differing viewpoints for consideration. Years ago someone taught me a valuable lesson about respect that impacts how I go about presenting opposing perspectives. I imagine the proponent of that viewpoint sitting before me in the class, listening to every word, and ensuring that I present the topic with integrity. While I may vehemently disagree with the perspective, I have approached the matter with respect.

My approach to disparate viewpoints in the classroom is quite different than the story of a distant relative of mine who allowed her children to run roughshod over her. On one occasion she was even told to leave the dinner table so the dog could sit in her place. Despite her best efforts at being a mother, her children looked upon her with disdain. Their disrespect rang its final toll when she took her own life.

I was once asked to pastor a wonderful Quaker church in Iowa. Having been exploited so many times before by sanctimonious church leaders, I submitted an inquiry that must have seemed odd to them. The clerk of session responded, "Terry, we are Quakers, and we always honor our word." I couldn't believe what I was hearing. Here was a group of committed believers pursuing forgotten virtues and actually honoring their word. It was a breath of fresh air to my weary soul.

While in high school, a gentleman from my church invited me to attend a Harlem Globetrotters basketball exhibition. He bought my supper at a local hamburger joint beforehand, and in typical teenage fashion, I must have crammed five good-sized burgers into that bottomless-pit stomach of mine. Here was a man concerned about a teenager's welfare, saw something of value in me, and modeled kindness. After his coworkers finagled cans of soda out of the pop machine at work without paying for them, I am told that he would put his own change into the machine to cover their theft. That's the kind of man he was. That is kindness. That is integrity. That is inspirational!

Recently, a university Dean sent an email to students that read, "Wishing each of you a joyous holiday filled with peace, love, and prosperity. Best wishes for a healthy New Year!" Many students responded with kind words of appreciation and extended similar greetings to the sender. One student, who happened to also be the CEO of a hospital, wrote a stinging rebuke for using the term "joyous holiday" instead of Merry Christmas. I imagine it was his knee-jerk reaction to the extreme craziness of political correctness we put up with in today's world.

This was a secular university comprised of Jewish, Muslim, Christian, Mormon, and atheist students, along with a mixed bag of other religious beliefs. The Dean's holiday greeting was sincerely extended to all, and yet, this Christian student wrote a nastygram belittling the joyous greeting. It reminds me of those who ardently oppose the killing of another human being while being strident supporters of the death penalty. The incongruity is obvious to all. Maybe we should just celebrate Jerry Seinfeld's "Festivus for the Rest of Us" and call it a day, but even then, someone would be offended. Why couldn't this student have expressed his view with a kind note exemplifying Christian love instead of a rude reply in the name of Christ?

In 2016, the movie *Hacksaw Ridge* was released—a true story about a drafted soldier who refused to bear arms for religious reasons during WWII. Although he would later receive the Congressional Medal of Honor, his fellow soldiers initially ridiculed and ostracized him for his pacifist stance. During the Battle of Okinawa, however, he risked his own life, and without firing a single bullet, saved the lives of seventy-five men. His selfless act of bravery earned him the respect of his fellow soldiers. Virtue like this still exists, and we yearn to see it more often.

Kindness Matters

Has simple thoughtfulness also gone by the wayside? A daughter frequently brings her two-year-old son to visit her mother, and a mini-disaster ensues with toys strewn all over the place. She picks up her son to leave but never thinks to pick up the mess left behind by her tiny human tornado. This happens over and over again, even after she is politely asked to help. Unfortunately, the pleas for thoughtfulness fall on deaf ears. This disrespectful behavior reminds me of my teenage years when my parents asked why I didn't help mow the lawn given how tall the grass had grown. I told them that I didn't even notice such things, and I apologized. From that day forward, my assistance with lawn mowing was routinely offered.

I once dated a woman from the South who taught me that opening car doors for women was a courteous thing to do. It has now been ingrained in me, and the other day, while taking my mother out to lunch, I opened her car door as a matter of respect and kindness. Manners can be taught, and they can also be "caught" when modeled by others. I never returned shopping carts to their parking lot bins, thinking that the store paid people to do that—and besides, I had a busy schedule to keep. Now, I am careful to put the cart in its rightful place as an act of kindness. Sometimes I even corral stray carts left behind by others. No longer do I frantically scope out the shortest, most strategic checkout line; instead, I readily allow others to go ahead of me. I find myself looking to perform random acts of kindness that bless others. It is amazing how a little kindness releases stress and makes you a nicer person. After all, as Taylor Swift notes, "Why you gotta be so mean?"

Kindness has that effect upon us—the ability to soften our heart and move us on the inside. Jesus was so stirred by the needs of others that he experienced a visceral reaction in his gut. The New Testament word "compassion" literally means to be moved in the bowels, the place where strong emotion is often felt. Jesus loved so deeply that it unsettled his stomach. He could be strong and stand up to the religious elite of his day, as in Matthew 23, where he lambasts the Pharisees for their external focus and warped religious perspective, or when he upended the tables of the moneychangers who were exploiting worshippers for profit, but most often, he was soft and kind, and others found him to be winsome and caring.

When a woman was caught in adultery, for instance, and brought before him for condemnation, he challenged the false piety of her accusers and responded in kindness, "I do not condemn you" (Jn. 8:11). The compassionate heart of Jesus is also revealed in Matthew 11:28–30: "Come to Me, all who are weary and heavy-laden, and I will give you rest. Take My yoke upon you and learn from Me, for I am gentle and humble in heart, and you will find rest for your souls. For My yoke is easy and My burden is light." Being kind to others often means stepping into their mess, and they can be very messy. We exhibit greater kindness when we walk in their shoes and try to see the world through their eyes.

The Priority of Character

Let me touch upon two key virtues that make our journey more graceful and gracious. Character is the first virtue, for it is foundational to so many other excellent qualities. Magnificent cruise ships roll into beautiful ports of call and though we marvel at their size, what lies below the waterline is more important than that above. Without a solid hull to withstand the pressures of the sea, the ship would take on water and sink. A breach in the hull could be disastrous. It is the same with gigantic icebergs floating in icy waters. Considering their mammoth size and elegance of white, we rarely think of what extends below the waterline—their most dangerous feature, and what breached the hull of the Titanic causing its deathly descent to the ocean floor.

When we talk about character, we are talking about building below the waterline and strengthening that which is so essential to keeping us afloat. Character is who we are when no one is looking. It is the consistent alignment between our words and our behavior. The Greek word for character refers to an engraved mark. Character, then, is something that is engraved upon us—an internal set of principles and moral qualities that bridges the gap between what we say and do with who we are as individuals. Recognizing the significance of this engraved mark, Scripture encourages the appointment of elders within the church who are of good character. This makes perfect sense. Surely we want, and need, spiritual leaders who are engraved from within with a consistent set of good principles and moral qualities—those who have built a strong foundation below the waterline.

Character comes under scrutiny when our behavior is in conflict with our values. Others see this, and trust is destroyed. When we publicly condemn certain behavior but engage in it ourselves, we have a character problem. When our actions and words are out of alignment, we function from a place of internal disharmony. The cracks in our hull begin taking on water, and nobody wants to be on that ship.

Our character is tested when we are forced to choose between our values and what might personally profit us. These testings become defining moments, for the choice we make reveals the engraver's mark upon us. Jesus experienced this very situation in Matthew 4:1–11.

After being baptized, Jesus was led by the Spirit into the wilderness to be tested. His public ministry was about to begin, and this test would unveil his character. A test reveals what we know and is a way to get on the outside what is on the inside. Fasting for forty days and nights will make anyone hungry and vulnerable, and though Jesus was tested multiple times over this period, Scripture records three specific incidents where a lapse of character could have easily occurred. Much could be said about his wilderness experience, but for our purposes, suffice it to say that Jesus passed all tests with flying colors.

The Father was calling forth from Jesus what was already present on the inside. Were there cracks below the waterline? Jesus' outward response to his wilderness testing was a direct result of his internal character. He revealed on the outside what was on the inside. If I had been in his shoes, I am afraid that my results would not have been so positive. When faced with a choice between expediency and doing the right thing, Jesus always chose the latter. He successfully drew upon the deeply held principles and moral qualities that guided his life. There was harmony between his inner life and his outer life— who he was and what he did. That's what testing reveals—what is below the waterline.

Every day we are faced with our own tests, and while they may not involve a lonely forty-day fast, they certainly involve critical choices between our values and our desire to advance self-interest. They become defining moments that forge character and reveal what we are made of—testing for cracks below the waterline. Life is full of these wilderness moments. What is the engraver's mark on your own heart? Will you pass the test with flying colors?

Christians come with varying depths and commitment levels. In other words, the hull of some ships are made of different strengths and thicknesses. This means that many pass simple tests that don't require much of them— where the waves of life may be challenging, but not daunting. However, when the test becomes too great and the heat in the kitchen becomes too hot, they leave or give in. These are the plants that spring up in Jesus' parable of the sower (Mt. 13) and are scorched by the sun because they have no roots. During the Nazi uprising of WWII, two main German churches existed (Lutheran and Catholic). Under the pressures of the Third Reich, a significant choice stood before both churches—a choice between a principled stand for values or a choice for self-interest and self-preservation. Unfortunately, they gave in far too often, and even today, this cultural stain colors Germany's past.

When people let us down, disillusionment and sarcasm can easily set in. It happened to me. I have been cheated out of thousands of dollars, lied to, and lied about. As a pastor, I have experienced the shadow side of church life, and it isn't pretty. I am not picking on others, for I have failed so many tests that I often wonder how God puts up with me. I not only become disappointed in those who let me down, I am also a terrible self-critic when I let myself down. Yet, I have put in the hard work of building below the waterline. Inch by inch, the hull of my ship is stronger today than it was yesterday. I seem to fail less often, have grown in my faith, become stronger and better, and am now able to navigate deeper waters instead of floating in the kiddie pool.

That's the thing about character—additive in nature and built over time, it is forged through the critical choices we make during those defining moments in life. The road that leads to steadfast character is fraught with trials, testing, tribulation, suffering, and failure. This winding path has a way of breaking us down, in a good way, so that what is left is a hull able to withstand the pounding of deep seas as we sail through life. We often learn more from our failures than our successes, and though extremely painful, the result is strength below the waterline.

Character rests squarely on the shoulders of our values, and values are built into us, taught to us, caught by us, and learned from experience. We dare not neglect the power of parenting in this regard during young, impressionable years. During my junior and senior high school adventures, it was the church youth group that became so instrumental in setting my life with deeply held values. I am forever grateful for the church's influence. Family and church can be powerful pathways for planting deeply rooted values that yield a plentiful harvest in later years.

Our habits also affect character, for what we do and how we do it on a daily basis is often an expression of what we consider to be important. I once worked with a youth pastor who equated his big personality with being big in character. Nothing could be further from the truth, as his booming personality was utilized to cover up the embezzlement of church funds. Personality is different than character. Personality is more like the *style of ship*—a sailboat, a cruise ship, or a speedboat—whereas character focuses on the *strength of the hull* below the waterline regardless of the type and size of boat.

Self-monitoring helps to ensure that our outside activities align with our internal values. Since character is based on values, it is essential that we engage in a process of personal introspection. Self-inquiry asks, "Who am I? What kind person do I want to be? What matters to me? What do I stand for?" These types of questions help align our life with values that matter. If honesty matters to you, for instance, then your speech will align with your values, and over time, this virtue will be tested on numerous occasions. Will you choose honesty, or will you fudge the truth? What kind of man or woman will you be in such circumstances, especially when fudging the truth personally benefits you? What choice will you make? Will you pass the test? What will be drawn forth from you? What will your character reveal?

The Priority of Humility

The second key virtue worth mentioning is humility, a quality that is counter-intuitive to a modern mindset that places greater importance on self-sufficiency, success at all cost, fame, fortune, looks, accomplishments, and self-adulation. Displaying humility in this environment is challenging, and we often feel like fish out of water. Humility can wrongfully be interpreted as a glaring weakness, when it is actually a sign of inner strength. Humble individuals are often viewed as weak, passive, insecure, submissive, wimpy, and unable to stand up for themselves. In reality, the exact opposite is true. Humble people are typically self-assured, confident, competent, strong, and secure. Their confidence is such that they seek to help others without any unction to brag about themselves or engage in self-promotion.

We don't view Jesus as a weak, passive, insecure individual, and yet, he describes himself in Matthew 11:29 as "gentle and humble in heart." The word "meek," a military term, referred to the taming of horses. Wild horses from the mountains were captured and trained for various uses. The best of the best were trained for war. Picture a large, muscled stallion, filled with spirit, courage, and unbridled power now brought under the control of a trained rider. They had been "meeked" while still possessing their amazing power. Meek individuals know when to be assertive and when to lay low, when to rise up and defend values and when to allow others the spotlight. Their emotions do not hijack their reason, for meek individuals operate under the control of the Spirit master. Much to our surprise, meekness isn't some wide-eyed, insecure, wimpy person out picking daisies, but a chiseled stallion filled with spirit, courage, and power under the control of God's Spirit.

This changes our picture of meekness, doesn't it? Instead of something to avoid, we now realize it is a virtue worth pursuing. 1 Peter 2:23 has this to say about Jesus: "and while being reviled, He did not revile in return; while suffering, He uttered no threats, but kept entrusting Himself to Him who judges righteously." This is power under control—knowing when to move with thunderous response and when to remain silent. His humble side is also seen in Philippians 2:5–9:

> Have this attitude in yourselves which was also in Christ Jesus, who, although He existed in the form of God, did not regard equality with God a thing to be grasped, but emptied Himself, taking the form of a bond-servant, and being made in the likeness of men. Being found in appearance as a man, He humbled Himself by becoming obedient to the point of death, even death on a cross.

Humility isn't low self-esteem but rather a self-understanding that translates into power under control, just like Paul practiced in his own life and urged others to practice: "Now, I, Paul, myself urge you by the meekness and gentleness of Christ—I who am meek when face to face with you, but bold toward you when absent!" (2 Cor. 10:1). Jesus taught the same thing in Matthew 5:5: "Blessed are the gentle (humble or meek), for they shall inherit the earth."

We easily recognize *non-humility* when we see it—it is called pride. Pride is typically thought of in the singular, as though it were merely one item, but it may be best to see the plurality of pride, for it manifests itself in so many subtly different forms such as arrogance, vanity, conceit, pretentiousness, boasting, egotism, snobbery, self-righteousness, dominance, disdain, contempt, never accepting help from others, and the like. Pride isn't one narrow, singular offense, but a multiplicity of transgressions, and it may be more appropriate to speak of the many vices of pride. This not only accounts for the many evil faces of pride but also allows for healthy aspects of pride to exist such as self-respect, self-confidence, and pride in family, church, and country.

If meekness is power under control, then the fruit of such control produces the exact opposite of the vices of pride. Simply put an "un" in front of each vice, and we get a clearer picture of humility—un-vanity, un-conceit, un-pretentiousness, un-boasting, un-egotism, un-snobbery, un-self-righteous-ness, un-dominance, un-disdain, un-contempt, and the like.

It takes a healthy view of yourself to express humility with these "un" characteristics. In many ways, humility begins with self-acceptance as opposed to self-aggrandizement. Too often, we set before us the goal of perfection, and when we don't attain this impossible standard, we berate ourselves and feel as though we don't measure up. Well, I might as well break it to you now—welcome to the human race. You fail. I fail. We all fail. It is called being human, so we might as well get used to it. Oh, and don't worry, everyone else is in the same boat as you. One of the most damning things we can do is hold ourselves to the impossible standard of perfection. When will we finally understand that our self-esteem should not be tied to our looks, our finances, our personality, our accomplishments or shortcomings, or our past? Some folks walk perilously close to the cliffs of depression and their self-esteem bottoms out simply because they didn't get the expected number of likes on their social media posts. How sad!

Attaching our self-esteem to temporal and constantly shifting targets makes for one nauseous ride through life. Healthy self-esteem, on the other hand, is securely attached to God, and since we are created in His image, we both reveal and reflect our Creator. From our head to our toes, we are forever grounded in Him. We are loved by, for, and in ourselves by the lover of our souls. There is no need for self-esteem issues, for we are not beneath anyone. Instead, we are equal with others in glory, purpose, and being, each shining forth and reflecting the Creator. It is time we embrace our humanness!

Once we firmly grasp that our very DNA traces back to our loving Creator, there is no longer a need to strive for perfection and compare ourselves to others. Our intrinsic worth comes from being securely attached to Him. We are what everyone else is, the beautiful creation and image of God. Humble people don't engage in pretense, aren't overly self-conscious, insecure, and have no need for competition with others in this space we call life. The opinion of others doesn't ruin their day or inflate their ego. In other words, they know who they are, who their Creator is, are comfortable in their own skin, and have arrived at self-acceptance. With open arms, they embrace their humanness, warts and all, and perfection is no longer the impossible standard that guides their life. Rather than being a sign of weakness, humility is an outward sign of inner strength and self-acceptance.

With its full array of ups and down, this life can be challenging to our pursuit of humility and our quest to return forgotten virtues to their rightful place. What follows are some key tips for practicing humility and restoring forgotten virtues.

Mitigating the Vices of Pride

Mitigating the vices of pride comes easier when the art of gratitude is practiced—when we value other people and express appreciation to, and for, them. This takes the focus off of ourselves and places it on others. Keeping a gratitude journal can be a great way of tracking our many blessings. Each year I focus on one key aspect of living that will bless others and improve my relationship with God. One year, my key concept was gratitude, and I made a special effort to say "thank you," write letters of appreciation, give credit where credit was due, and offer intentional prayers of gratitude to God for the many ways I am blessed. Humble people are grateful people, and gratitude reinforces the practice of humility.

In addition to gratitude, exchanging judgment for compassion also assists in the practice of humility. As much as I think my way of "seeing" is typically correct, I realize that I am filled with all sorts of prejudices, contradictions, and inaccurate perspectives. For humility to take root and grow, I must confront my many prejudices and erroneous viewpoints, and yet, my firm grip begrudgingly refuses to release them, knowing that I will be expected to venture away from what has been my treasured and longstanding security blanket. Releasing judgment and grabbing hold of compassion, however, is what I must do. So, I loosen my grip on comparing myself with others. I loosen my grip on my expectations of life and others. And, most importantly, I loosen my grip on what I expect of myself. It is a painful release but also a freeing release—a feeling of fear, pain, and indescribable joy, all at the same time.

By confronting my prejudices, even toward myself, I let go of the many trappings that hold me back. Now that my hands are free, I grab on to positive things that promote humility, like self-compassion, gratitude, service, self-acceptance, and focusing on others. My fear was in letting go of my security blanket. My joy was in living life without one. By confronting our prejudices, we become more compassionate toward others and ourselves.

Another way to pursue humility is to practice "otherliness" or maintaining an outward gaze rather than an inward focus. When life becomes all about me, then I have surely missed what the good news of Scripture is all about. The practice of "otherliness" means that I put others first, listen, and become situationally aware so that I might be a joy and blessing to others. Humble people are not self-referential but rather self-aware, situationally aware, teachable, open to feedback, and realize they are not the center of the universe. Their gaze is always focused outward toward others. They can do this because they are comfortable in their own skin and securely attached to their Creator.

Along with an outward focus comes a spirit of service. Service has a gentle way of reminding us that humility matters. Unfortunately, there are those who never give a dime to charity, never freely share a moment of their time to assist others, or offer their talents without cost for the benefit of those in need. This is in stark contrast from the practice of Jesus, who fed 5,000 hungry mouths on a mountainside for free, healed others without charging a penny, and who demonstrated the spirit of service even to his disciples as he wrapped a towel around his waist and began washing their feet.

A rank-and-file servant would have typically washed their feet prior to eating the Passover meal together. Yet, none was available on this occasion and the disciples wouldn't lower themselves to perform the menial task, so Jesus took it upon himself to serve them, and he thereby demonstrated the power of humility. After displaying a servant's heart, Jesus states in John 13: 14–16, "If I then, the Lord and the Teacher, washed your feet, you also ought to wash one another's feet. For I gave you an example that you also should do as I did to you. Truly, truly, I say to you, a slave is not greater than his master, nor is one who is sent greater than the one who sent him." An outward focus and a spirit of service enhances our journey toward humility. Restoring and practicing forgotten virtues makes us kinder and gentler on the busy highway of life. After all, "Why you gotta be so mean?"

Wisdom for the Journey

In our trek through life, it is often *how* we journey that makes the road more or less enjoyable. By restoring forgotten virtues, we make the trip more pleasant for ourselves and others. Soak in the wonder surrounding you and discover awe in the beauty of others. Cultivate forgotten virtues by building below the waterline so that when the testing of life comes your way, solid character will be drawn forth from you. Cultivate humility with a secure attachment to your Creator so others will experience you as kind, grateful, civil, loving, service-minded, and other-oriented. You will not only be better able to live with yourself and others, but also with the great mystery of life itself.

chapter nine

A Different Kind of Me

Life has changed for me over the years in so many ways—some for the good and some for the bad. I am not quite sure what to make of many of the changes, for they don't readily fall into my positive and negative categories. With the dizzying speed of life nipping at my heels, I don't have time most days for such pondering. I get caught up on life's frenzied freeway and ride white-knuckled with the flow of traffic. It is stressful. Exiting the fast lane for some cherished down time puts a smile on my face, slows my heart rate, and releases stress. I yearn for it.

The vast changes in technology, for instance, have mushroomed during my lifetime. The computer club photograph in my high school yearbook consists of a few students standing by a great big box—the computer. I had no idea a computer club even existed, and all of my college papers were turned in using an electric typewriter. My first doctoral degree was completed on a Leading Edge Model D computer with DOS operating software and a 9-pin dot matrix printer that I upgraded to an 18-pin model. Things are much different these days with smaller, more powerful computers, an Internet, and even cell phones that act as a camera, recording device, clock, calculator, flashlight, gaming apparatus, music player, movie screen, web browser, and so forth. The convenience of technology makes my life a little easier. I can't imagine reverting back to the days of punch cards, mimeograph machines, typewriters, multi-party telephone lines, and the like. Though technology has its drawbacks, I can handle this kind of change.

Every time I travel back to my home town in Iowa, I take a little drive down memory lane. I want to see where I grew up, the houses I lived in, the schools I attended, and the familiar baseball fields where little boys dream. I seek to remember and treasure the past. In elementary school, I was voted captain of patrol and one of only two students to represent my school at the all-city track meet (I placed fourth). This was where I received my immunization shots, played tetherball, wrinkly Mr. Campbell was the principal, and a classmate experienced the death of his sister. But the physical remnant of my past is no longer standing. The city tore my elementary school down. Fortunately, I took pictures before it was demolished and spent time in the parking lot reminiscing about years gone by.

My junior high school has been demolished and replaced with soccer fields. The church of my youth removed the sanctuary pews and transitioned to a contemporary service. My home town is not the same. Schools have consolidated, roads are deteriorating, downtown is untidy, and, quite frankly, I like the way it used to be so much better.

Constant Change

Change happens. We all experience it—some for the good and some for the bad. My father once said that children step on your toes when they are young and step on your heart when they are older. My mind imagines a little girl placing her tiny feet on top of daddy's shoes and dancing about the room with him in pure delight. Grown children, however, go about walking on their own two feet while parents are often forgotten or neglected.

My children are grown, and I have experienced the "step on your heart" phenomenon my father referenced. Now that they are on their own, things aren't the same, and as much as I anticipated the empty nest syndrome, I am still reeling from its wake. I now know firsthand what my father was talking about. It is painful at times, but it is change that I must deal with, as millions of other mothers and fathers have had to do. I wish I was more mature in my younger days so I didn't step on dad's heart, but as he used to say, "You can't put an old head on young shoulders." Blessed wisdom from a simple, down-to-earth, blue-collar repairman. He has since passed on, another change to cope with, and I miss him dearly.

Intellectually I grasp that change occurs and, in one sense, that it must occur. I get it. Yet, I struggle emotionally. My elementary school was demolished, and though I understand why, I experienced a loss. My hometown is not the same, and though I understand the economic issues surrounding its decline, I wish it wasn't that way. It is this emotional element that is most difficult to bear.

You know what else has changed over the years? Me. I am still me, but a different kind of me. Some days I like the different kind of me and am grateful for the changes, and other days not so much, wondering if I should revert back to the way I once was. As difficult as change is for some, I find it much easier to identify and deal with external developments such as technology and school closings than to figure out internal changes.

The River Flows

The ancient philosopher Heraclitus spoke of ever-present change and noted that we cannot step into the same river twice, meaning that when we put our foot into the river, pull it out, and dip it in a second time, we are not stepping into the same river since the original water has already flowed past. The very nature of life is ever-present change—a river constantly flowing. Change happens because of us, in spite of us, to us, and without us; there is not much we can do about it. We live in a time when change is so rapid that reinventing ourselves is a necessary and constant adjustment, not to mention an added stressor to life.

What is difficult to ascertain, however, is how I have changed over the years. In reflecting upon my own metamorphosis, I think intently about the kind of person I am today compared to the person I was, want to be, and should be. Have you ever taken the time to think about you—how you have changed, what kind of person you want to be, or should be in light of who you are today? I do. I think about it a great deal. Life is an experienced teacher, and its lessons are often learned the hard way. There is much to ponder.

Positive Change

One way I have positively changed over the years is my ability to critically think through issues and evaluate the various options available. My dearth of experience hampered me in my younger days, not to mention my lack of interest in doing so. Now, with significant education under my belt and years of experience at both failing and succeeding, I know what questions to ask and how to assess or create alternatives. I see potential pitfalls and am well-versed in creating strategic pathways for success. This is a positive change in my life. I listened to the wisdom of experience and the advice arising from failure. Now, others look to me for assistance in sorting through issues and moving forward. I like this change. It makes me feel good that I can offer support to others when called upon.

Tolerance of divergent viewpoints is another aspect of my life that has changed for the better. Listening to perspectives in stark contrast to my own is something I enjoy. Previously, listening to others was largely about noticing kinks in their armor, faults in their logic, and mentally preparing for how I could persuade them toward a superior view. Their outlook, in my mind, was merely a competing and deficient paradigm. Nowadays, I seek to learn, understand, empathize, and pursue win-win outcomes. More importantly, I listen to their passion and why their perspective is so important to them. It tells me a great deal about who they are, and as I get to know them as persons, not viewpoints, greater empathy arises. It causes me to better love them and reconsider my own view. This change brings me joy, and I embrace it wholeheartedly. I have matured and become a better person so others' experience of me can be positive. I have changed for the good in a million ways and am grateful for God's patience despite my slow learning curve. I am different than I was. The river has flowed by, yet, I have become a different kind of me—a gentler, kinder me.

Negative Change

As much as I have improved for the good, there are many changes that are not so positive. I am, and always will be, a work in progress—always journeying toward living in a manner worthy of my Creator while never fully arriving at my destination. In fact, I think this is how God intended it, that we journey with Him. In one sense, life is a long walk with God, and we experience Him best when we are moving, climbing, encountering hills, valleys, mountains, ravines, and obstacles. The journey also comes with the enjoyment of shade trees, resting places, refreshing water, friendship, and communion with the living God.

Sometimes I wish there were more shade trees and less sticker-filled ravines, but that type of thinking is short-sighted. We seek to jettison the very things God uses to change us, for they are often painful. It would mean, however, doing away with the journey itself. We need the journey, for it is how God shapes us, leads us toward maturity, and how we experience Him. It is difficult to experience the full satisfaction of a classic sports car, or any car for that matter, just by sitting in it. The greater thrill comes from driving it.

A not-so-positive change in my life has to do with cynicism. Like a war-torn soldier coming home from the front, I have seen and experienced so much during my years in ministry that I feel a bit shell-shocked—an open door for sarcasm to enter my life. The idealism of my youth has vanished. This isn't unusual, as adolescents grow up to realize the world is much more complex than they had ever imagined. At times I prefer the days of my youth where we frolicked as cowboys and Indians in the ditch behind my house or played baseball with the neighborhood kids. No worries—just simpler times.

Unfortunately, any idealism I had of the church quickly waned as my experience grew. Church was important to me as a kid. It not only kept me out of trouble while in junior and senior high school, it actually mattered to me. Church is where God became a reality in my life and where I first sensed His presence. It was instrumental in shaping me and calling forth my commitment to serve in full-time pastoral ministry. I am grateful for its formative impact in my life.

I suspect, however, that fading idealism has infected more Christians than we might imagine. Many are exiting the church at an alarming rate because they can no longer tolerate the conflict, backbiting, hypocrisy, power plays, judgmental attitudes, and the like. They still love God but strongly dislike the current state of church affairs. As a teenager, I remember lying in bed listening to dad speaking softly with mom upon arriving home from the monthly board meeting. It was late and they didn't want me to hear, but I could make out the fact that drama and church board meetings were intricately connected.

On one occasion, our youth group raised $500 to purchase a foosball table, the "in" thing at the time. Since we raised all the money ourselves, the funds weren't coming from the church coffers. One board member was upset that we were purchasing the game table and made a big stink about it. I am uncertain what the real issue was—whether he felt it was a waste of money, didn't want such "worldly" games housed within hallowed walls, or wanted the money spent differently—but I do remember from my father's late-night whisperings that it was a source of contention. We got our foosball table, but at what cost? Tension arose between board members over a lousy table game, and the seeds of disillusionment were planted in the life of a young man whose tender heart was tugging at the calling of God.

A Front Row Seat

As a pastor and senior executive in Christian higher education, I have had a front row seat to the very things that cause good people to drop out of organized religion. While at an outdoor church function, a young lady with tattoos and piercings all over her body approached me. Knowing that I was the pastor and attempting to shock me, she stated, "I can't stand organized religion." I gently replied, "I know. I can't either." It wasn't the response she anticipated, but it prompted a healthy conversation about the shortcomings of the church and the heart of Christianity. I understood her disillusionment and pain. In fact, I bore the brunt of this as a pastor, having been cheated, lied to, scorned, manipulated, slandered, yelled at, shunned, called Satan, and the like. The stories are numerous, funny, and sometimes unbelievable. Each time I endured such ill behavior, a piece of my heart was being stripped away and replaced with concrete. Cynicism worked hard to become a permanent fixture in my life.

Upon arriving at my second full-time pastorate, a female parishioner instructed me to become best friends with her husband. He was loosely connected to the church and my role, as relayed to me, was to be his best friend and lead him to a closer relationship with God. Although I really liked this couple, her husband and I did not become best buddies; that is something you cannot force upon individuals. But it was the Christmas gifts I received from them that revealed her disappointment in me. The first year of my tenure, I received a box of steaks—a substantial gift for a young, poor pastor. Those were, after all, the days when you prayed that some gracious family would invite you to lunch after the morning service (and pay for it, of course). The second year of my tenure, I received a fruit basket. The third year, I received nothing.

It was nice to receive gifts of appreciation from loving parishioners during the Christmas holidays, but in this instance, the steaks loudly proclaimed, "I am glad you are here, Pastor. Now go be the best friend of my husband and change him into a godly Christian man for me." The fruit basked screamed, "You are doing a lousy job of changing my husband. I am disappointed that you haven't met my expectation. Now get on with it." When the Christmas gifts ceased, the clear signal was, "You have failed to meet my expectation and are a bad pastor. You haven't changed my husband, and I am done with you."

This is how organized religion seems to work out for some folks. Church is exciting for a time, and it meets a deep need in their life. It is the season for steak. Then life happens, they experience the shadow side of congregational life and the initial excitement wanes. This is the season of disillusionment—the season for fruit. Over time, as the fruit dries up and barrenness sets in, they are left with nothing. No steak, no fruit, only disappointment.

I could feel the change stirring within, from steak, to fruit, to nothing, but I didn't know how to deal with it, and most days I didn't want to. My "I love God with all my heart and want to serve Him" attitude didn't seem to cut it, and the protective barrier provided by such a mindset quickly deteriorated. Time and maturity have brought about a more reasoned perspective. The scars remain, but my attitude has changed. I no longer view difficult circumstances with such cynicism, and instead, realize how important they are to my growth. I now have a better understanding of ministry, people, relationships, church dynamics, and the like. I also have a better understanding of myself.

I wish I could report that my sarcasm has completely disappeared, but it hasn't. Though diminished, and I have greatly matured, I wrestle with its damning presence in my life more than I care to admit. I am not an eternal optimist, but I have moved from sarcasm to realism. Like a pendulum, I swing from seasons of realism to flashes of optimism and back to moments of sarcasm. I have changed from the young idyllic me to a realistic me with short stints in both optimism and sarcasm. Though I much prefer the youthful, without a care in the world me, I skidded off the road into sarcasm, found it wanting, and have climbed out of the perilous pit into the world of realism. It's a journey—remember?

A philosophy I adhere to maintains, "When life kicks you in the butt, make sure it kicks you forward." Hey, now there is a bit of optimism shining through! This philosophy has served me well. When you get kicked so many times like I have, veering into sarcasm seems inevitable. While my backside is sore and bruised, I know that sarcasm, as fun as it is sometimes, is not a long-term solution for genuinely experiencing God. I needed to ensure that life kicked me forward.

Everyone Has a Story

Everyone has a story to tell, and I suspect that you have been kicked around, too. You may be disillusioned with organized religion and a current member of the Church Alumni Association. Immeasurable physical or emotional anguish may have knocked you to your knees and become an unwanted bedfellow. Pain is an inevitable reality in this world and seems to hurt more when it comes from the people we love and invest in or when something is taken from us, like a loved one, when we believed God was perfectly capable of sparing us from such agony.

Life is full of changes. Some we bring on ourselves, but others just happen with no reasonable explanation to give. As you survey your life, you can probably identify many positive ways you have changed over the years. You like the new you. On the other hand, you can probably highlight areas where bitterness, anger, sarcasm, disillusionment, you name it, has set in. You don't like what it has done to you. Its ugly presence is unhealthy, and you don't know how to rid yourself of it, or even want to. Sometimes we enjoy wallowing in self-pity as a protective blanket insulating us from further harm. Unfortunately, it is not a long-term solution to wholeness.

Some years ago, I attended a retreat where the author of several books on spiritual formation led the church in quieting our hearts so we could commune with God. She shared the story of blind Bartimaeus sitting alongside the road who hears that Jesus is passing by and cries out, "Jesus, Son of David, have mercy on me!" We were asked to meditate on this story, consider our own needs, and place ourselves in the shoes of the blind man.

After a time of reflection, she asked participants to declare their own cry to Jesus. As others shared what they would have said to the itinerant prophet, I realized that I wasn't even at that point in my life. Spiritually speaking, I couldn't cry out. I couldn't stand. I couldn't speak. I was unable to form words, articulate a sentence, let alone diagnose my own illness. I could only sit by the wayside hoping that Jesus would somehow come close enough to notice me, for I had no ability to raise my voice. I have walked where the sting of disappointment is so sharp that the only thing you can do before the Father is groan deeply from within, or mumble "Oh God" while struggling to breathe. Been there, done that, and don't like it one bit.

Wouldn't it be nice if I possessed a magic wand that could turn all of life's circumstances into positive and happy experiences that bypass the difficult and painful change in our lives? Dream on! We have to deal with the fact that change occurs whether we like it or not, whether we approve of it or not, and whether its outcome is positive or negative. I am sorry, but that's just the way it is.

Sometimes folks get perturbed when they discover that I don't have all the answers and can't walk on water. I have met pastors who truly enjoy being the "go-to" person—the one who "speaks for God" and doles out spiritual directives. Many have the training and experience to be effective, but others simply enjoy the power rush. Counseling, for instance, is one of those areas where I feel underprepared. Sure, I can, and do, offer a certain level of wisdom, but I lack essential training in the subject to go much deeper. Recommending others who are better qualified is beneficial for the seeker and prevents me from wading into waters too deep. Unfortunately, some ministers simply quote a few well-known Bible passages for everything that ails us and dumb down complex issues while telling us we need to do more to receive God's blessings. It is shameful and says more about the psychological needs of the minister than the seeker.

I readily admit that my answers these days are few and my questions are many. That doesn't stop me from loving God and living for Him. I continue the journey, because it is in the journey that I experience God, and wherever that path takes me, I want more than anything to know the reality of His presence in the depths of my being. Is it okay to *not* know all the answers? Absolutely! An important element of successful Christian living is the ability to walk closely with God amidst the ambiguities of life that swirl about like a shaken snow globe—to somehow reach beyond all that we *don't know* and still follow hard after God. After all, it is a journey of faith.

Self-Examination

Though I am not the "answer man," a few insights from my journey may prove helpful to your own travels. Recently, I was fortunate to reconnect with a high school friend from over thirty years ago. I commented, "Been a long time since high school, hasn't it?" to which the reply came, "Heck yes. I look in the mirror and see somebody else, not me."

Looking in the mirror has a way of revealing what is. Yet, it is a positive thing to do. For some folks, every time they walk in front of a mirror, they pause to admire themselves in vain glory. That kind of mirror-watching is useless, unless of course we really do have a piece of broccoli stuck between our front teeth. The reflective nature of mirrors helps us to view ourselves more accurately. In a similar vein, examining our lives helps us in the evaluation process.

Self-examination acts like a mirror, not for vanity's sake, but for essential introspection. In reality, I don't believe we do this enough or to the depth that is truly helpful. For many, the extent of self-examination is an annual, superficial New Year's resolution that rarely exhibits the depth required on a journey to wholeness.

Prior to participating in the Lord's Supper, Paul urges the Corinthians to examine themselves so they don't partake in an unworthy manner. This is mirror work. In 2 Corinthians, readers are encouraged to examine if they are even in the faith. More mirror work. Realizing the difficult days to come, even Jesus engaged in mirror work while in the Garden of Gethsemane. On this momentous occasion, he sought confirmation that the path of suffering he was about to endure was in alignment with the Father's will: "My Father, if this cannot pass away unless I drink it, Your will be done."

Jesus' ministry was about internal transformation—looking inward and allowing God's Spirit to change us from the inside out. He lambasted the Pharisees in Matthew 23 for their outward focus and for thinking that God was impressed with their stringent rule-keeping and copious external rituals. Jesus demonstrates that God is most interested in the inner transformation of the heart.

Introspection takes courage and honesty. Looking in the mirror is scary. Yet, the very act of self-examination is also freeing—a feeling of being honest and clean before God as the author of Psalm 51:10 desires: "Create in me a clean heart, O God, and renew a steadfast spirit within me." Have you ever come clean before God? Did He immediately strike you down with a thunderous bolt of lightning from the heavens? If you are reading this book, I am guessing the answer is no. Yet, sometimes I try to trick God, manipulate Him, and regurgitate half-truths to hide my shortcomings before Him. It doesn't work. We acquire our bearings when self-examination is conducted with authenticity. Once we know where we are, we can look back to see how far we've come and look forward to where we want to be. Honest introspection helps us gauge where we are along life's journey.

Like most individuals, some changes bring a smile to your face. They are good and positive changes, and you are better because of them. On the other hand, there may also be jagged edges in your life that require further attention. Either you haven't moved in the right direction yet, or you have changed in a negative way that must be corrected. Why is it that many elderly folks are sweet, kind, and adorable while others are bitter, biting, and angry? I wonder if the difference between bitterness and joy is an honest self-evaluation and the strength to simply say, "I am not going to be like that anymore." In the absence of honesty, the changes we experience in life can take a turn for the worse. When done with honesty, self-examination is a valuable exercise for understanding ourselves and keeping track of our faith. It helps us gauge whether the "different kind of me" is the right kind of me.

A Grateful Heart

Hearing the still, small voice of God has not been easy for me. Do I turn right or left? Should I move forward, sideways, or just sit tight? My mind seems far too active to hole up in a pup tent for a month searching for God in seclusion from the rest of the world. I enjoy sanity breaks designed for listening and reconnecting (I do that often), but I want God to be with me in the here and now. What good is it if His presence can only be found in a wilderness pup tent off in the hills somewhere? It is in the daily grind that I need Him.

The problem is that while I yearn to feel His presence, I don't always experience His leading the way I want to, especially in the heat of the moment. Is God with me? Are the impulses I feel in my gut Him or me? While I desperately desire to experience Him in the present, I often struggle to do so. Instead, I see His hand in my life more clearly by looking in the rearview mirror. Driving farther on up the road of life requires faith, but keeping an eye on the rearview mirror reminds me of all the tough spots I came through while arriving at the "different kind of me" I am today. Looking back helps me remember God's great work in my life, and I am grateful. A retrospective approach is helpful to following God in the present. As the psalmists recall the wondrous ways God moved in their lives, they stretch forth their hands in praise and long for Him like a parched land crying out for rain.

Psalm 143: 5–6

I remember the days of old;
I meditate on all Your doings;
I muse on the work of Your hands.
I stretch out my hands to You;
My soul longs for You, as a parched land.

Psalm 77:11–15

I shall remember the deeds of the Lord;
Surely I will remember Your wonders of old.
I will meditate on all Your work
And muse on Your deeds.
Your way, O God, is holy;
What god is great like our God?
You are the God who works wonders;
You have made known Your strength among the peoples.
You have by Your power redeemed Your people,
The sons of Jacob and Joseph.

Amidst the perpetual ebb and flow of change, both positive and negative, I seek to maintain a grateful heart. When we see beauty among ashes, we have reached a level of spiritual maturity in which God can be seen in the unlikeliest of places. On numerous occasions, such as Psalm 33 and 138, the psalmist's pen is filled with gratitude. The most familiar, however, may be Psalm 100:

> Shout joyfully to the Lord, all the earth.
> Serve the Lord with gladness;
> Come before Him with joyful singing.
> Know that the Lord Himself is God;
> It is He who has made us, and not we ourselves;
> We are His people and the sheep of His pasture.
> Enter His gates with thanksgiving
> And His courts with praise.
> Give thanks to Him, bless His name.
> For the Lord is good;
> His lovingkindness is everlasting
> And His faithfulness to all generations.

I Thessalonians 5:18 is similar: "In everything give thanks; for this is God's will for you in Christ Jesus." In the Old Testament, a man named Job paid a heavy price despite his upright and blameless stature. Although he lost his family, his health, his possessions, and became a broken and humbled man, we find him proclaiming, "Though He slay me, I will hope in Him" (Job 13:15). A grateful heart frees us to live with joy in an ever-changing world. In light of the "different kind of me" we have become, an attitude of gratitude helps us accept ourselves, warts and all.

Potter-Clay Perspective

We are bothered by our lack of control and would more readily embrace change if we could regulate its nature, speed, and impact; but we can't. Wouldn't it be nice to control the aging process—to slow it down, or stop it altogether? Control of the stock market could help us profit from our investments. What about our teenage children? Ever want to control the sharpness of their tongue? In reality, we don't control much of anything other than our own reaction to the change within and around us. That alone is enough to consume us.

Instructed by the Lord to visit a potter's house, the prophet Jeremiah sees a marred pot on the potter's wheel and watches the artist remake the lump of clay into another pot. The Lord then asks Jeremiah, "'Can I not, O house of Israel, deal with you as this potter does?' declares the Lord. 'Behold, like the clay in the potter's hand, so are you in My hand, O house of Israel'" (Jer. 18:5–6). Paul's words in Romans 9:20 reflect a similar sentiment: "On the contrary, who are you, O man, who answers back to God? The thing molded will not say to the molder, 'Why did you make me like this,' will it?"

In this life, we are the clay and God is the potter, not the other way around. Resisting this reality is an express lane to bitterness and disappointment. Much to our chagrin, we don't get to call the shots, and the sooner we get over this, the better off we will be. By misunderstanding our proper place in the potter-clay relationship, we attempt intimacy with God *in spite of* Him, not *because of* Him. There is a big difference. Instead of yearning to usurp the potter's role, an attitude of gratitude serves us much better. Despite the plethora of changes we experience, there is much to be thankful for in this life, and finding meaning and beauty becomes easier when we realize our clay status.

Potter and Clay

God is the Potter.
I am the clay.

God is the Creator.
I am the created.

God is the worshipped.
I am the worshipper.

God is the leader.
I am the follower.

God is the Father.
I am the child.

God is the King.
I am the servant.

God is the Shepherd.
I am the sheep.

God is the initiator.
I am the responder.

God is the lover.
I am the beloved.

God is the owner.
I am the steward.

God is the vine.
I am the branch.

God is God.
I am not.

Faith for the Road

Like an exhilarating rollercoaster ride, life can be both exciting and uneasy with its surprising twists and turns. For some, life is akin to sitting in the dentist's chair—an unfortunate necessity endured with clenched fists. For others, life becomes a lazy afternoon slumped in the rocking chair with a faithful dog by their side and a refreshing beverage in their hand—life is good.

Whether life for you is symbolized by a rollercoaster, dentist's office, or rocking chair, I hope you learn to celebrate you and enjoy the journey with all of its challenges. Life is one big walk with God—a journey taken together. The greater joy, it seems to me, is that God wants to walk with us, and while no path is the same, His presence is comforting no matter the route. I do not know why some travel to the right, and some veer left; why some climb mountains and others explore flatlands, or why unbearable pain is the hallmark for some while others seem to skate through life unscathed.

In our temporal existence, we search for specific answers to unanswerable questions. We seek explanations from God for the changes that have deeply marked us. This is where faith enters the picture. The only viable response is to place our trust in a Creator who knows more than we do—who is the potter while we remain clay. Our unique journey makes little sense without a Creator. Believing in a benevolent higher power and walking the way of Christ while in a constant state of "not-knowing" is the substance of faith. We walk hand-in-hand with our Creator without always knowing the why or where of our journey, and this is called faith.

Wisdom for the Journey

When life happens, change occurs, and we become a "different kind of me." During this lifelong process, squeeze the hand of God a little tighter if you need to, talk a little longer, and share more deeply. And though the journey may make little sense to you, remember that it is the journey that God is most interested in. It is the walk, the conversations, the holding of hands, the deep sharing, and the intimate communion shared with the living God that becomes the essence of the journey. We become a better "different kind of me" by realizing that the journey itself is the means God uses to commune with us. In this life, travel is required for experiencing God. It's okay to be a "different kind of me." Embrace it; embrace you! The changes within you indicate that you have lived life—that you have journeyed. Now the question is, did you journey with God along the way?

— chapter ten —

Second-Chance Loving

Put on some Blues guitar music and my soul is raptured into pure bliss. If there were such a thing as reincarnation, which I don't believe there is, I would come back as a Blues guitar player, for I certainly can't play my guitar very well in this life. I follow some of the great Blues guitarists, and when their tour schedule brings them close, I make an effort to see them. I attended a Walter Trout concert as he played the iconic Surf Ballroom in Clear Lake, Iowa, the last venue Buddy Holly performed at before he died in a tragic plane crash in 1959. Walter was performing songs from his award-winning *Battle Scars* album—music written about his near-death experience with liver failure and the second chance he received through a life-saving transplant. Each song reflects some aspect of his haunting ordeal.

I don't know much about Walter Trout the man—his character, what he stands for, believes in, and all of that—I just appreciate his music and enjoy listening to his guitar skills. His near-death experience, however, reminds me that second chances bring hope and life—we all need fresh opportunities and plenty of do-overs. I have been given numerous second chances for which I am extremely grateful, and I have extended second chances to others, as well. Never underestimate the power of a do-over. Just ask Walter Trout.

All too often, however, I find myself being what I call a "jumper"—someone who jumps to conclusions far too quickly without embodying proper doses of patience and compassion. I jump when I should offer life-giving second chances. I hate it when I engage in knee-jerk reactions, and though they occur less often these days, I wrestle with it on a daily basis. For those with trigger-happy tendencies, it is always easier to jump. Judging is effortless; loving is hard. Jumping is reactionary; loving is thoughtful. To be the kind of person I want to be, I must pursue the path of second-chance loving.

Unconditional Love

Unconditional love is a concept that has occupied my thoughts over the years. The term literally means to love without conditions. Is it even possible to do this, I wonder? Does this kind of love even exist? Would we want it to? We are called to love like He loves, and love is the premiere characteristic of the Christian life (Jn. 13:34), but I can't find a single verse of Scripture that refers to God's love as unconditional.

All of life seems to be conditioned in one sense or another. For instance, if you don't eat, drink, or sleep (conditions), you die (result). In fact, it is difficult to imagine doing anything without some sort of condition attached. Even when we attend church in corporate worship or engage in various acts of service, we do so believing that it is in our best interest to do so. There seems to be a gap between our created image-of-God status (our position) and actually living out that likeness (our practice). Without conditions there would be no relational boundaries, and without boundaries love morphs into something other than love. The closest thing to unconditional love may be the parent-child bond, but even then, backs have been turned upon one's own flesh and blood.

Realizing that unconditional love may simply not be possible, any dogged insistence upon the term forces us to redefine its meaning into something other than "without conditions." Some take offense that unconditional love is even questioned. In their minds, to strip the term from their vocabulary is akin to attacking the very nature of God. The wagons are circled and weapons are drawn in an effort to protect their fragile faith. Still others give it a casual nod, though they talk more about wrath, hell, damnation, and judgment. Their punitive actions and hateful words convey their true beliefs.

Various arguments can be advanced for or against the concept of unconditional love, depending, of course, on which biased perspective one prefers to promote. After all, when you have already arrived at a verdict, only those data supporting your conclusion seem to be valid. For the purpose of this chapter, debating the merits of such arguments takes us off course. Some folks talk about love, argue about its definition, write great treatises on the subject, and so forth, and at the end of the day, still never love—the one thing God desires that we actually do.

As a young Christian in the late 70s, I strummed my guitar to the lyrics of a popular Christian song: "And they'll know we are Christians by our love, by our love, yes, they'll know we are Christians by our love." We didn't debate the definition of love; we just loved. It never occurred to us to dissect it, put it under a microscope or argue about it. We just knew that we should love God, love others, and love ourselves. The more we argue about love, the less loving we become, whereas the more we love, the more loving we become. People innately know what love is and recognize it when they see it, so let's just do it. Love is the practical outworking of our relationship with God—an automatic byproduct of our communion with Him. When you are intimately connected to the source of love, there is never a lack of supply since it flows to us, in us, through us, and out from us.

Selfless Love

Rather than *talk* about unconditional love with its various entanglements, I opt for a different word altogether that makes sense to me—a concept that gets to the heart of love without the trappings of argument. I prefer "selfless love," a term we can all relate to, visualize, experience, and do. Selfless love prevents jumping and encourages second-chance loving.

If you have ever been loved deeply by another human being, you know what love feels like. Love expresses itself as both feeling and action. Some stress the *feeling* aspect, while others downplay the emotional element and focus on *acting* lovingly. From my experience, love seems to embrace both, and depending on the circumstances, may emphasize one over the other. Even Jesus, prompted by love, experienced strong emotions that resulted in compassion. Yet, he also acted lovingly toward others by healing the infirmed, sharing his wisdom, washing the disciples' feet, mentoring the Twelve, and listening to the hearts of his followers.

In my own life, I have acted lovingly without the accompanying feelings of intense emotion, and at other times, I engaged in loving acts simply because my emotions were stirred at the core. At times, both emotion and intellect are in alignment, and sometimes they aren't. The underlying drive for both, however, is love. Whether our hearts are stirred by pure emotion or prompted by rational thought, it is important to recognize that these are merely channels by which love is initiated toward its rightful end—actually loving. Unfortunately, our tendency, as with so many other good things God has for us, is to fall into the snare of cheap substitution—that is, rejecting true love and settling for counterfeits that selfishly promote our status, our goals, and our interests ahead of our beloved.

To experience selfless love is to be loved well, for it causes us to feel valued. We experience what it feels like to actually matter to someone—to be treasured. Selfless love always has the best interest of others at heart and flows from who we are on the inside. It is not reliant upon personal benefit or expectations of reciprocity. This investment of love transcends the return of personal gain, is based upon the intrinsic worth of the individual, and is sourced directly from God, who is love (1 Jn. 4:8). It is through our communion with the infinite source of love that we are able to love others in themselves, by themselves, and for themselves. We love people simply because of who they are, rather than what they can do for us.

Imagine being loved simply because you are you—a love without filters upon speech and without jumping through hoops of expectation. Imagine a love that sees past your faults to your intrinsic value and seeks your best interest above all else. That kind of love can alter the trajectory of someone's life. If both husband and wife, for instance, would love one another in this manner, their experience of mutual selfless love would bring about radical transformation. Their deep affection would not be contingent on some required or meritorious behavior, but upon the treasured worth they see in one another. When this occurs, mental and emotional barriers vanish, allowing God's love *within* them to flow out *from* them so each of them is blessed.

When we love someone simply because we want something from them, we are, in essence, paying for love. A transaction occurs whereby love is exchanged for some favor, status, dominance, act, and so forth. That isn't selfless love, but a mere business transaction. It is nothing more than a cheap imitation that tricks us into thinking we have truly loved well when the very heart of the exchange was personal gain. I remember saying to one of my best friends, "I don't need or want anything from you; I only have your best interest at heart." It was said with great sincerity, was demonstrated in my interactions, and he was shocked to discover a friend who loved him so selflessly. It was my attempt to love another human being without expectation of return.

See Good in Others

Selfless love sees the good in others. Far too often, relationships consist of comparison, judgment, criticism, disappointment, and the feeling of never measuring up. These types of relationships are destructive, bring us down, and cause us to question whether selfless love will ever be experienced. It doesn't help when much of Christianity views humankind as flawed beyond repair, depraved at the core, and unable to do any good whatsoever—what Martin Luther and John Calvin called total depravity.

Others, however, take a metaphorical approach to the serpent and forbidden fruit episode in the book of Genesis. Instead of fixating on how bad humans can be, they accentuate our original image-of-God status (imago Dei). After all, it is asserted, God created humankind as the crown jewel of His creation, and when all was said and done, He looked at His handiwork and declared it to be very good: "God saw all that He had made, and behold, it was very good" (Gen. 1:31). In fact, God declared His creation "good" six times in the first chapter of Genesis. It is difficult to see how we can be both a "very good" image of God and at the same time totally depraved and flawed to the core. The two concepts don't play well together. Which perspective will guide your interactions with others? Will you see them as very good and filled with intrinsic worth, or will you attempt to fix them before you extend an offer of love and acceptance?

When we look at others and think to ourselves, "You are flawed to the core and must be fixed," we convey non-acceptance until a requirement is met. Selfless love, on the other hand, says, "You are the 'very good' creation of God, accepted and loved for who you are, and filled with intrinsic worth by the hand of your Creator. I will love you just as you are." Is it possible to love others this way despite their failures, foolish mistakes, and penchant for irritating and disappointing us? These are two fundamentally different ways of viewing others. One sees people as flawed and in need of a fix, although there is no universal agreement on what that fix is, and the other views people as the "very good" creative work of God—crafted in His image. I choose to focus on the latter, for the journey of inner transformation begins when we feel accepted, valued, and loved. We love well when we recognize the good in others.

Sacrificial Love

Selfless love is sacrificial love. Its demands upon our heart can be taxing, for rarely is it the easier road to travel. When we use people for our own ends, we may accomplish goals much faster, but at what cost? The trail of carnage left in our wake is devastating to those who get in our way. It is a heavy price to pay. I am reminded of a song B.J. Thomas sang on his 1979 *You Gave Me Love* album, titled "Using Things & Loving People":

Using things and loving people
That's the way it's got to be
Using things and loving people
Look around and you can see
That loving things and using people
Only leads to misery
Using things and loving people
That's the way it's got to be

Being loved is in the giving
All we have is what we share
Loving life is for the living
You have to have a heart to care
And loving things and using people
Only leads to misery
Using things and loving people
That's the way it's got to be

So put your hand inside my hand
I don't know where the road will lead
We may not find the things we want
But we will find the things we need
And all we need is love

Using things and loving people
Brings you happiness I've found
Using things and loving people
Not the other way around
Cause loving things and using people
Only leads to misery
Using things and loving people
That's the way it's got to be
For you and me
For you and me
Written by: Hal David and Archie Paul Jordan

Who are we kidding? Some folks are just plain hard to love, including our-selves at times, but everyone is *worthy* of love. Herein lies our internal dilemma: do we love everyone, even those who have deeply wounded us, or do we love only those we deem worthy of such love? Scripture is pretty clear on this; we are to love even our enemies. For Jesus declared, "You have heard that it was said, 'You shall love your neighbor and hate your enemy.' But I say to you, love your enemies and pray for those who persecute you" (Mt. 5:43–44). Created in the image of God, all humans are of immeasurable worth. They are, after all, cherished by their Creator and seen as "very good," just as we are.

To love selflessly, a choice is forced upon us, and like so many other paths we pursue, there is always a decision to be made. Do we turn left or right when we come to the fork in the road? Instinctively, many choose the wider, well-beaten path of least resistance, for it requires very little of them. They get to *proclaim* the way of God without actually *walking* in the path of God, and in doing so, settle for cheap imitations, bypass the essential work of internal transformation, and prevent their heart from being thrilled beyond measure.

Others realize that loving well requires personal sacrifice and still choose to pursue selfless love. From their perspective, how could they choose any differ-ently? Selfless love is not only the way of God, it is also the way God thrills their heart. Fresh out of seminary so many years ago, I remember shoveling snow from my neighbor's sidewalk. It was a long, corner-lot walkway and took some time and effort to complete. I kept glancing at their large front window, hoping they would notice what a magnanimous gesture this was on my part. The humility of their neighbor, Mr. Pastor Man, was on full display, like a proud peacock fanning his iridescent plumage.

I wanted my neighbor to notice me, thank me, and see my humble-servant attitude. Much to my chagrin, they never said a word. It is probably best they didn't, for my shoveling gift was nothing more than a selfish publicity stunt designed to make me look spiritual in the eyes of others. My immaturity and insecurity sought out accolades for humility rather than being genuinely humble. My love had a catch to it and was conditioned upon receiving some-thing in return. This wasn't an act of true love, but a cheap self-serving imitation. Selfless love has a purity about it that acts solely for the benefit of others, expecting nothing in return. For this kind of virtuous motivation to exist, we must jettison pride and the dangerous me-first mindset. Selfless love is about seeing intrinsic value in others who are worthy of love—our love.

Jesus knew that his message of internal transformation would face stiff resistance from the religious leaders in Jerusalem, and yet, he traveled there anyway, and at great personal cost. In wrestling with what was to come, he spent a lonely night in the Garden of Gethsemane. Abandoned by his sleeping disciples and sweating drops of blood under the weight of this historic moment, he would face the sting of betrayal from a member of his inner circle, undergo a sham trial, be mocked and spit upon, and eventually nailed to a cross like a common criminal. Jesus paid the ultimate price of crucifixion for follow-ing and proclaiming the path of inner transformation.

While most of us won't pay the ultimate price for our faith, loving others selflessly always involves some degree of personal sacrifice, for it is not our own interest we seek to advance, but that of others. Ironic, isn't it, that love has this double-edged quality about it, for you cannot be both selfish and selfless at the same time. One trail takes us down a narcissistic approach to life, and the other leads to personal sacrifice on behalf of others. One choice follows the path of God, while the other pursues expediency and personal gain.

To leave love hanging on the cliffs of personal sacrifice doesn't tell the full story, and it seems rather depressing until we remember that after the sacrifice comes renewal; after the dying comes resurrection. This is the great cycle of life and a significant element in the teaching of Jesus: "Truly, truly, I say to you, unless a grain of wheat falls into the earth and dies, it remains alone; but if it dies, it bears much fruit. He who loves his life loses it, and he who hates his life in this world will keep it to life eternal. If anyone serves Me, he must follow Me" (Jn. 12:24–26a).

The Wheat Principle

In one sense, each time an old way of thinking, seeing, acting, or being is buried in the ground to die like a seed of wheat, new understandings and new ways of seeing rise up. It is the wheat principle at work, though it is never easy to let go of the things we once clenched so firmly. But as old paradigms die, surprise awaits us, for it was in the letting go that we were freed to see things differently. Rising up from the soil is a harvest of renewal that moves us ever closer to the Lord. Each time the death and resurrection cycle occurs, we allow more of God's image to shine forth. We experience a resurrection of sorts—the very thing the wheat metaphor was designed to convey. The message Jesus proclaimed was one of letting go—releasing old, worthless, and selfish ways of seeing so the inner transformation of God's Spirit can bring forth much fruit, renewal, and new ways of seeing and experiencing God.

This wheat principle is seen throughout nature and seems to be a universal principle of life. Seed is buried in the soil, and from its burial comes an abundance of fruit. Resurrection comes after death. According to Paul's great resurrection chapter of I Corinthians 15, Jesus' own resurrection becomes the first fruits of all who die—an example to the rest of us. We see this cyclical principle in Israel's relationship with Yahweh. Israel walked in the ways of God, slid off the marked path, traveled down the road of pain and hardship, finally came to their senses, and renewed their vows to follow God. This great wheat principle is everywhere—the idea of letting go, burying and dying in order to experience renewal.

Personal sacrifice can involve a loss of prestige or status, a loss of financial resources, experiencing pain that is difficult to bear, or giving up time and effort that could be directed elsewhere. Doing the right thing may not always be easy, but it is always right to love selflessly. On that fateful day of September 11, 2001, I was in Washington, D.C. when an Islamic terrorist group hijacked four commercial airliners in coordinated attacks upon America. Two planes flew into the Twin Towers of the World Trade Center in New York City, one slammed into the Pentagon in our nation's capital, and the fourth, courageously subverted by heroic passengers, crashed into a Pennsylvania field, far short of its intended target.

Flights across the nation were cancelled, rental cars were unavailable, and I was stranded. But, there was my friend, a former student of mine and missionary to the Micronesian Islands, who loved me closer than a brother. Without a second thought, he hopped in his jeep and drove from his home in North Carolina to pick me up in D.C. and bring me to the front door of my house in Indiana before turning to make his way back. It cost him time, money, effort, and the delay of other pressing items. Before my very eyes, selfless love was modeled by a man whose heart was thrilled with the ways of God. I am reminded of John 15:13: "Greater love has no one than this, that one lay down his life for his friends." Loving well often involves personal sacrifice.

While selfless love is typically oriented toward others, we do well to remember that it radiates out from us. In other words, to give love away, we must possess it ourselves, for we cannot share what we do not have. The good news is that all human beings possess the love of God within their heart, as Paul makes clear in Romans 5:5: "the love of God has been poured out within our hearts through the Holy Spirit who was given to us." Praying for God's love is a waste of time. Why ask for what has already been given to us? There is no greater love to seek or obtain than the love already poured into our hearts by God Himself. The issue isn't getting more love, but simply releasing the love within us. This is a significant point worth pondering. There is no obstacle preventing us from sharing the love already poured into our hearts.

A Deep Flowing River

It may be helpful to picture God's everlasting love as a wide and deep flowing river that never runs dry. Think of yourself as a five-acre plot of land a mile away from the river and the Holy Spirit as the underground pipeline that connects the river water to your acreage. All the water you need to grow your garden, water your livestock, wash your clothes, and drink to your heart's content is readily available. You can soak in a hot bath any time you like! The issue isn't getting more water, for you already have all you need and want. The issue is simply utilizing the water that has been provided to you. Turn the faucet on! This never-ending resource sustains selfless love because it is constantly connected to the source of God's everlasting river of love.

Love isn't so much about what we do as it is first and foremost about who we are. John 15 notes that we are the branches, Jesus is the vine, and God is the vinedresser. As image-bearers of His divine nature, we also partake of His love—the love that has been poured into our hearts. We love selflessly because it is who we are and how God made us to be—a part of our nature because it is a part of His nature. When the love of God flows through us and out toward others, we reveal and reflect our Creator. How can we be any different if we are truly branches connected to the vine? God's love is bigger than us, larger than we can imagine, and more expansive than we could ever dream. Yet, this vast reservoir of love becomes a part of us. By simply turning on the faucet and allowing the river to flow to us, in us, through us, and out from us, our own capacity to love enlarges and expands.

A Three-legged Stool

That God's love flows through us toward others is one thing, but allowing His love to envelop us is another matter. We tend to shy away from the notion of self-love, and yet, Jesus notes its necessity for loving God and others well. Intricately entwined together, Scripture indicates that we love in a three-fold manner: love God, love others, and love ourselves. When one of these three legs is missing, we spend more time trying to balance ourselves on a two-legged stool than actually loving well.

In his summation of Scripture, Jesus notes that the greatest commandment is to love God with all of our heart, soul, and mind. The second great commandment is to love our neighbor as we love ourselves (Mt. 22:34–40). We easily grasp our need to love God and others, but when it comes to loving ourselves, we feel unworthy and consider it a selfish act. But unless and until we learn to love ourselves in a healthy manner, we can never love God and others the way we were meant to. It is like trying to solve a math problem with missing parts to the equation. Our three-legged stool loses one of its necessary legs.

Plenty of individuals become lovers of themselves in unwholesome ways. This is simply narcissism at its finest—a pleasure-seeking, "me-first" mindset that is far from the respectful love God intends for us. To love well means that we love ourselves selflessly, not narcissistically. Is selfless love only meant for others, or does God intend that we also selflessly love ourselves? God absolutely delights in you—just for being you, for existing, for being His creation. Yet, we struggle to delight in ourselves and give ourselves the gift of second chances. We love others one way and love ourselves in a lesser way—two different standards. Do you insist upon perfection in your own life while charitably giving others a pass? Out of love, do you readily extend forgiveness to others while stubbornly refusing to forgive yourself? Do you generously love others for who they are, yet can't seem to love yourself until you measure up? You get the point.

Most of us are better at selflessly loving others than extending that same selfless love to ourselves. This, however, is precisely what God requires of us, for it allows us to love more fully. Loving ourselves is a necessary part of the equation to loving God with everything we are. The concept of healthy self-love may be new to you, and if so, you have come upon a fork in the road. Will you choose the path of God though it requires a change in perspective—that you selflessly love yourself? Are you willing to implement the wheat principle and bury your old way of thinking about yourself in order to experience a resurrected perspective—a new way of valuing yourself whereby greater fruit is produced? When your love mirrors a two-legged stool, loving God and others seems unnatural, forced, and steers us to the brink of exhaustion. Loving ourselves with the same selfless love we extend to others is a necessary element to a three-fold approach to love.

Modeling healthy self-love is a precious gift to others, especially to our family. Teaching our children to love God, love others, and love themselves is a powerful three-pronged approach to increasing their chances of becoming well-balanced, loving adults. There are healing properties in the power of love. I have seen abandoned and abused dogs respond overwhelmingly to affection, even after being treated so inhumanely. Children, friends, family, and acquaintances all seem receptive to love, and hardened enemies may also be softened by its winsome qualities. A proper love of self can restore our own beaten-down soul and assist in the healing of days gone by. Love is a powerful, positive, and restorative way to influence others. Stop berating yourself and inciting negative self-talk, for it is not of God. We must extend selfless love to ourselves if we wish to experience the fullness of God's precious love.

Selfless love isn't about perfection, and it doesn't diminish the emotional ebb and flow of normal relationships. There is a thing called life and being human that we cannot escape. Selfless love isn't engaging in never-ending people-pleasing without ensuring our own needs and desires are met, for that would be an unhealthy way of loving ourselves. Selfless love doesn't cast aside all boundaries, for boundaries are healthy and necessary. We wouldn't allow a beloved family member to abuse another family member while nonchalantly shrugging our shoulders and saying, "I love you to the moon and back; abuse who you want, when you want, for there are no boundaries to my love for you." That is sheer lunacy. Finally, selfless love isn't about losing our individuality by fusing to another in relationship. In other words, rather than merging into one, we maintain who we are and how God made us while at the same time recognizing, celebrating, and respecting dissimilarities. We choose to love across our differences.

Dip in the River

Comparing God's love, the source of our own love, to a river that never runs dry is my attempt to convey that the river's depth and width is big enough for all—even you. Come to the river, no matter what you have gone through or what you have done or haven't done. God's love is big enough to receive you. Come drink from the river, swim in the river, bathe in the river, float in the river, and bask in its abundance. Get wet, splash about, go under, play, ponder, and be alive. This is the great invitation of Christ who calls you to himself: "Come to Me, all who are weary and heavy-laden, and I will give you rest. Take My yoke upon you and learn from Me, for I am gentle and humble in heart, and you will find rest for your souls. For My yoke is easy and My burden is light" (Mt. 11:28–30). How could we not love ourselves when Christ loves us so deeply?

The river flows from the very nature of God Himself and is one aspect of who He is. In fact, He cannot be any other way. His river of love is differentiated from sexual love, familial love, friendship love, any other kind of love we can think of. Agape love is the term specifically used by New Testament writers to set God's love apart from all other loves. His love is expansive, incomparable, and pure. It is the highest form of love possible and is the type of love God has for all of His creation. In fact, it is the type of love Jesus exemplified, as well. We see God's great love demonstrated over and over again in Scripture, and our own experience affirms its truth. The water in the endless river is agape love straight from the heart of God.

The most wonderful aspect of this agape love is that it cannot be earned. It is not merit-based, but grace-given, and extended to all. There is not a thing you can do to make God love you more or love you less. It is this amazing, expansive, incomparable, pure, endless love—the highest form of love possible—that God has poured into our hearts. Having His love within us is part of what it means to be "partakers of the divine nature" as noted in 2 Peter 1:3–4. This kind of love is seen in Ephesians 2:4–10:

> But God, being rich in mercy, because of His great love with which He loved us, even when we were dead in our transgressions, made us alive together with Christ (by grace you have been saved), and raised us up with Him, and seated us with Him in the heavenly places in Christ Jesus, so that in the ages to come He might show the surpassing riches of His grace in kindness toward us in Christ Jesus. For by grace you have been saved through faith; and that not of yourselves, it is the gift of God; not as a result of works, so that no one may boast. For we are His workmanship, created in Christ Jesus for good works, which God prepared beforehand so that we would walk in them.

Wisdom for the Journey

As we journey through life, it takes great courage to pursue a three-fold approach to love (God, others, and ourselves), for it requires that we spurn conventional wisdom and choose a less-travelled footpath, such as loving ourselves with the same second-chance, selfless love we extend to others. It will take the never-ending river of agape love to flow to us, in us, through us, and out from us to positively interact and influence others. Remember that God's love has already been poured into your heart and you are forever connected to the source of love—God Himself. Don't overthink love; just do it. When you see a need that you can meet, do it. When a hug would calm a fear, give it. When you are treated poorly, love in return. Embrace the wheat principle without fear and courageously bury old paradigms so that God can bring renewal to your heart from the inside out. Just as winter comes before spring, so must death arrive before renewal enlightens the heart. To journey in love is to travel well. It is worth the pursuit.

chapter eleven

Catching Flies

The facility hadn't been updated for years and was as inviting as a dreary hospital wing with its speckled linoleum floor tiles and dismal wall color. I felt like distributing personalized sick bags emblazoned with the school's logo to incoming students while welcoming them to our shoddy facility. We didn't have the funds to hire a contractor to freshen up the place, so we decided to do it ourselves, along with the help of generous volunteers. Every Friday was remodel day as staff took time to paint, scrape, repair, and clean. The final outcome was breathtaking and brought us into the twenty-first century. No more perpetual testing of our gag reflexes. Now, students were enjoying the space, drinking coffee, and gawking with delight at the transformation. I was proud of the staff for accomplishing this important goal together.

There was one incident, however, that is forever etched in my memory. I allowed frustration to get the better of me and criticized a valuable member of the team in front of others—an absolute no-no. On Friday work days, I typically arrived several hours before employees in order to lighten their load. On this day, we were to paint classrooms. I arrived at 5:00 a.m. to paint trim lines so they could roll on paint without slowing down for this tedious chore; this eased their workload and more could be accomplished in less time. I didn't mind arriving early to assist them. On many occasions, I journeyed the extra mile to be a caring and compassionate leader. For instance, other schools closed for Labor Day while ours remained open. I allowed staff to "work from home" so they could spend the holiday with family and friends without taking time off, while I manned the phones and front desk.

In preparation for the upcoming work day, the staff promised to complete several tasks ahead of time so that our painting efforts would be productive. However, they did not do what they had promised. Because I was forced to complete their tasks from the night before, I was unable to accomplish the necessary trim work. This wasn't the first time this had occurred. When the crew arrived, I openly shared my frustration and became critical of a key staff member in front of the others. Because of my outburst of public criticism, our anticipated fun-filled day was transformed into an awkward environment.

Yes, a foolish move on my part. It is frustrating when you give of yourself to others and they don't appreciate your efforts or come through on their end. Even so, there is no justification for publically criticizing team members. It merely revealed my frustration, was a bad leadership decision, and demeaned the staff. I have since kicked myself a hundred times and wish I had a "do-over," but instead, I settle for a valuable lesson learned—praise in public and correct in private.

Criticism

I share this story because we have all spoken harsh words and have also experienced the disparagement of others. I have been the recipient of caustic criticism that left behind its blemished mark, and I have also dispensed my share of tongue lashings that wounded others. Knowing the destructive nature of criticism, it is fitting that we expose its despicable work, label it as such, and move on to more productive approaches, like encouragement.

You have heard the well-known saying, "You can catch more flies with honey than with vinegar." If flies were worth $500 each and we were in the fly-catching business, would we experience greater success by using sour or sweet in our catching efforts? The answer is obvious, as is the saying itself, which might be rephrased this way: you can influence others more positively with encouragement than with criticism.

Generally speaking, criticism destroys while encouragement uplifts. Criticism triggers defense mechanisms, while encouragement elicits openness. Criticism focuses on the negative, while encouragement emphasizes the positive. Criticism poisons relationships, while encouragement fosters strong relational bonds. Criticism scars, while encouragement heals. Criticism diminishes self-worth and self-image, while encouragement protects and values both.

We have all received our fair share of criticism and know firsthand its destructive nature. In all honesty, we have also played the role of judge and jury in the lives of others with devastating results. We have been hurt, and we have hurt others. When we criticize, we choose the path of least resistance—the easy way of handling issues. Whether born out of frustration or arrogance, the end result is the same. There has got to be a better way.

The term "constructive criticism" often becomes a lazy justification for spewing harsh words. By putting "constructive" in front of "criticism" we attempt to turn something that is inherently negative into something that is positive. This, however, makes no sense and confuses one's *response* to criticism with criticism itself. Criticism by its very nature is negative. There is no such thing as "positive criticism," for the terms are polar opposites. It is like saying "non-pregnant pregnancy," or a "dead living" specimen. The two words don't play well together. Positive comments are called praise or encouragement, not criticism.

We know that people are always better off when a learning posture is maintained and life is viewed as a teacher, no matter what the circumstances. Difficult conversations or harsh words *can* be turned into something positive, but we dare not confuse our *response* to criticism with any inherent quality within criticism itself. Individuals who learn and grow from a bout with cancer don't believe that cancer is a good thing. Rather, *how* they manage the situation influences their perspective despite the debilitating nature of the disease. It is the same with criticism; any constructive outcome is due to our positive response to it, not because there is such a thing as constructive or positive criticism.

Criticism is no stranger to those of us who have served in full-time pastoral ministry. One pastor was censured for crossing his legs while sitting on stage. Apparently, a tiny gap of visible skin between his socks and dress pants brought about the charge of indecency. With his tail tucked between his legs, he now wears socks extending up his calf so as not to arouse the ire of holy "skin-peepers." Upon arriving home from the worship service, I received a phone call from a woman who felt compelled to criticize me for a particular illustration I used in my Sunday sermon. Who does such things?

Pastors live in glass houses under the scrutiny of congregational members, all with their own perspective of how ministry ought to be conducted. While singing for a traveling evangelist, I was criticized for my choice of shoes, and for not sounding like George Beverly Shea, a soloist for Billy Graham's crusades. I was criticized for having my eyes open while leading congregational singing and for closing them when belting out a solo. I was criticized for not preaching like celebrity television ministers. You name it; I have been criticized for it.

Silencing the Canary

In many ways, I am like the canary who happily sang day after day until its owner decided to clean the bird cage with the vacuum cleaner hose and accidentally sucked up the bird. Pulling him from the dirt-filled sweeper bag, the owner brushed him off and set him back on his perch. The traumatized canary doesn't sing much anymore, and now sits quietly in his cage listening intently for the terrifying intake of the vacuum cleaner. In this life, criticism is unending—relentless and overwhelming at times. It has the capacity to silence our beautiful voices and keep us on our perch.

We can muster the strength to deal with occasional criticism, but withstanding an avalanche of negativity is exceedingly onerous. Being subject to caustic jabs on a regular basis can be debilitating. I know a woman who has endured the onslaught of her alcoholic husband's critical words for over thirty years. She doesn't dress right. He can't stand the boots she wears. She brushes her teeth incorrectly and is considered lazy for using an electric toothbrush. She takes too long to run an errand, and even her lovemaking skills are belittled. Sick and tired of being beaten down day after day, she filed for divorce—the inevitable result of unending criticism.

It has taken me a long time to realize that critical people have a problem, and most of the time it isn't me, although I am often the target of their pernicious verbal thrashings. When criticism reigns, we begin to think that something is wrong with us, when all along the critical spirit lies within our accuser. Criticism reveals a great deal more about the person criticizing than it does about us.

There was a time in my life when I placed too much emphasis on what others thought of me. We all want to be liked, and there is nothing wrong with that, but we must realize that pleasing everyone is impossible. And when we don't, we cannot be so crushed as to stop singing like the traumatized canary. There is a saying that goes something like this: in our twenties we worry about what everyone thinks of us; in our forties we don't care what others think of us; in our sixties we realize they were never thinking of us in the first place. In essence, we put too much stock in the opinion of others.

Best Interest Relationships

There are situations where we ask for feedback, both positive and negative, from others whose opinions we value. My son took pitching lessons from a professional baseball player and eagerly sought critical evaluation from his coaching expertise. By placing ourselves in mentoring situations, we invite correction from others. Joining the Army implies listening to the drill sergeant's sharp words. Employment brings about performance standards and assessments. In these situations, the evaluation of others is readily forthcoming and expected. Yet, relentless criticism from anyone, especially those who have no business serving that role in our life, diminishes self-worth and demeans self-image. Constant criticizers are poison to the proper functioning of the community of faith.

Touted in support of the constructive criticism bandwagon is Proverbs 27:6: "Faithful are the wounds of a friend, but deceitful are the kisses of an enemy." This verse says nothing about constructive criticism. Yet, it is important to note that the wounds arise from a friend. In deep and abiding friendships, anything can be said and discussed without filters. That which is paramount to the relationship is the best interest of the other person. Such discussions can occur within deep friendships because someone's heart is faithful to you, loves you, and desires only what is best for you. Words arising from a place of trust, love, and respect can be life-giving, but not everyone deserves that place in your life. Most criticize to advance their own interests, not yours.

Notice the second part of the proverb, "Deceitful are the kisses of an enemy." False praise is equally devastating. As a tactical advantage, many deploy strategic flattery in an effort to get what they want from you. They are not your friends because deceit is involved. They say what you want to hear in order to betray your trust. Jesus experienced s similar phenomenon when Judas Iscariot betrayed him in the Garden of Gethsemane with a deceitful kiss upon the cheek. Pretending to be his friend, Judas turned on him for thirty pieces of silver.

In a chapter contrasting the upright with the wicked, Proverbs 15:31 notes, "He who listens to the life-giving reproof will dwell among the wise." A truly wise individual, Scripture reveals, treasures the instruction and advice of faithful, friendly reproofs that have wise living as its aim. Proverbs is filled with sayings to this effect, such as the following: "He who neglects discipline despises himself, but he who listens to reproof acquires understanding" (Prov. 15:32); "He who walks with wise men will be wise, but the companion of fools will suffer harm" (Prov. 13:20); "Give instruction to a wise man and he will be still wiser, teach a righteous man and he will increase his learning"

(Prov. 9:9). Ecclesiastes 7:5 strikes a similar chord: "It is better to listen to the rebuke of a wise man than for one to listen to the song of fools."

These verses make perfect sense. Those who walk in the light of God listen to life-giving instruction. Being attentive to wisdom makes us wiser, while ignoring or resisting instruction is the way of a fool. Some mistakenly believe that verses like these justify the onslaught of nasty criticism, and well-intentioned dragons feel it is their life-duty to point out your shortcomings. Fortunately, this is not the meaning or intent of these verses. They are not a license to maim, but a plea for maintaining a learning and listening posture so we can become wiser ourselves. It has the effect of being life-giving, rather than life-draining.

I am not some rosy-cheeked, wide-eyed, naive child living in a fantasy world. I realize that difficult conversations must sometimes occur regarding our thinking, behavior, and speech. This is part of the maturation process. Yet, I am a firm believer in authentic, loving relationships that become fertile soil for welcoming such conversations. Our hearts are receptive to "wounds from a friend" when our best interest is at heart. In these kinds of relationships, both encouragement and reproof flow from hearts that love deeply. The nature and intensity of criticism that prevails today is unparalleled and destructive. It often produces the very opposite effect of its intended design.

Encouragement

There was once an elderly church woman known for her constant encouragement. The youth and inexperience of the church's pastor was obvious to all as he struggled in his role. Yet, Sunday after Sunday, after every botched message, the elderly woman had nothing but encouraging words for him. The congregation noticed her kind demeanor towards the young man, and one particular Sunday, after his pulpit delivery was bungled in a most egregious and obvious way, congregational members wondered what positive remarks could possibly be made. As she exited the sanctuary, the elderly woman shook the young man's hand and commented, "Pastor, what a wonderful passage of Scripture you chose for us today!" She knew of his struggles, but chose to offer honest encouragement rather than criticism.

This sweet woman's disposition is summed up in the following quote from an unknown source: "A word of encouragement during a failure is worth more than an hour of praise after success." Words are powerful—having the ability to build up or destroy. As a young man, I realized the potency of words for good and evil and penned this little poem:

Words

Words are knives,
sharp as can be.
Slicing through hearts,
ruining lives.

Words are healing,
soothing as they flow.
Dressing wounds, and
binding hurts we're feeling.

Words are irons on fire,
directly from the coals.
Branding some for life,
a searing from liars.

Words are water clear,
from a bubbling brook.
Quenching deepest thirsts, and
bringing comfort near.

Words are this way,
my tongue feels shame.
Hurting and healing,
all in the same day.
© Copyright Terry S. Wise 4/6/1988

Harsh words stir up anger (Prov. 15:1), and rash words are like sword thrusts (Prov. 12:18). It is the fool who loses his temper (Prov. 29:11). The tongue, according to James, is "a restless evil and full of deadly poison" and likened to a small flame that can light an entire forest on fire (Jas. 3:5–12). Jesus taught that what comes out of the mouth proceeds from the heart, thereby exposing the true nature of a critical spirit (Mt. 15:10–19). Realizing the tongue can set a forest ablaze or encourage the lowly of heart, we are instructed to watch over our heart with all diligence, for from it flow the springs of life (Prov. 4:23). Our remarks can be life-giving and impart energy and goodness to others. They can be life preserving as Proverbs 13:3 notes: "The one who guards his mouth preserves his life."

Encouragement is vastly different than criticism in both quality and outcome. While criticism is inherently negative, encouragement is by nature positive. The outcome of constant criticism is the continual chopping at the root of self-worth while encouragement becomes the building block for positive growth. The Bible has much to say about building one another up. While the modern church could be a bastion of encouragement, it is often anything but that. When hurting individuals seek healing and positivity, all too often they receive criticism, judgement, and condescension. Instead of embracing the love of Christ with open arms, they run for the hills—an understandable response. Too often, the Christian message of love and acceptance is hindered by its messengers. It is sad to watch the church stumble over its own two feet. This is a far cry from the message of Jesus who said, "Come to Me, all who are weary and heavy-laden, and I will give you rest. Take My yoke upon you and learn from Me, for I am gentle and humble in heart, and you will find rest for your souls. For My yoke is easy and My burden is light."

To my knowledge, I have never read a verse of Scripture that says, "Therefore, criticize one another, for this is pleasing to the Lord." There are no such passages in the Bible. Thank goodness! In fact, we discover just the opposite. We are asked to love and encourage each other. All one has to do is read the "one another" verses in the Bible to be convinced that criticism is not a positive pathway. Approximately one hundred "one another" verses exist in the New Testament. For instance, we are not to judge one another (Rom. 14:13), but bear one another's burdens (Gal. 6:2), encourage and build up one another (I

Thess. 5:11), accept one another (Rom. 15:7), bear with and forgive one another (Col. 3:13), and seek the good for one another (1 Thess. 5:15). The Lord's garden leaves no room for the weeds of criticism.

Weaponizing Scripture

We are instructed to speak the truth in love to one another as Ephesians 4:25 notes, but this verse is mistakenly quoted by the uninformed to support their critical spirit. Sometimes the very tools God provides for relational harmony are fashioned into weapons. I can't count the number of times critical Christians have bludgeoned me with this verse, in love of course! It seems that when others don't like what I do, what I say, or how I say it, I am usually invited out to lunch so they can "share their love" with me! This verse becomes a convenient method for disguising what they are really after. They want to control me, change me, or use me to further their agenda. Wouldn't it be nice if someone actually invited me to lunch simply *because* they loved me, not as a means to advance their personal agenda?

We know we are living in a warped reality when loving someone equates to criticizing them. One gruff parishioner, whom I will call Big Al, didn't like anything about me. He criticized me up and down for everything in the book. He criticized my sermons, my family, my office hours, my personality, and I am sure he would have criticized my breathing if he had thought of it. Big Al was a challenging individual and a constant burr in my saddle. He took me out to lunch to criticize me, and when he didn't receive the desired response, he handed me a book to read. If his "love" couldn't get through to me, maybe this handy paperback would set me straight.

A few weeks went by before he sought the return of his treasured book meant to whip me into shape. Although I didn't read it, I discovered a powerful quote within its pages that touched my heart. It went something like this: "Don't let others create your world, for when they do, they will always make it too small." Big Al realized he couldn't control me, couldn't manipulate me, and couldn't love me with his brand of criticism. He wanted the right to wound me as a friend without the essential ingredient of friendship. He sought his own interest ahead of mine. For Big Al, "truth" was nothing more than his way of seeing things. His perspective on any given topic was always "truth," and "love" was merely a euphemism for criticism. In his mind, if he could convince others by criticizing them that his way was the right way, then he was fulfilling Scripture by speaking the truth in love. What a convoluted way of seeing things!

It never ceases to amaze me when folks claim to possess the truth for you but never seem to apply that same truth to their own life. I am reminded of Paul's words in Romans 2:1: "Therefore you have no excuse, everyone of you who passes judgment, for in that which you judge another, you condemn yourself; for you who judge practice the same things." Again, in Romans 2:21–23, "You, therefore, who teach another, do you not teach yourself? You who preach that one shall not steal, do you steal? You who say that one should not commit adultery, do you commit adultery? You who abhor idols, do you rob temples? You who boast in the Law, through your breaking the Law, do you dishonor God?" Some go to great lengths to pinpoint the speck in our eye while neglecting the log in their own, something Jesus highlighted as two-faced in Matthew 7:1–5:

> Do not judge so that you will not be judged. For in the way you judge, you will be judged; and by your standard of measure, it will be measured to you. Why do you look at the speck that is in your brother's eye, but do not notice the log that is in your own eye? Or how can you say to your brother, 'Let me take the speck out of your eye,' and behold, the log is in your own eye? You hypocrite, first take the log out of your own eye, and then you will see clearly to take the speck out of your brother's eye.

When issues arose in the newly formed church in Rome, Paul wrote, "But you, why do you judge your brother? Or you again, why do you regard your brother with contempt? For we will all stand before the judgment seat of God" (Rom. 14:10). Instead of looking down on another, one stands or falls before the Creator, not based on our judgment, but upon God's.

It appears that judgmental attitudes were commonplace in the early church, for James also addresses the issue in his epistle (Jas. 4:11–12): "Do not speak against one another, brethren. He who speaks against a brother or judges his brother, speaks against the law and judges the law; but if you judge the law, you are not a doer of the law but a judge of it. There is only one Lawgiver and Judge, the One who is able to save and to destroy; but who are you who judge your neighbor?" We must refrain from judging another, for when we criticize, we invite judgment upon ourselves (Jas. 2:13).

Even Jesus, perhaps the greatest of all teachers, denounced the catching of flies with vinegar in Matthew 7:1–2: "Do not judge so that you will not be judged. For in the way you judge, you will be judged; and by your standard of measure, it will be measured to you." The critical nature of the early church may have been a contributing factor for Paul's well known words in Philippians 4:8: "Finally, brethren, whatever is true, whatever is honorable, whatever is right, whatever is pure, whatever is lovely, whatever is of good repute, if there is any excellence and if anything worthy of praise, dwell on these things."

Positive Influence

Instead of judgment, criticism, and fault-finding, which is destructive to the Christian community, we are to pursue the way of encouragement. Paul's pen would again write of such things in I Thessalonians 5:11: "Therefore encourage one another and build up one another, just as you also are doing." He discovered a bright spot in the church of Thessalonica and encouraged them to continue the positive practice of lifting each other up.

According to the prophet Jeremiah, the heart of humankind is "more deceitful than all else" (Jer. 17:9) and when too many words flow from our lips, an opportunity for transgression exists, "When there are many words, transgression is unavoidable, but he who restrains his lips is wise" (Prov. 10:19). The bottom line seems to be this: in light of our propensity for spewing forth criticism, we should be careful with our words. Instead of judging another, encouragement is the better pathway.

Think about those who have positively influenced your life. Were they negative individuals or did they exude love, kindness, and encouragement? My bet is that they were the kind of people who had your best interest at heart and provided uplifting nudges toward progress. According to Romans 8:1, not even God condemns us: "Therefore there is now no condemnation for those who are in Christ Jesus." I have kept this outstanding verse close to my chest ever since I was a teenager. Think about the implication of such teaching. If our Creator does not condemn us, then we are free to live, free to change, free to grow, and free to risk. His posture toward us is positive, loving, kind, gracious, and encouraging. We can give ourselves wholly to loving Him and loving others without danger of divine retribution.

Barnabas

As the early church began to blossom, Barnabas became one of its greatest encouragers, and he is a wonderful example to us. His very name means "son of encouragement," and in Acts 4:36, he encouraged others by selling a tract of land and donating the proceeds to those in need. It was Barnabas who encouraged Paul after his Damascus Road experience and convinced skeptical disciples in Jerusalem to fully accept a man who had earlier been hell-bent on persecuting followers of Jesus: "When he [Paul] came to Jerusalem, he was trying to associate with the disciples; but they were all afraid of him, not believing that he was a disciple. But Barnabas took hold of him and brought him to the apostles and described to them how he had seen the Lord on the road, and that He had talked to him, and how at Damascus he had spoken out boldly in the name of Jesus" (Acts. 9:26–27). It was the encouragement of Barnabas that allowed Paul and the Jerusalem disciples to unite together for powerful ministry.

To equate encouragement with someone who is timid and dull would be a mistake, for nothing could be further from the truth when it comes to Barnabas. He traveled with Paul on many occasions, defending the faith right alongside one of the most prolific writers of the New Testament. During Paul's second missionary journey in the book of Acts, Barnabas desired that John Mark accompany them, while Paul resisted this arrangement since John Mark had earlier deserted them in Pamphylia. Paul's ministry went one way with Silas while Barnabas sailed to Cyprus with John Mark. Paul, the great thinker and powerful spokesman for the faith, was unwilling to give John Mark a second chance. Barnabas, the son of encouragement, however, was always looking to uplift others. He encouraged John Mark, believed in him, and provided another opportunity to shine, much like he did with Paul years before (Acts 15:36–41). Barnabas was the consummate encourager and provides a strong example of the positive impact encouragement can have in the life of others.

Jesus

Jesus was also an encourager. His warm and inviting words inspired others to hope in God. Tired of the legalistic burdens placed upon their shoulders by religious leaders, Jesus encouraged the weary to follow him, for he is gentle and humble of heart. His yoke is easy, his burden is light, and rest can be found in following his ways (Mt. 11:28–30). Rule-keeping is burdensome; following God is refreshing.

A woman caught in adultery was brought before Jesus in John 8, and a strict view of the Law of Moses demanded her death by stoning. A judgmental Jesus could have promoted such harsh treatment, but instead, he responds to her accusers, "He who is without sin among you, let him be the first to throw a stone at her (vs. 7). Hearing this, the accusers leave, one by one. Turning his attention to the adulterous woman, Jesus said, "'Woman, where are they? Did no one condemn you?' She said, 'No one, Lord.' And Jesus said, 'I do not condemn you, either. Go. From now on sin no more'" (vs. 10–11). Realizing the turmoil his disciples would experience after his death, Jesus encourages them with these words: "In the world you have tribulation, but take courage; I have overcome the world" (Jn. 16:33). The uplifting words of Jesus are winsome, and many today are still attracted to his inspiring message.

A Thousand Tiny Acts

Though I have walked through fires of criticism, I have also experienced kind words of encouragement that served as a healing salve upon open wounds. Encouragement breathes life into our weary souls and is always positive. As I ponder how others have encouraged me, I become overwhelmed by the sheer number of little acts of kindness that have uplifted my soul. Tears of gratitude fall from my eyes remembering those precious moments when I felt the hand of God upon my shoulder through the positive influence of others. God moves in so many ways in our life, and often through a thousand tiny acts of encouragement rather than one great big kindness.

I am grateful for Joanne, a retired parishioner with numerous health problems, who regularly invited me over for lunch so I could take a break from church work. She made some of my favorite foods, including fried bologna sandwiches. Her support and constant encouragement made a difference in my life. I remember Nicolas and Ana, key church leaders, who took me out on their boat in an effort to help me relax during a tumultuous time in the life of the congregation. Unfortunately, it was a gusty day and as the Gulf waves were wildly thrashing about, I became seasick and gloriously emptied my stomach contents into the ocean, to the dismay of their teenage children. I performed the sideshow a second time with even greater acclaim. We all had a good laugh, but it was their encouragement that touched my heart.

I remember the church custodian and several administrative assistants who became comforting anchors to my family during tough days. I remember Greg, a heaven-sent attorney, who took me under his wings. We became good friends who challenged and encouraged one another in the faith. When the master cylinder gave out on the old green Buick given to me during my seminary days, Greg paid to have it repaired, realizing that I had no discretionary funds for such expenditures. I remember the encouraging words of my district superintendent and the joy of hugging a hospitalized parishioner wired up to all kinds of contraptions who told staff, "I can't calm down until I get a hug from my pastor." The list could go on and on.

It was not uncommon for me to write notes of encouragement to parishioners on a regular basis. After all, they were on my mind, and I cared deeply for them. My role was to serve, and I wanted to be like Barnabas, an encouraging example to the community of faith.

Gifts for Edification

According to Scripture, the Spirit of God endows each person with special gifts and abilities, including you. These gifts are given for the encouragement of others. "But to each one is given the manifestation of the Spirit for the common good" (1 Cor. 12:7). In 1 Corinthians 14, the edification of others becomes an important theme in Paul's teaching: "So also you, since you are zealous of spiritual gifts, seek to abound for the edification of the church" (vs. 12); "But one who prophesies speaks to men for edification and exhortation and consolation" (vs. 3); "Let all things be done for edification" (vs. 26).

Paul goes on to say in Ephesians 4:11–12, "And He gave some as apostles, and some as prophets, and some as evangelists, and some as pastors and teachers, for the equipping of the saints for the work of service, to the building up of the body of Christ." Our spiritual gifts become one pathway for doing this. Encouragement is a powerful tool for marking others—for building them up and helping them change from the inside out. In a thousand little ways, encouragers become the very hands and feet of Jesus to a hurting world.

The words attributed to Aristotle ring true: "To avoid criticism, say nothing, do nothing, be nothing." The only time in my life when criticism fell silent was when I lived in the back of a funeral parlor during college. At times, I would break out my sound system and backup tracks, set equipment up in the viewing area after hours, and sing to a subdued crowd of embalmed individuals. I sang my heart out for them, and they didn't say one unkind word!

Causes of a Critical Spirit

The tongue, unfortunately, can be a dangerous weapon, and though it lacks the anatomical structure of bones, ligaments, and tendons, it possesses the power to break a heart, wound a spirit, or ruin a life. Words carry weight, and while

I have never heard of anyone committing suicide or a homicide as the result of too much encouragement, there are those who have taken this path because excessive criticism diminished self-worth and demeaned self-image. Criticism can be deadly. Why do we continually use vinegar to catch flies when Scripture exhorts us to use honey? Why do we criticize?

While there may be a myriad of reasons why a critical spirit establishes itself in our heart, several key causes come to mind. First, we criticize as a method of comparison. Pointing out the faults of others makes us feel like we are better. Placing others on a lower rung of the ladder makes us feel pretty good about being one rung above them. Have you ever met individuals who stop by for a visit and wind up criticizing your paint colors, your carpet choice, the arrangement of your furniture, and proudly note that your pictures aren't hung at the correct height? It isn't the "proper" way to decorate, and they certainly wouldn't have done it the "wrong" way. Obviously, the glaring fact that it isn't their home escapes their notice as they elevate themselves one rung up on the ladder. They know how to decorate, but you don't. This is an act of comparison, "one rung-manship," designed to elevate their status as the knowledgeable one.

A second reason for criticism is due to self-interest. Big Al, whom I previously mentioned, used criticism as a method for getting his way. He was uninterested in me as a person and clearly didn't have my best interest in mind. Instead, criticism became his tool of choice for bludgeoning others into acquiescence. A third reason arises from frustration. When life doesn't go our way, we can lash out at others in an attempt to hide our resentment. A final reason for criticism is spiritual in nature. One may be running from God, angry at God, disappointed with God, bitter, unforgiving, or resisting the Spirit's leading rather than dealing with heart issues. Criticism spews forth as a smokescreen to mask underlying problems.

I am tired of the gatekeepers in my life who stand at the top of the stairs proclaiming to the world all my imperfections. It gets old. It is draining. It is demoralizing. It is time for those who are too holy for their halo to make way.

No more nasty naysayers in my life, Christian or otherwise. Good riddance! The older I get, the less I appreciate nosy fruit inspectors scrutinizing whether my fruit is worthy of their approval. The church is in dire need of encouragers. Will you answer the call? Growing in our faith is much easier and more appreciated when we surround ourselves with good people who are good for us, good to us, healthy for our soul, and have our best interest at heart.

Honest Self-Examination

To get there, honest self-examination is essential. We cannot judge ourselves by our intentions and others by their actions. We don't want to be too holy for our own halos, and we don't want to be fruit inspectors in the lives of others. We do, however, want to gauge ourselves accurately so our lives are lived in alignment with Paul's words in Ephesians 4:29, "Let no unwholesome word proceed from your mouth, but only such a word as is good for edification according to the need of the moment, so that it will give grace to those who hear" and Colossians 4:6, "Let your speech always be with grace, as though seasoned with salt, so that you will know how you should respond to each person." As we work to perfect the art of fly-catching, our efforts find greater success by using honey rather than vinegar.

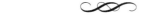

Wisdom for the Journey

Like fields overgrown with weeds, the road of life is replete with criticizers, nay-sayers, and fault-finders who long to zap our energy and lock our gaze. By focusing on such negativity we can easily lose our way and become soured wine. Life is lived with greater joy and satisfaction when we make up our minds to become like Barnabas, a son or daughter of encouragement. By choosing to love rather than judge, we become a ray of hope in the darkened world of others. Life is easier when we encourage and are encouraged.

— chapter twelve —

The Journey

Because we think the grass is always greener on the other side of the fence, our discontented souls yearn to be someplace else. This leads to a dissatisfied feeling of being shortchanged, and it prompts our continual search for mile-markers that indicate we have finally arrived. Yet, when we finally get to where we think we want to be, we quickly scan the horizon for other destinations to assuage our wandering hearts. We jump from one quest for internal assurance to another, and it is this search-land-jump mentality that is problematic.

We never seem satisfied with our various landing spots, and it isn't long before we pull up stakes and initiate a new search. When traveling, on the other hand, we can't wait to find a place to land, even though our chronic anxiety ensures that it will inevitably serve only as a temporary resting stop. What is with this roller-coaster quest of ours? Life, for many, is like a whirlwind vacation to Europe, rushing from one place to another in an attempt to squeeze in as many sights as possible. For others, a more leisurely approach is preferred.

A Journey—Not a Destination

If you haven't already figured it out, life is a journey. We had absolutely nothing to do with our initiation into this excursion since we didn't "cause" ourselves, and if we had our way, we wouldn't allow ourselves to experience death, either. The beginning and ending of life isn't ours to decide, but from the very beginning we were meant to journey. There are no set destination points we are meant to reach in this life; there is only the journey itself. Life would be far easier if the goal was to all congregate, let's say, in Texas. If we could just make it to Texas, we would be assured, beyond a shadow of doubt, that we had reached a point of inner security knowing that of all people, we turned out okay. We were in Texas while others weren't. This is just like us; instead of relishing the journey, we scramble for external markers that affirm our worth in comparison to others.

Cocooned for nine months in the safety of our mother's womb, things were very comfortable. The temperature was perfect, even when it was cold outside. We were cared for, didn't have to eat or breathe, and life was cozy and secure. Our birth initiated a journey we couldn't stop. Ousted from our sheltered abode, we began breathing on our own, eating on our own, adjusting to unfamiliar surroundings, and learning how to survive in a hostile world. Our birth initiated a process whereby we are both living and dying at the same time—a journey that will last about seventy-eight years, if we are lucky. Whether black or white, rich or poor, male or female, Jew or Gentile, our migration toward death is never halted or delayed. Birth and death become the bookends of life with only the journey in between.

As a teenager, I imagined success as owning a home and driving a Jeep Wrangler with a Golden Retriever in the back seat. My adolescent mind thought that if I could reach these milestones, I would be a successful human being. There I was, early on in life, believing that a specific destination determined my worth. It never occurred to me that I was already treasured by God, or that life was a journey, or that how I journeyed actually mattered. My dad's saying, "You can't put an old head on young shoulders," certainly applied to me.

There is nothing wrong with a Jeep Wrangler, a home, or an adorable Golden Retriever. We have to live, own things, do things, and be things. The distinction, however, is that they are not ends unto themselves—not final destinations—but merely aspects of a larger journey into the mystery of God. Landing spots become a part of our story, but they are neither the story itself, nor the purpose and meaning of the book. The quality of our journey is a matter of perspective, priority, and purpose rather than the attainment of perceived external markers of self-adulation. Our journey is about becoming, evolving, and transforming rather than amassing power, status, possessions, and titles.

As our journey commences, the end is too far down the road to see with much clarity, and we are unconcerned with our approaching demise. As we progress through life, however, the very opposite occurs. The end comes into greater focus while the remembrance of earlier years is shrouded in forgetfulness. Allow me to share several key insights from my own journey in an effort to aid yours—since, after all, I am on the downhill side of life.

Transformation

First, it is paramount that we understand that life's journey is about transformation—becoming all that we were meant to be. The journey of change and growth lasts a lifetime, for there is always room for personal development. Transformation is a matter of progress—a metamorphosis of incremental steps rather than instant arrival. The core message Jesus proclaimed was one of transformation from the inside out. The Spirit's revolutionary work in our lives moves us in the direction of living abundantly, loving boundlessly, and becoming all that God desires us to be. It is an internal evolution of the heart whereby we more accurately reflect and reveal our creator.

It is possible to be financially secure without want or worry and still be naïve and numb to the importance of journey. On the other hand, a homeless person living on the streets of San Francisco may possess greater firsthand knowledge of the challenging work of transformation. Status, wealth, and possessions are not part of the equation; instead, they are often nothing more than roadblocks to the renewal process, for they are merely temporary landing spots, not the substance of lasting internal change. The art of becoming isn't about the accumulation of "things," whatever those things might be, but rather, fine-tuning our sensitivity to the Spirit. Changing from the inside out is an ongoing process of learning, growing, and becoming, and it may be similar to chasing the horizon—something we always seem to be running after but never quite catching.

To move from one level of self-understanding to another often involves pain. Looking in the mirror and seeing our shortcomings staring back at us is never a pleasant experience. How do you move from alcohol addiction, for instance, to sober reality and become the kind of parent and spouse you were meant to be? This kind of radical about-face takes courage, effort, and constant diligence. Moving from the sad existence of addiction to a new reality is a life-changing process. You are becoming a new you—the real you. This is the art of becoming, changing, and moving from where you are to what God wants you to become. It is the work of growing up and maturing on the inside—the very heart of our jaunt through life. Recognizing the importance of journey is a foundational perspective that allows us to courageously travel the path of revitalization, or what Jesus called the narrow way.

I possess an insatiable determination to learn and achieve. This drive is a part of who I am, and like a fingerprint that is uniquely mine, it is hardwired into me. Learning and achieving are positive attributes, but like all personality traits, they come with a downside. This thirst for knowledge places me on a quest to understand, conquer, and wrap my arms around whatever I set my mind to study. Every time I try to master the intricacies of God, however, I hit a brick wall. He is just too complex for me to figure out. All intellectual roads lead to an eventual dead-end as I realize the huge gap between my finite abilities and His unlimited being. In essence, I am unable to do what I was designed to do—understand. Living in this intellectual limbo can be frustrating.

God cannot be "solved." He is a glorious mystery that cannot adequately be captured by our symbols, knowledge, and language. In some way, I had to come to grips with my drive to understand and my inability to know. Being too conservative in my understanding of God meant placing limits on His abilities. Being too liberal nearly did away with Him, reducing life to only that which can be known and controlled. Both approaches seemed off-kilter. The answers I craved were hidden from me. I had to learn to live without certitude, and yet, allow for the expansiveness of God. A gradual transformation took place in my thinking so I could be true to myself and at the same time live within the mystery of God. That may not sound like an exciting transformation in your eyes, but for me, it was huge. One aspect of Christian maturity is the ability to live joyfully in an imperfect world and to trust in a God we are only able to experience, never fully explain.

After many years of marriage, a close friend of mine went through a divorce. An arrogant, know-it-all side of him was on full display, and his well-rehearsed religious doctrine came across as judgmental and self-righteous. Over time, he had gained weight, refused to get things done around the house, and neglected his wife and marriage. She was deeply wounded, and he refused to accept responsibility for his role in the deterioration of their vows. In time, the inevitable occurred—she divorced him. This wasn't how things were supposed to wind up. The ordeal drove him to his knees. He didn't want a divorce and certainly didn't expect it, but here he was sitting on the corner of loneliness and despair. As is often the case, we don't appreciate what we have until it is gone.

What else is there to do but seek the Lord when your back is up against the wall? Pain has a way of softening our heart in earnest preparation for our search for answers. As Scripture notes, when we seek God with all our heart, we find Him (Jer. 29:13–14). The arctic ice encasing our heart begins to melt and break apart so that a renaissance within freely flows. The Spirit's searchlight began its illuminating work, and my friend saw himself in the light of Christ—as he really was rather than with the jaded spectacles of self-deception he was used to wearing.

With clear-cut resolve, he asked God to make him a better man, and God obliged, as He always does. It was a painful process but one full of promise.

He committed himself to reducing the vast chasm between who he was and who God wanted him to become. It was the right move—a step of faithful courage. Today, my friend is a changed man—transformed by the Spirit's power. When we give God the key to our life, He enters the premises, cleans house, rearranges things, and strips us of the belly-button fluff we once considered so precious. He makes real men and women out of us. Much to my friend's surprise and joy, he and his former wife are now happily remarried, a wedding ceremony that I performed. In a sense, I had a front row seat to a revival of the heart.

Our trek through life is never static, and though our travels take us to many ports of call, our goal is never to reach a destination, sit on our laurels, and wait to die. No, life is a journey into the mystery of God—winding and weaving, over and under, but always moving forward, always progressing, and always becoming. It is futile to engage in all kinds of religious activities, as many do, with the high hopes of earning God's favor. Transformation isn't like that. Changing from the inside out is not a method of earning God's approval; instead, it securely basks in the knowledge that God already approves and delights in our very being. The dawn of inner renewal emanates from a deep connection to the living God. It is a result, not a task; a byproduct, not an activity designed to appease a demanding deity. As the very ground of our being, God is the source of all that we are. His call upon our life is to fully experience His love, immerse ourselves in His life, and live abundantly in His being. Transformation is the natural outcome of allowing our Creator, the source of our existence, to encompass us, flow to us, through us, around us, and out from us.

God is in the Journey

The first thing to know about life's journey is that it is the journey that God is most interested in, for it becomes the fertile soil of transformation. The journey is about movement and progress, and it involves our entire being. It is a journey of relationship with the living God, and like Abraham who left Ur of the Chaldees in search of a new land, our odyssey also involves faith. God uses the circumstances of everyday life to teach us and draw us closer to Him. Walking with God does not occur without a journey, and this thing called life is where we roll up our sleeves and experience His presence. Growth doesn't happen in a vacuum. The world becomes our classroom. If life is all about the journey, then *how* we journey becomes all-important, and this becomes the subject of our second important insight: How we journey impacts the rate of transformation, the depth of transformation, and whether we transform at all.

How We Journey Matters

From my own travels, I can affirm that our trek through time is constantly filled with choices, often opposites in perspective that make all the difference in the world. For instance, journey or destination becomes an important choice that determines a good many things about our sojourn. Choosing journey over destination is the right choice, but there are other decisions to be made. Allow me to share a few of them with you.

Embrace or resist, peace or panic, fear or courage, joy or sadness, optimism or pessimism, forgive or avenge, gratitude or entitlement, and the like are some of the choices we encounter. We don't get to choose a good many things in life, such as our genes or the actions of others. The choice left to us is *how* we journey. We get to choose our attitude, perspective, interpretation, and response to the state of affairs in which we find ourselves.

For instance, community or individual becomes an important choice. Will we involve others in our journey, or will we go it alone? Scripture places high value on community as a source of encouragement and growth. We were meant to walk this planet with others. Of course, this means more drama, headache, and irritation, whereas individualism avoids most of these negative aspects. Traveling with others always involves surprises, both good and bad. From a scriptural perspective, however, walking alone is never an option, and though it is the easier path to follow and avoids the predictable pitfalls of human interaction, it is not a path God intends for us. In community, we learn to patiently love and serve others. It is in the presence of others that we learn about ourselves. This is a choice you get to make. Will you journey alone, or will you journey with others? Community or individual?

Imperfection or perfection is another decision thrust upon us, and this one is rather tricky. We strive to be perfect, expect others to be perfect, and continually seek perfection in an imperfect world. We chase after an impossible goal, wear ourselves out trying to attain it, and fail to realize that it isn't even a goal we should pursue.

Have you ever noticed that Jesus never became upset with sinners? He invited the imperfect to himself. He loved them, ministered to them, and saw the life of God in them. Jesus seems to be far less concerned with our shortcomings than about the life of God already within us. The religious elite of his day pursued perfection, even meticulously tithing mint, dill, and cumin. They were caught up in sin management and with their giant magnifying glasses, became expert fruit inspectors who enjoyed mandating, controlling, and inspecting the fruit production of others. This wasn't what captured the heart and passion of Jesus, and it certainly didn't occupy his time. He only seemed to be upset with those who *thought* they were perfect. God is fully aware of our shortcomings, and He loves us anyway.

We search for God in the perfect when He reveals Himself through the imperfect. Sin management is a distraction and a quick route to missing God. We are surprised to see Him in the leper, in the despised Samaritan, and in the lowly sinner. Whether we wear designer jeans or tattered hand-me-downs, we are all naked under our clothes. If you want to see God in this life, don't look to those who proudly proclaim their own holiness; instead, look for Him among the lowly, the marginalized, and the poor (Mt. 25: 42–45). God associates with imperfect people—like you and me. As we discover His presence in unlikely places, He has a way of surprising us. Why continue the fruitless search for perfection and run ourselves ragged?

God or religion is another important decision we make. This is the choice between real gold and fool's gold—between the shadow and the shadow-maker, and between symbol and reality. In our trek across time, we can easily get caught up in the insignificant, all the while deceiving ourselves into believing it is important. The difference between experiencing God and doing religious things for God is a line that can become blurry.

The issue is one of substitution whereby we mistake religious activity for experiencing God. We may encounter God while doing just about any task, religious or not, but the deed is separate and distinct from the experience of God. The pursuit of religion is exhausting, whereas the pursuit of God is inspiring and life-giving. Believing that God is somehow impressed with our many religious endeavors and that those endeavors earn us favor in His sight is nothing but fool's gold. It is the experience of God that we long for, and while our symbols, our churches, and our rituals may point to Him, they are not God. This distinction alone helps to separate the wheat from the chaff in choosing God over religion.

Once we understand that God is interested in and experienced through the journey, we realize that our daily decisions take on greater significance. While making wise choices enhances our experience of God, there is yet another aspect to our journey worth mentioning—our journey home.

The Journey Home

For the last eight years, I have lived out of boxes. I jokingly refer to my place as a tiny storage unit with a bed. Though my recent travels have taken me to various places, I don't think of any of them as home. I seem to have a gift for diagnosing dysfunctional and declining institutions and strategically nursing them back to health again. Once they are fixed up and placed on the right track, I am off to restore another ailing organization. This is good work, but my heart longs for home, a place where I can unpack my things and stay a good while. My father worked for the same company for forty years. He knew a stability that I have yet to experience. Living out of boxes is no fun.

When I say that we are on a journey home, I am not referring to a physical home, although I long for that in my own life. Neither am I referring to heaven, the place many Christians believe is our final resting place when we die. I use "journey home" as a metaphor. We could call it a sense of spiritual self-actualization, feeling comfortable in our own skin, finding our true selves, or being and living according to our God-given blueprint. In this sense, we all long for that sweet spot where life is lived from a recognition of who we are and whose we are.

In my own life, this journey has been rather fascinating. Complicated, confusing, and fraught with obstacles, I wouldn't trade it for the world for the simple reason that I finally came home. I am truly comfortable in my own skin—with how God made me. I now realize that God is even within me. This is a powerful realization I would not have embraced had it not been for the journey. For me, like so many others, my realization was a second-half-of-life occurrence. With significant experience under my belt and worn out from living behind the façade of a false self, I was finally ready to come to terms with myself.

Discovering our true self is a process that only the journey can produce. The true self is within you, waiting to be revealed, treasured, and embraced, yet it struggles to break free since it is covered in layers of ego-driven falsity that has accrued over the years. The journey home is the discovery of deeply knowing who you are and allowing that beauty to shine forth for all to see. We think we know who we are, but merely thinking something doesn't make it true. Without a deep awareness of our true selves, we exist as mere posers, living according to how we think others want us to be or how our false self defines us. We hide behind scaffolding that projects an image we strive to protect. We are like the giant marble slab from which Michelangelo sculpted David, his Renaissance masterpiece. Most see only the massive block of rock, but Michelangelo saw a precious work of art within. His role was to reveal the seventeen-foot showpiece by chipping away at all that covered it up.

Our lives are similar to the statue of David. Finding our way back home involves chipping away all that covers up our deepest, truest self. Each blow of the Master's hammer is designed to free us, to reveal our true self until we realize our own magnificence.

I don't care much for the blows of the chisel. I feel it reverberate throughout my entire being. It is noisy, painful, and it seems to take forever. The journey, however, became the process by which my statue of David was being freed from the marble slab. Over the years, a gnawing feeling grew in the pit of my stomach that annoyed me. There was more to life, wasn't there? More to me? The religious answers of the past seemed insufficient to meet the needs of my present journey. They didn't work in the real world of my second-half-of-life reality. The answers I was touting to others no longer worked for me. In my mind, I wasn't living honestly and truthfully. There seemed to be a difference between the façade I was hiding behind and the real me that yearned for freedom. The scaffolding looked good from the outside, and it helped me to play nicely in the sandbox of life, but I longed to sail across oceans of knowledge and discover who I really was.

Over time, I realized that I didn't fit in very well with the rest of the religious crowd. Was I the only one who saw the façade for what it was? Did no one else see the scaffolding around their lives? My early faith and religious belief helped get me to this point, but it was unable to propel me farther along on my journey. For many, religion is about correct belief, and in this sense, it is no different than any other club where conformity of thought becomes the entrance ticket. But Jesus didn't emphasize right belief as the prerequisite for knowing our Creator; he merely invited others to follow God—to follow the narrow path, and to simply love God and love others. His was a practical Christianity—an experiential one, not some ideological litmus test.

I might say it this way: my first car, a 1966 Chevy Impala, was falling apart and finally broke down along the side of the road. I was unable to put it back together again, and even if I could, it would eventually break down again. It was, after all, from an era gone by, and a newer, different vehicle would have to transport me from here on out. Transformation simply means to change forms. I exchanged a 1966 Chevy Impala for a new set of wheels. One took me so far, broke down, and necessitated my entry into a newer vehicle. Our journey is meant to transform us. We start out in a 1966 Chevy Impala, but we change, we grow, we mature, and we become. The marble slab is being chipped away at by the Lord's hammer until we stand tall and proud, freed from the cultural crude that holds us back. We change from a slab to a masterpiece—from a 1966 Chevy Impala to a newer vehicle. Our motivation changes, our goals change, as does our outlook. We begin to see the world through the heart of God. We finally come home. This is the process of transformation—the very purpose of our journey.

For transformation to occur, we must unlearn many things we once thought we knew. Coming home is about unlearning and freeing. We are, after all, chipping away at the slap and getting rid of everything that impedes our statue from being unearthed. As we drive our 1966 Chevy Impala down the road, layers of dirt, grime, and filth accumulate, and eventually the car conks out from wear and tear. Unfortunately, we hold on to worthless items that become a part of the scaffolding around our heart. It turns into slab material. When we realize the façade is just that, a false front, it begins to crumble and chunks come crashing to the ground. When what we once believed, even if it is a religious belief, leads us away from transformation, it becomes part of the problem, and further chipping at the stone is necessary. This is the heart of transformation—changing forms and freeing ourselves to live authentic and truthful lives.

Unlearning is absolutely essential for the renewal process to have its resulting effect. We place the seed of faulty perspectives into the ground so that it can die and morph into something else—a new way of being and seeing. The outlook we once held onto so dearly has broken down on the side of the road like my 1966 Chevy Impala, and it is time to jump into a new set of wheels. We acquire a new reference point from which to operate because the old one no longer works. We thought that life was about arriving at various destinations—the more, the merrier. But, with each destination we attained, the thicker the façade became. We were building our house on quicksand—a foundation incapable of sustaining our journey over the long haul. When the house begins to sink into the ground, we start looking for a new reference point to guide us—a new foundation upon which to build our life.

The irony is that we looked elsewhere for God as though He were some object "out there" to be found, when all along we see His presence within us. We are not God and will never be God, but God is certainly within us, for the mystery of Christ is in us, the hope of glory (Col. 1:27), and according to Acts 11:28, "in Him we live and move and exist." When we recognize that He is the very source of our being and is within us, around us, moving out from us, and at the same time beyond us, we realize that the journey of finding God is a journey of coming home. We look for him "out there" when all along He is within us. We are already home.

This recognition alone leads us to a renewed sense of awe for both God and ourselves. The weight of trying to measure up is lifted from our shoulders. Because we are loved and valued for who we are—for just being—we can dance with delight knowing that home is within ourselves. We are the statue of David that has been freed from the marble slab. Think of it—the One who is so far beyond us is also within us. The transformation we experience is realizing that we were home all along. We just had to find ourselves—a process of chipping away and freeing our own masterpiece. The floodgates are now open, so the life of God within us can flow out from us. Our souls can finally rest, for we are home.

Communion with God

The final aspect of our journey is communing with God in our travels. This is taken for granted so often that it frequently becomes a forgotten. We neglect the silencing of our life in order to hear His still, small voice whispering to our soul. The prophets, the mystics, and even Jesus subdued the heart so the Father's voice could be heard.

The gospels demonstrate that Jesus peered behind the veil of life to experience another dimension—the spiritual dimension. For Jesus, there was more to our existence than the physical here and now. He saw visions. He prayed intimately to his Abba Father. He recognized the Spirit upon him. He engaged in healing and miracles. He taught with wisdom and authority. The gospels portray him as a Spirit-filled individual in whom God's power flowed. Even his enemies recognized this.

We find Jesus alone in the desert, engaged in prayer and fasting, and seeking solitude from the crowds. He purposefully sought to quiet his heart in order to sense the moving of God upon his soul. The ministry of Jesus, according to the gospel of John, was directed by the Father (Jn. 5:19; 8:28; 12:49). He knew where to go, what to say, and what to do because he spent time in intimate communion with God.

Quieting my heart enough to sense the Spirit's leading has always been a personal struggle. My mind is active, always thinking, planning, and figuring things out. In my attempts to hear the whisper of God, I often don't know what to do or how to go about it, so I simply remove external distractions and say to my Creator, "Lord, speak to me. I am listening. Help me to hear." I shut up and listen. That's it. There is nothing fancy about it. Like Jesus, I desire to peer behind the curtain and experience the Spirit world. My soul longs for His whisper, and in the silence of the moment, I crave His presence. I don't want to merely journey to God; I want to journey with God. I don't want to merely believe in God, or believe things about God; I want to know God, experience Him, and be sensitive to the Spirit's guidance. I am still learning to do this while traveling on my own journey.

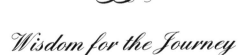

Wisdom for the Journey

The most fundamental aspect of our trek through life is that it is God's method for transforming us from the inside out. Our tour-of-duty is not to be shunned but experienced and embraced, for transformation occurs because of life, not in spite of it. How we journey becomes all-important since it enhances our move from what is to what can be—from who we are to who God wants us to become. This expedition reveals God's presence in uncanny and unexpected ways. There is nothing so liberating as climbing out from under the rubble to discover our true selves, and to sense God's delight in our very being. It is the feeling of finally coming home. Buckle your seat belt and hold on tight—the journey of a lifetime is upon you. Allow God to thrill your heart from the inside out.

— chapter thirteen —

Lost Hope

❧

What? Really? Are you serious? You've got to be kidding me! These thoughts rise to the surface during moments of frustration. In fact, sometimes I roll my eyes and sigh in disbelief. Making fun of our communal uphill swim within the organization, my employees created a sign for my office wall that read, "It's always something!" Some days I just shake my head and mutter under my breadth. Do you ever have moments like that?

Frustrating incidents occur every day, and though we sigh and grunt with displeasure, we deal with them, overcome them, and work to minimize their disruption to our life. Like gnats on a hot day, we swat them away and move on. But there are instances where we experience such trauma, such disillusionment, and such deep disappointment that we totally deflate like a popped balloon. Because the wounds are so painful, we are in jeopardy of losing our way, losing our hope, and feeling that God has abandoned us.

During these difficult moments, life seems like a smelly dung heap. These aren't the kind of annoying incidents you just swat away and be done with;

instead, they occupy our heart and mind while an internal wrestling match ensues to make sense of it all. We sometimes arrive at solutions that allow us to move forward, and at other times, we continue the silent search for answers. When the sting of disappointment is severe, we become like ships on turbulent seas, aimlessly tossed about by waves of meaninglessness, all the while desperately searching for solid ground upon which to stand.

I just got off the phone with a young lady who is experiencing a sudden job loss, a lack of income, mounting debt, and a boyfriend who called it quits. She might have been able to swat these annoying issues away had it been her first trip drifting on the high seas, but this was her third go-around with trauma and loss. Losing hope after striking out so often brings us face-to-face with disillusionment, an ever-present danger lurking in the shadow of pain. Just this last week, hopelessness hit me like a brick, and I had to take time to get my mind right—again. We often experience disappointment in people, organizations, politics, religion, and are especially sensitive to its influence during times of loss, trauma, and uncertainty.

Disillusionment

People can be huge letdowns, can't they? That may be the biggest understatement in this book! I am not a Debbie-downer; instead, I am a realist. People fail us every day, and we let others down, too. It is the nature of being human and living in relationship with others. Yet, sometimes these failures are so egregious that they take our breath away and stop us in our tracks. An unfaithful partner, an intentional hurtful act, or being used and manipulated by someone we care about can send us into a tailspin. No matter how far we progress as a civilization, our past is likely to be relived in future generations if we are not careful. Since the creation of life, humans have been disillusioning one another. Needless pain and suffering occurs because of the disappointment caused by others.

Organizations can also let us down, and while they are made up of people, it is often the policies, practices, culture, decisions, and expectations that can bring about despair. When organizations hold employees responsible for accomplishing goals without providing the resources or authority for success, dysfunction prevails and disillusionment is sure to follow. On countless occasions, I have been asked to transform declining institutions into thriving entities, all with insufficient finances, entrenched personnel, outdated technology, dreadful policies, dysfunctional processes, and a resistant culture. I was expected to accomplish transformation without altering the political landscape or hurting anyone's feelings. In other words, I was expected to bring the results of change without actually given the freedom to change anything. They wanted a god, and I was a mere mortal. How can a thoroughbred win the Kentucky Derby with its front two legs tied together?

Years ago, as I interviewed for a university faculty position, the President proudly whipped out an architectural master plan revealing his next big building project in hot pursuit of a presidential legacy. Realizing that faculty worked several jobs outside of the university just to make ends meet, spending millions on new construction while dedicated faculty were barely eeking out an existence didn't seem right to me. In my young mind at the time, a chasm existed between the values proclaimed and the values practiced. I saw a disconnect between proclaiming to value faculty and paying them non-livable wages, and disavowing material items while redirecting funds for a multi-million dollar facility. Obviously, there is nothing wrong with building new facilities, but in those days, the juxtaposition made me think about organizational integrity.

Several new administrative positions were being created in a restructuring move at one institution I served. Sitting in a leadership meeting, the key decision-maker, my boss, stated, "I already know who I want. Do we advertise the positions internally so people feel like they were considered for the position?" What? If you already know who you want and the decision has already been made, why go through a sham process where others don't have a prayer? Though it was a faith-based institution, this manipulative move undermined integrity. People see right through these disingenuous actions, Christian or otherwise.

The political and religious arenas also engender extreme disillusionment. One's personal worldview, for instance, may not be reflected in government policies or by the party in power. Merely reading the daily news can discourage the heart. As the human population continues to increase and cultural and geographical boundaries shrink, religions collide with one another, and much of what is done in the name of God is puzzling and discouraging. Many are disillusioned by the evil they see in this world and a God who, in their mind, is unwilling or unable to do anything about it. For those who have endured extreme hardship, the thought of a benevolent higher power is nothing but an illusion.

Larger domains beyond my own insulated world exist that I also consider. Recently, I heard of a young woman who escaped the brutal North Korean dictatorship, only to watch her mother being raped at one point in their journey to China. As the story is told, she walked across the Gobi desert to Mongolia in search of freedom, all the while carrying a knife, ready and willing to kill herself if she were caught. Better to be dead than return to the horrors of a brutal regime. I envision war-torn refugees fleeing their homeland with nothing but the clothes on their back. The life they once cherished has been stripped from them. I contemplate those living in economically depressed nations with nothing to look forward to except the emptiness they have known all of their lives. Though our own sense of lost hope seems to pale in comparison with those who have lost so much, disillusionment is relative to one's own situation, wherever and whatever that is. In other words, all can experience lost hope to one degree or another.

When things are going well, life is good and we are happy. But when uncertainty, trauma, or loss parks on our doorstep, disillusionment is within striking distance. Losing hope is real. Disillusionment is real. Our journey can be painful, and we don't always die with a smile on our face. Sugar-coating these difficult seasons of life only serves to imprison us in a false reality. It is far better to acknowledge their presence and openly discuss how to hit the reset button. One of the best ways to ward off disillusionment is preclusion—to hold it at bay rather than expend precious emotional energy constantly digging ourselves out of the pit of despair. The focus is on prevention rather than correct pit-climbing techniques.

A common way people deal with foreboding disillusionment is to lower their expectations, believing that if they don't have any, they won't be disappointed. With this approach, they either become indifferent and detached or they work to become king of the jungle in a dog-eat-dog world and learn to play the game better than others. Either extreme is no way to live life with fullness and joy.

Engaging in top-dog jungle fights is far removed from the teaching of Jesus. Even if we adopted this cutthroat perspective, disappointment would still seek us out, as there is always another dog stronger, faster, and wiser than us. There is nothing wrong with being strategic, but viewing life as a sick game whereby we jettison our values in order to outmaneuver others before they outmaneuver us doesn't align with Scripture. Whether the disillusionment we experience causes us to become withdrawn or self-absorbed, neither result is acceptable. We must find a better way—a way that is reasonable, practical, and positive.

I know a man who succumbed to the "game" mentality early on in life after experiencing the sting of disillusionment. His job became a paycheck. He stopped caring. His goal was to have everyone *think* he was the consummate employee, while he was merely building a façade of perceived reality. He participated in the least amount he could strategically get away with. He took on a defensive posture and thought, "I will outplay you, outsmart you, use you before you use me, and you will never know it. I will not get screwed over again." At times we must implement measures of self-protection, but living life this way becomes a roadblock to the abundant life Jesus desired for us.

Disillusionment often *tests* us, and if we are wise, it can also *teach* us many valuable lessons. We learn when to hang on and when to let go. We sometimes give up too early and lose out on blessing and growth, and at other times, we hang on too long and experience greater pain. Wouldn't it be nice to live with such inner tranquility that nothing outside of ourselves upsets our equilibrium? Is it possible? Is it worth pursuing? An all-important pathway for experiencing rock-solid inner peace is maintaining a healthy outlook. Correct perspective acts as both an anchor and a compass in our life. It grounds us when threatening winds blow and guides us through difficult terrain. We need both.

Overcoming the Disillusionment Factor

Let me share some important perspectives that have assisted me with the disillusionment factor. While these broad-stroke perspectives have helped me drastically reduce the frequency and depth of my own disappointments to manageable levels, feel free to add to them or make up your own. Like all of us, I struggle to implement these healthy outlooks in my own life, but the more I consciously choose them over other alternative thinking, I not only cope better, but I seem to thrive. The point is to discover healthy ways of dealing with severe disappointment. I prefer to live with outlooks that preclude and reduce disillusionment rather than exert energy digging myself out of one hole after another.

Manage Me

The first thing I do is manage me. Though this may seem elementary, it is extremely difficult to do well. It may even be that one of the reasons we lose hope so often is that we haven't learned to regulate our mind and emotions; we haven't mastered the art of "managing me." Though it isn't easy, it is a necessary and foundational element for living well.

I began managing myself when I realized my own finiteness. It hit me one day that I couldn't fix every person, solve every problem, and that I was unable to be and do everything I desired, let alone meet others' expectations. The issues were bigger than me. I also realized that just as I was disillusioned with others, I disillusioned people, too. The deflated-balloon feeling of disappointment in the pit of my stomach was the same feeling I sometimes caused in others. What a vicious cycle, to be both the recipient and the cause at the same time.

There's not much we can do about our own finiteness. It just is. We can mope, pout, stomp about, lash out, or punch a wall, but nothing changes. Though we struggle to accept our limitations, we are better for recognizing them and moving toward perspectives that better our journey through life.

We are complex beings with spiritual, physical, emotional, intellectual, and social dimensions. We hold our aspirations high, possess biased perspectives, are susceptible to influence, and possess certain personality traits and skill sets. How could we ever possibly entertain controlling others when we struggle to manage ourselves?

Though it is a daunting task, we must turn our face toward the wind and engage in the onerous work of dealing with ourselves. Controlling life's circumstances is a myth, but if we manage ourselves well, our biggest disappointments can ultimately become our greatest gain. No matter the situation, I divert attention from my surrounding environment to the kind of person I want to be. What character traits am I after? What is the gold standard by which I measure myself? How will I hold myself accountable in thought, word, and deed to the kind of person I seek to become?

I recognize my limitations and focus on living within my own sphere of influence. I seek to be the change I desire to experience in others. I set my own path, create my own journey, and establish my own timetable. In other words, I unswervingly follow the path God has set before me. I seek to narrow my focus on the goal of becoming the kind of person God desires, rather than wasting energy trying to gather the stars of the universe together. In essence, my efforts go toward self-management instead of trying to control what cannot be controlled.

Establish Boundaries

In addition to managing myself, I establish boundaries designed to protect my heart against those with a propensity for irritating others. When we are in the presence of folks like that, there is always some degree of disappointment that occurs. In these situations, my boundaries limit the contact, content, and consternation of my interactions. I have learned the art of self-respect and saying "no."

A "favorite" relative, for example, who always seems to generate anxiety and discomfort during family get-togethers may be in need of boundaries. In this case, you determine when to show up at family gatherings, what topics of conversation are off limits for you, who you want to surround yourself with, and how long you stay at the event. In this way, you are sociable and present, while negating the disastrous effect of the "favorite" relative's demeanor.

My friend, a healthcare employee, works with a medical doctor who brings a cloud of disillusionment wherever he goes. To survive this daily barrage of negativity, my friend created emotional boundaries to ward off the doctor's effect of demoralizing those around him. By erecting emotional barriers that others were not allowed to cross, including the doctor, she was able to establish a more harmonious work environment. Her countenance brightened, and her behavior became much more measured.

Pastors are easy targets for criticism by well-intentioned dragons within the church's hollowed walls. One of the best boundaries that church leaders can establish for their minister is to become a buffer zone between the endless stream of criticism and the pastor's compassionate heart. This buffer zone becomes a line of safety whereby disillusionment is not allowed to cross.

Boundaries can be emotional, physical, or a combination of both. Wisdom dictates that we not scream in confrontation, "You are a big disappointment to me. I am creating a barrier between us so I won't be disillusioned by you anymore." Common sense knows better than that. Done in the proper way, boundaries are healthy and necessary for abundant living; they become protective barriers that guard our motivation, our kind-heartedness, and our joy.

When we manage ourselves well, we become mindful of destructive situations and people that have an adverse effect upon us. Armed with this knowledge, we can establish appropriate boundaries that enable us to thrive. We learn when to walk away, speak up, control our emotions, and what our limits are. We become responsible for ourselves and for our own self-care. We should always be kind to others and abandon our judgmental attitudes, but we are free to create necessary boundaries for preserving our sanity, lowering our stress, and maintaining positive energy flow.

Focus on Joy and Peace

The third perspective in my arsenal of disillusionment stoppers is to focus on what brings me joy and peace. Though I must accept the limits of my own finiteness, I am in full control of this aspect of my life. There is something about being in-tune with our Creator that brings joy and peace deep into our soul. Jesus said it best in John 14:27: "Peace I leave with you; My peace I give to you; not as the world gives do I give to you. Do not let your heart be troubled, nor let it be fearful." Paul echoes a similar thought in Philippians 4:7: "And the peace of God, which surpasses all comprehension, will guard your hearts and your minds in Christ Jesus." He goes on to say in Romans 14:17 that "the kingdom of God is not eating and drinking, but righteousness and peace and joy in the Holy Spirit."

Motorcycle rides on paved country roads bring me peace. Taking in the beautiful landscape and lively wildlife of a nearby lake brings me peace. Soaking in a hot bath and reading a good book brings me peace. Enjoying good conversation with friends brings me peace. Knowing that I am loved and accepted by my Creator brings me peace. Engaging in the things I am gifted and skilled at brings me peace. My inner tranquility is something I treasure. No one can take that away from me, and no circumstance has the right to steal it from me. It is mine, and I guard it closely.

Discovering the beauty of God in places where others only see desolation brings me joy. As I become more sensitive to the pain of others, joy and gratitude blossom in my life. Rather than focusing on what I don't have (control of all things), I intentionally draw my gaze toward those things that bring me peace and joy, things that can never be taken from me. What we focus on determines the meaning we attach to the circumstances in our life, as noted in Proverbs 23:7: "For as he thinks within himself, so he is."

What grabs our attention consumes our energies. I intentionally focus on joy and peace because I want to expend my energies on something that produces positive results in my life. If I long to see positive change in this world, that change must begin with me. For that to happen, I must operate from a position of strength, where energy arises from deep within my soul and sustains me for the long haul. As disillusionment seeks access to my life, the twin pillars of peace and joy deny entry.

Live Your Principles and Values

Another perspective that drives my approach to lost hope is a desire to always live by my principles and values. Despite the shifting circumstances of life, and life often shifts frequently and seismically, I stand firm in who I am, what I am, and how I choose to live my life. It becomes the bedrock upon which my life is built.

Some folks attempt to alter their personality, their beliefs, their values, and their character depending on the situation and what is in their best interest at the time. I can't live with that kind of schizophrenic outlook, and find it extremely debilitating. Who am I? What am I? What do I stand for? Well, with this outlook, it all depends! In a world where I don't control much of anything, I *can* control the principles that guide my life and the values upon which I am determined to live.

What principles and values guide your life? Many haven't given serious thought to this question, and rather than being anchored to a foundation of bedrock, they simply react according to how they feel at the moment. They are emotional roller coasters, and life becomes a constant series of highs and lows, ups and downs. I encourage you to think deeply about how you want to live your life. What principles will guide you? What will you stand for, and what will be your bedrock values? Will integrity be a top priority? Is being a person of your word important? Will kindness be a prized character trait? Will you cherish others, even though they see things differently? Will you give of yourself in service? Will you pursue joy, peace, compassion, and cultivate an attitude of gratitude in your life? Who are you? What are you? What kind of person do you want to be?

Pursue Friendship

The final perspective worth pursuing is friendship. The support of loving friends who have our best interest at heart is life-giving. The words of Ecclesiastes 4:9–12 ring true:

> Two are better than one because they have a good return for their labor. For if either of them falls, the one will lift up his companion. But woe to the one who falls when there is not another to lift him up. Furthermore, if two lie down together they keep warm, but how can one be warm alone? And if one can overpower him who is alone, two can resist him. A cord of three strands is not quickly torn apart.

Friends help us weather the disillusionments of life. They confront, console, counsel, and clarify our thinking and behavior. They become solid support mechanisms in an otherwise slippery slope of disappointment. In contemporary Christianity, a questioning spirit and independent thinking is rarely encouraged. Sadly, we are expected to have already arrived at some predetermined state of holiness. Life, however, isn't about arriving, but about journeying, learning, growing, and becoming. It is about transformation from the inside out, and that involves thinking, questioning, readjusting, and wrestling with the difficulties we encounter.

The account of Jonathan and David in the Old Testament is an inspiring story of friendship that withstands the test of time and circumstance. A strong friendship bond exists between David, the hero shepherd-boy who slew Goliath, the Philistine giant, and Jonathan, the great archer-warrior and son of King Saul.

In light of David's rising fame, King Saul became jealous and sought to kill David on numerous occasions. He was bent on tracking him down like a common criminal to ensure his demise. This caused David frequent hardship and many sleepless nights. It is in this context that David and Jonathan formed a covenant of lifelong friendship arising from their mutual respect for one another. Jonathan's valuable friendship must have brought gentle reassurance to David's soul and helped him overcome discouraging and disillusioning thoughts while constantly on the run.

We need people like that in our lives—Jonathans who will covenant with us, stand by us, and offer their support and encouragement. Life's journey isn't as easy as picking daisies on a sunny afternoon with songs from *The Sound of Music* blaring in the background. Instead, it is often an arduous trek, filled with constant pitfalls. It is best to travel with the help of friends. If one falls, the others lend a helping hand. A cord of three strands is not quickly torn asunder.

Some folks, like me, are introverts, preferring a smaller number of close friends with the ability to go deep. The danger, of course, is being left alone when the wagons are circled. Extroverted individuals, on the other hand, enjoy a wider circle of support. The concern here, however, is shallow relationships and feeling alone while surrounded by a crowd. Whether extroverted or introverted, my advice remains the same; find friends who can strengthen your cord so it is not easily broken. When trusted others become your Jonathan, disillusionment struggles to lodge itself in your life.

Let me close this chapter by bringing up the issue of expectations again. While some try to live without them in order to avoid disappointment, it seems to me that we do, and we should, have expectations in this life. The key to warding of disillusionment is not in doing away with all expectation, but in honestly evaluating the expectations we hold. Too high, and we easily come crashing down. Too low, and we become unfulfilled. If we expect of others what we are unwilling to do ourselves, we set ourselves up for disappointment. If we skew our perspective or only accept selective data, our expectations are off.

In reality, we must consistently be asking ourselves if we are viewing our circumstances correctly. Are my expectations in alignment with reality? How can I see things more clearly? And most importantly, what do my expectations say about me?

───※───

Wisdom for the Journey

As you journey through life, disappointment will seek you out. It happens to all of us. Rather than wait until you get to the mountain before learning to climb, I suggest you prepare now by implementing perspectives that will help you avoid the highlands of doom altogether. These perspectives include managing yourself, creating appropriate boundaries, focusing on what brings you joy and peace, living by your principles and values, and establishing a network of supportive friends. Finally, examine your expectations often to ensure you are viewing things correctly.

— chapter fourteen —

Stand & Sit

Scientists, philosophers, and professors debate the purpose and meaning of life, as do farmers, business owners, and religious folks. Why are we here? Is there meaning to life—some reason for our existence? Is our purpose to worship God, procreate, oversee the planet, or grow in the human and spiritual maturation process? The debate, I imagine, will not be settled any time soon.

Though I enjoy these deeper discussions, I am far too practical to get sucked into the quicksand of what may never be fully known. I am concerned with today, for this is where life is lived—in the present. How shall I live right now? What will capture my attention in this temporal journey of mine? What will be my focus, my purpose, and my values? Instead of becoming entangled in abstruse debates, I want to keep things real—things that actually help me on a daily basis. I don't mind having my head in the clouds, but my feet must also be firmly planted on the ground.

This chapter discusses two important items—standing and sitting. By standing, I mean substantive issues that matter so much that we are willing to

203

take a stand for them—whenever and wherever. For some, taking a stand for issues of magnitude can become a life's work. Discovering consequential issues worth dying for shapes our lives with purpose and meaning.

This chapter also addresses a second important item—sitting, by which I mean taking time to rest and replenish energy reserves. Sometimes we get so wound up in standing that we forget to sit down. By sitting, I am talking about margin—the difference between the amount of energy available and the load exerted upon us. In other words, we need time for ourselves. Call it personal space, margin, or the ability to stop and smell the roses—our addiction to the hamster-wheel of life can no longer consume us. Pushing the pause button is healthy for us in so many ways. As we journey through life, there is a time to stand and a time to sit—hence, the title of this chapter.

Standing

The things I am willing to stand for have changed over the years—not in a drastic way, but in a deeper, more nuanced way. It is part of growing up, maturing, and viewing life from the vantage point of experience. I stand for my belief in God, for instance, but my understanding of who He is has deepened over the years. I now know the difference between form and substance—between the shadow and the shadow-maker. As a freshly minted seminary graduate, I was prepared to debate theology in an effort to convince you that I was right. Now, however, I could care less about debating and convincing. For me, Christianity isn't about right belief, but rather, a vibrant relationship with the Creator. From a theological perspective, I am no longer willing to die over "correct" doctrine—whatever that is. After all, which "correct" doctrine is correct? Instead, I stand for experiencing my Creator, a far more important issue—a real, "rubber meets the road" kind of issue that matters.

Our days upon this earth are numbered and fly by far too quickly. We only live once, so we might as well make it count. Why live someone else's dream? Why invest in the insignificant? Why get caught up in issues that don't really matter? Why allow contemporary culture to define who we are and what should matter to us? Our best interest isn't what motivates corporate America's marketing strategies. Why not live according to what matters to you? This seems to make much more sense, and it is far more comfortable and rewarding.

Years ago, while pastoring a church in sunny Florida, my ship's anchor had broken off into the sea and I was drifting aimlessly, or so it seemed. I was still afloat, of course, but where was I headed? Day after day, I lived the same old lonely existence with lack of energy and no dry land in sight. I needed to re-imagine myself, re-negotiate with my own thinking, and get back to my center of gravity. In essence, I needed to find me again.

This is the point where well-meaning but naïve Christians spew forth unhelpful clichés that are nothing more than shallow bumper-sticker religion. I understand their intent, but it can come across in accusatory tone, insinuating that the fault lies squarely at our own feet. It is like saying to a young mother who just lost her stillborn baby girl, "Your baby is the angel of God now. She is a star twinkling back at you in the dark of the night." Wow. What in the world does that mean, and how is that even helpful? Though it originates from a well-intentioned heart, what we really need is time for serious reflection—a way to take stock, process what just happened, and sort things out in a way that asks, "In light of my circumstances, how will I proceed?" This is what I asked myself during my aimless drifting.

My energy reserves were low, and my mind was preoccupied. Deep within, I knew I had to reorient my life—to get back to who I was and how God made me. So, I did just that. After conducting the Sunday church service, I changed into comfortable clothes, jumped on my motorcycle, and cruised the streets to clear my head. Riding in the Florida sunshine is quite relaxing, especially with the neighborhood alligators sunning themselves on the banks of nearby ponds. I stopped at a local restaurant and slipped into a quiet, corner booth where I could process my thoughts without interruption. I ordered a salad and a beverage, whipped out my trusty yellow legal pad, and began putting down on paper what was racing through my head.

Corner-booth processing is empowering. I scoured through my life experiences and began to see patterns of what motivated me, what I was good at, and what impassioned my heart. I revisited my failures and my learnings. A reconnection with myself was taking place, and I relished every minute of it. It was the kind of rejuvenation I desperately needed. In those hours alone with God, a legal pad, a salad, and a glass of iced tea, a sorting occurred in my life where I began to catch a glimpse of God's glory within me. I did possess gifts. I was skilled in specific ways. There was life left within me, and I could sense the embers being stoked once again. Like a rising tide, the breath of God was rushing back into my soul.

This kind of winnowing process can help us better understand ourselves and God's good work within us. From that day forward, I have kept the fires stoked and focus on the things I discovered that day. Let me give you an example of what I mean by not being distracted from the focus of what makes our heart beat.

At age fifty-six, an opportunity arose for me to attend medical school. It wasn't the traditional path to medicine, but it was a viable option for someone like me who was older than most medical students. This would have been my fourth doctorate in a new field of knowledge. How exciting! My intention was to spend the rest of my life providing medical care in the South Pacific Islands where the need was great and the beaches were enticing. I had already been involved in ministry and education; now I could finish my career with medicine. This was pretty lofty thinking, especially at my age.

Had I put my mind to it, I may have been successful at this new challenge. But then again, it may have been too much for me. I turned from this opportunity for numerous reasons, and though it was certainly a worthy endeavor, it wasn't the best route for me. It wasn't who I was or how God made me. I needed to pursue my passion and giftedness instead of changing course for such an arduous trek at this point in my life. It was, in reality, the chasing of rabbits and losing my way to an interesting distraction. We must know what is important to us and take a stand for it, even when it entails a choice between good, better, and best. I took a stand for who I was and how God made me. I rebuffed this potential opportunity so that I could be true to myself.

What Matters to you?

Why don't we take a stand more often for the things that truly matter? One reason is that we don't know what we stand for. Like a silver ball in an arcade pinball machine, we get knocked around from one place to another without a clear path of direction. If we don't know what we stand for, we wind up falling for just about anything. Focus is often the outcome of personal assessment—a valuable tool for helping us sort things through. You can ride your motorcycle to a local restaurant and hole up in a corner booth like I did, or you can travel a slower route where self-realization occurs over time. The emphasis is not so much on the process as it is the outcome. Christians are adept at telling the world what they are against, but they struggle to articulate what they are for. What is it that you stand for? Have you taken the time to sort out who you are, how God made you, and what is important to you? What will you value in your journey through life?

To resolve large questions of higher purpose, it is often helpful to address other, smaller questions first as useful stepping stones toward the larger point. These smaller questions help us focus with laser-beam quality so that we are driven by what inspires us rather than simply being knocked around like a pinball. This sorting process can feel quite lonely, for only you can do it. Rest assured, however, all of us go through it at some point. Once you gain clarity around what you ought to do, what you want to do, and what God desires of you, doing anything else seems wholly unnatural.

Stepping-Stone Questions

The first stepping-stone question that helps us identify what we stand for is this: what thrills your heart? What is it that puts a big smile on your face and makes your heart happy? Deep down, we are pretty intuitive people. Our heart knows a great many things about us if we will but listen to it. When we are honest with ourselves, we have an inkling which path is best to travel. There is something within each of us that enlightens our soul, and yet, we argue with it, hold it at bay, and allow our minds to talk us out of a good many things. By quieting the mind, the heart can speak. We are directed to our purpose when we listen to our heart.

We yearn for involvement in something bigger than ourselves—something that gives our life meaning. Unfortunately, we rarely arrive at that place without the full commitment of the heart. Without engaging the heart, we merely go through the motions of a cold intellectual exercise. What makes you come alive on the inside? What breathes life and energy into your weary bones? What puts fire in your belly and prompts you to stand for something greater than yourself? Only you can answer the question that often comes only after careful reflection.

Answering the "why" question is another useful, but severely neglected, self-diagnosis tool for ascertaining what matters. From both textbook knowledge and firsthand experience, I have learned that no matter what people are arguing about or what position they tenaciously hold, we can discern the reason behind their position by asking "why" questions. Nobody likes to be pushed off a stance once it has been publicly declared, for that would entail losing face. By talking about interests—the why behind the position—we peel the layers away until we reach the heart of the issue, and by doing so we can move toward mutually agreeable solutions. Pretty simple concept, isn't it?

By asking "why" questions, we begin sorting out the underlying motivation for our actions and launch an exploration into deeper levels of self-understanding. You might ask, for instance, "Why do I seem to gravitate toward challenging positions or roles that involve serving others? Why do I always find myself sticking up for the underdog? Why do I seek out positions of leadership?" These sample questions merely illustrate the point, that asking the "why" behind our thinking and behavior can help us discern what we stand for.

Another helpful tool for determining what we stand for is discerning our strengths and abilities. We are born with a bent—a toolkit of strengths, aptitudes, and gifts—that is intrinsic to whom we are as individuals. We are most fulfilled, I believe, when we engage these qualities, for they allow us to express our very identity as human beings. People notice that we are in our element, and when we are in our element, we add value to any group or circumstance. We are at our best when we are expressing our true selves.

The quest to discover our passion often leads back to our innate, God-given strengths and abilities. It is possible to be passionate about things for which we have no natural abilities, and it is equally possible to possess God-given strengths in areas where we are passionless. The two, however, must work together. Most of us are drawn to areas in which we have the natural talent to achieve. Knowing your God-given strengths and abilities helps sort out what is important to you.

Another question that helps make things clear is this: what would you give up everything for? What matters so much to you that you would willingly sell everything you own to attain and protect it? Does anything really matter that much to you? Americans live in a culture where affluence, achievement, and appearance are highly esteemed. Do you treasure what culture values, or are you able to think for yourself about what is important?

My guitar collection is a good example. I enjoy guitars, especially electric ones. I love their sound, their looks, their feel, and how they make me feel. I currently own seven of them, and every year I find myself admiring new models. I would love to play my guitars with the skill of a great blues guitarist, but that would entail time, practice, and attention. It would require sacrifices in my life that I am unwilling to make. I would be forced to say "no" to other important endeavors in order to become a more proficient musician. Who am I kidding? The truth of the matter is that collecting guitars seems to be more important to me than actually playing them well. In essence, I am unwilling to pay the price to be a talented guitar player, for other things are more important to me. In a practical way, I have chosen between good, better, and best. Unlike my guitar collection, the higher purposes of life are so substantive and so principled that I would sacrifice a great deal to see their fulfillment. When we know what we are willing to sacrifice everything for, we know what truly matters to us.

Another clarifying question worth investigating is this: where does your courage come from? Think of a time when you ventured from your comfort zone to stand for an issue that mattered. Did you speak up to protect someone else, prevent a wrong, or put a bully in his place? Maybe you simply decided it was time to face your fears and pursue a path that meant something to you—a path that initially felt awkward and uncomfortable, but at the same time, seemed so right. The point is that you displayed courage and overcame what frightened you. You conquered your fears and took a risk for something you believed in so strongly. What is it in your life that, when you pursue it, you have no fear? What gives rise to your courage is something you are willing to stand for.

A final question worth considering is this: how will you measure your life when all is said and done? This was the subject of a sermon series I preached many years ago. When your last breath is approaching, how will you assess whether or not your life was productive and meaningful? The answer you provide depends on the measuring stick you use. When we know what is important to us, we can align our life with the values that matter most. The accumulation of material items is not a proper measurement because that which matters isn't things, but relationships, principles, love, people, justice, service, etc. Are you going to measure your life by the modern cultural values of affluence, achievement, and appearance, or will you stand for more important matters? Your yardstick values provide significant clues to what matters in your life.

Contemplating these smaller questions can initiate a journey of self-discovery. Years ago, I remember telling myself, "Don't just take up precious space on this planet; make your life count for something." I want my journey to matter, to be meaningful, and to make a difference. May the courage of my convictions be on full display as Martin Luther King, Jr. once said: "The ultimate measure of a man is not where he stands in moments of comfort and convenience, but where he stands at times of challenge and controversy."

The Fear Factor

The first reason we may not take a stand is because we have not identified what matters to us. The second reason is because of fear, the universal restrainer that constantly suppresses our adventurous spirit. We are afraid of living because we fear dying. We are afraid to voice our opinion because we fear the opinion of others. We are afraid to forge ahead with God because we fear losing control. We are afraid to be, to live, and fully enjoy this life because fear holds us back. Surely there was a time when you took a stand—when something mattered so much to you that courage rose forth and overcame the restrainer's power. In fact, it felt right to take a stand and leave fear behind. Instead of cowering in the corner, you were a force to be reckoned with.

Now that I am on the downhill side of life, I am at greater risk for physical ailments than when I was younger. Cancer and heart disease are leading causes of death in America, and my chance of getting one of these ailments is high. I am being realistic, not morbid. It is what statistics tell us. Many well-meaning Christians, however, have chided me for talking this way and reprimanded me for my lack of faith in God's healing power and my failure to "name and claim" His desire and promise that no one be sick. Illness, they say, results from either a lack of faith or a failure to deal with sin in one's life. I don't buy any of it, and while my own beliefs do not align with their perspective for numerous reasons, my point is that I am closer to death today than I was yesterday. Sooner or later the Grim Reaper will impart unto me the kiss of death, and my time on this terrestrial ball will come to an end.

Moving closer toward the conclusion of life bothered me—as one of my elder parishioners used to say, "Growing old ain't for sissies!" I knew the eventuality of death would come knocking at my door, but I was reluctant to let him in. My own demise was something to be avoided and delayed for as long as possible. One day, however, my perspective changed. I began to see death as an integral aspect of life. At any given moment, we are both living and dying at the same time. In other words, we are always in the process of dying even as we live and living even as we die. My last breath will merely be the culmination of a process that began at my birth. My life started with God breathing His life into me, and it will end with that same breath returning to the One who gave it to me. Death is simply another moment of transformation—one form of life, a seed, being placed into the soil to die so that transformation can occur—rising to new life in God. This is the great transformation cycle that we see over and over again. Something lives, then dies, and then transforms into something new. The breadth of life given to me will simply return to the One who breathed His life into me.

With its 100-percent success rate, death has a pretty good track record. We all die, but I no longer fear death's arrival; instead, I see it as part of the great cycle of transformation. I don't want to be struggling with my own demise at the last moment while on my deathbed; I want to look death squarely in the eye now, and by doing so, free myself from its frightful grip. Trepidation has been replaced with courage, and I can live fully and abundantly every day of my life. I am willing to take a stand for those things that are important to me, for I fear nothing—not even death, the ultimate source of fear. The faster you come to terms with your own demise, the sooner you begin living fearlessly.

In a similar vein, I no longer fear the opinions of others, either. Though we desire their glowing endorsement and wish they would think highly of us, we often feel that if we can garner their approval, we must surely be okay. This, however, is like trying to hit a shifting target. You can be on the in-crowd one day and an outcast the next. Opinions fluctuate according to a "what have you done for me lately" mentality. I remember sitting next to one of the church elders who didn't care much for me back in the day, and I remarked, "Funny isn't it, how I can be a savior to some and a devil to others"—and I was his devil. If my self-esteem was based solely on the ever-changing estimations of others, my emotional well-being would become a swinging pendulum, consumed with chasing after fickle opinions to determine my worth.

In my younger days, I traveled with an evangelist while singing for his church meetings. Though I sang my heart out for God, there were those who loved it and those who hated it. That's the way life is, but in my case, I gave undue credence to the negative opinion of others which prevented me from doing what I enjoyed. Their criticism took center stage and restrained me from taking a stand for what mattered to me. Lurking just below the surface was a current of fear. My singing days are over, largely because of the scorching negativism directed my way. Know this—you will never please everyone, so stop trying. Live the life you want to live. Take a stand for what matters to you. Make your life count, and make it dependent upon *your* choices, not the shifty opinions of others. Bernard Baruch said it best in one of his well-known quotes: "Be who you are and say what you feel, because those who mind don't matter, and those who matter don't mind."

Standing for your values takes courage and can even become a way of living—a natural response to any given situation. My landlord committed in writing to replace the living room windows if I signed my lease for another year. I trusted this Christian woman to do what she said she would do, but the windows were never replaced. When I asked why she didn't honor her word to me, she turned into a Big But Christian full of excuses . . . "I would have honored my word to you—but . . ." For her, Christianity meant believing correct doctrine rather than pursuing a way of living—a doctrine to be adhered to, not a truth that transforms. When it was time for her to stand, she wilted. When I asked how not keeping her word honored our Lord, she had no response. There are specific moments where we need to step up and stand tall for what matters, and there is also a "way-of-living" aspect to standing. Are you willing to stand for the things that matter?

Sitting

Standing is a part of our journey but so is sitting. Life is short when counting the hands of time, and yet, I have found it best to think of my own journey as a marathon rather than a sprint. By taking the long view, I prepare for the mountains while I am in the plains. For years, I knew only one speed—breakneck speed—and it knocked me off track every time I hit a speed bump or approached a sharp corner. Life wasn't meant to be lived with such velocity, and now I take corners more carefully. I recognize speed bumps and slow down for them. If life is about the journey, as I believe it is, then stopping to smell the roses is difficult to do while traveling at warp speed. Slow down. Sit down. Rest. Chill. Take in the sights. Smell the roses. Drink a little coffee and enjoy the company of another. There is never a shortage of opportunities to stand, and yet, it is more difficult at times, to slow down, sit down, recoup our strength, get our mind right, and take in the sights before hitting the road again.

The stress and complexity of life seems to increase with each generation. My journey seemed slower and simpler when I was a kid growing up in the 60s and 70s. Presumably, the pilgrimage of my parents seemed less complicated to them during the 40s and 50s when they were growing up. Maybe life just seems more complex by virtue of being a grownup in a great big world of responsibilities. The advent of technology and the blossoming of hi-tech gadgets is one of the greatest changes my generation has experienced. Like you, I am personally acquainted with life's stressors and often feel like a fuse box constantly shutting down with overloaded circuits. Continually pushing the pedal to the floor and extending myself beyond the threshold of what is reasonable overcomes my defenses to the point of exhaustion. I am tired of nonstop overload and living beyond my abilities as a human. The problem is one of exceeding healthy thresholds, and like rain-soaked soil, we reach a saturation point—unable to take in anything more before short-circuiting our lives.

Even my finely tuned multitasking skills were unable to keep pace. I was besieged with information overload, media overload, work overload, responsibility overload, professional goal overload, and personal expectation overload, not to mention dealing with the noise of life, the speed of life, and the unprecedented pace of change. There are a thousand stressors that encumber our lives. It is time to slow down—time to live with margin.

Margin

In the business world, margin is the difference between income and expenses. In an electrician's world, it is the difference between the load required and the amount of power available. From the perspective of daily living, margin is the difference between the energy on tap and the energy it takes to get through each day. In each scenario, margin has to do with the necessary gap between what is available and what is needed. It is this excess—this margin—that gives us our much-needed reserves to carry on, recharge our batteries, and survive difficult times. Without reserve fuel in the tank, we run on fumes and eventually burn out. Even the Old Testament Sabbath rest helped to restore margin so life could be lived within the limits of what was good for people.

Drawing from my own life experience, there are five main areas where margin is needed: 1) Emotional energy, 2) Physical energy, 3) Spiritual energy, 4) Time energy, and 5) Financial energy. In each of these areas, when the load squanders the resources on hand, stress and burnout ensue. Finding margin in each of these pockets of energy helps us maintain a sense of balance and well-being.

Emotional Energy

Our psyche has the ability to produce vast amounts of emotional energy. When we feel good about things and our emotions are stable, we have strength to conquer most anything. When our sensitivities are wounded and we feel trapped, the energy that once sustained us through ups and downs is depleted. Without reserve fuel in our gas tank, everything goes downhill fast. Last weekend, my emotional energy was so depleted that I did absolutely nothing but lie around, watch movies, and eat more than I should. My goals sat idly on the backburner. That's not how I live my life on a daily basis, but this particular weekend I simply needed to replenish my emotional energy. I was exhausted on the inside from all sorts of things, and I took a much-needed break. It felt good, and the emotional energy in my reserve tank was restored. It worked.

How much reserve is in your gas tank? Like most, emotional energy rises and falls depending on whether you are restoring energy to your emotional system or withdrawing energy until there is none left at your disposal. Living within the threshold of what is healthy for us enhances emotional well-being. It allows for the restoration of energy reserves so that margin always exists.

Without some sort of emotional padding in our lives, depression, anxiety, and fear quickly overwhelm us.

Rest is an amazing energy restorer. We need it more than we think. A weekend of doing absolutely nothing helped to refill my emotional gas tank. Sometimes I take a nap, get away for the weekend, take a break at work, or find other ways to secure personal chill time. Music is a powerful restorative element for me, and I often lie on the floor with my headphones on listening to the sounds of pure energy. Sometimes I laugh or cry about things. Life gets a bit weird at times, and both laughter and crying releases pressure built up on the inside. It is good medicine for the soul. As I am depressurizing and de-stressing, I find that my emotional energy is being restored. Find ways to slow down so that energy can trickle back into your life.

When I wake up in the middle of the night longing for sleep, I find myself offering up prayers of thanksgiving to God. Despite the hardships in my life, those quiet moments of thanksgiving remind me of His constant presence and the many good things surrounding me. In the still of the night, this precious activity comforts my soul and draws me closer to God. From an emotional perspective, it helps to center my life upon Him. I not only live each day for Him, but I also sleep each night for Him. I rest in His calming presence.

Knowing *who* I am and *whose* I am also replenishes my energy reserves, for I have come to grips with how God made me. Working to be the best me I can be is not draining at all, but life-giving. I know what I stand for and what my intentions are in life. I am not a lost, wandering soul, but someone with purpose, meaning, and a role to play in service to my Creator. I am accepted by God, forever loved by Him, and live with and in His presence. This is one of the most important facets to restoring emotional energy that I can think of—know yourself, know God, and become comfortable in your own skin while basking in His abundant love for you. When your emotional energy is strong, you can live out your purpose with resolve.

Finally, the pursuit of love is an outstanding method for restoring emotional energy even though people and relationships are fraught with web-like complications. To be involved with people is to be in the business of pain and suffering. If dilemma and drama were all we had to look forward to in relational endeavors, then a solitary, hermit lifestyle may be preferred. But there is far more energy to gain from human interaction, if we allow it.

Relationships offer support, and through friendships, we become acquainted with empathy, wise counsel, encouragement, connectedness, and love—all emotionally empowering experiences. We learn to establish healthy boundaries, to forgive, to accept, and extend grace. Relationships become the fertile soil for living out our faith and can teach us a great deal about ourselves and about God. They can be draining and painful if we are not careful, but they can also be life-giving. Relationships help restore emotional balance to our life.

As I go about the business of loving God and others, I sense that I am doing what God would want me to do, and that in itself is emotionally uplifting. While the demands of love can be taxing at times, I view each day as sacred, and I see His reflection in others. Living life this way restores depleted quantities of emotional energy and helps me keep my wits about me in this turbulent world.

Physical Energy

The second area where margin is needed—physical energy—has been an ongoing struggle for me. My backside daily sits at a desk where I exercise my mind, not my body. This has led to numerous degrees, the writing of books, increased knowledge, and the ability to problem-solve complex issues. In short, my mind has strengthened, but my body has not, though I am getting better at recognizing life's speed bumps and taking intentional steps to harness greater amounts of physical energy. I like to keep things simple, so this is how my mind sums things up: First, get physical exercise. It takes energy to make energy. In other words, get up and move. The more I do it, the easier it becomes, and I always feel better. It is that initial burst of energy needed to get my duff off the couch that is the hardest. For physical exercise, I endeavor to do three things: 1) cardio for my heart and lungs (I walk a great deal), 2) weightlifting to create and sustain muscle mass which produces a higher rate of metabolism

(I would rather just walk), and 3) stretching which keeps my body limber (Did I mention that I would rather just walk?). While I much prefer to invigorate the mind, it is the exercise of my body that produces the physical energy I need.

In addition to physical exercise, I try to eat healthy. I unabashedly prefer burgers, fries, pizza, fried chicken, mashed potatoes, and the like, but these days I eat more from a plant-based, whole food perspective. It is far healthier, and I actually possess more pep when my eating habits are intact. Food is our body's fuel, and what we eat affects how we feel. What goes in the mouth is either helping us or hindering us from attaining the energy levels we desire. I know how hard it is—the mind is willing, but the body is weak. I long for the lean build of Bruce Lee, the great martial arts master, but instead, I feel more like Jabba the Hutt from *Star Wars*. The benefits of exercise are limited if it is not accompanied by healthy eating. Exercise and proper eating are often neglected elements in our quest for energy, but the two go hand-in-hand.

Finally, I try to get a good night's rest and de-stress as much as I can. The formula for increasing physical energy is pretty simple: exercise, eat well, and rest. The difficulty isn't in the understanding, but in the doing. Why wait for a heart attack to grab your attention? It is time to get off the couch and take care of yourself, and that goes for me, too!

Spiritual Energy

A third area of needed margin—spiritual energy—refers to our level of contentment with God. It is the part of us that feels connected to a higher power—that seeks to experience our Creator and affirm a meaningful relationship with Him. At times, aimlessness and feelings of discontent invade our thoughts. We become spiritually lonely and feel alienated from the One we desperately long to intimately know. This restlessness can deplete spiritual energy levels while hopelessness and despair backfill our lives. In this scenario, it is our understanding of God that may need to change in order to recoup spiritual margin.

From my vantage point, spiritual energy is generated from practicing a way of being rather than striving to attain some sort of status with God. Being involved in religious activity may provide short bursts of spiritual enthusiasm, but it isn't the sort of thing that sustains us for the long haul. The more doctrine I studied, the more religious tasks I engaged in, and the more I tried hard to believe, the further behind I got. I was spiritually exhausted until I discovered that all of these things were nothing but cheap substitutes for God. In essence, spiritual energy isn't found in the doing, but in the being. God doesn't need me to do things for Him. I am not some religious errand boy running to and fro fulfilling the whims of a spoiled deity; instead, God wants me to experience His presence each and every day.

When I realized that I was in God and that God was in me, my entire understanding of His presence in my life changed. He wasn't just a part of my life; He was my life, the very source of my existence. Acts 17:28 indicates that "in Him we live and move and exist," and according to 2 Peter 1:4, we partake of God's divine nature. Numerous verses indicate that Christ lives within us (2 Cor. 13:5; 4: 7–7; Rom. 8:10; Gal. 1:15–16; 2:20; 4:19; Eph. 3:17; Col. 1:27; 2 Thess. 1:10). God is not a celestial being sitting upon a throne in a far-away galaxy. No, He is always present with us, for He is in us, around us, under us, beside us, and over us. You don't get much more "present" than that!

We seek His presence when He is already here. The issue isn't getting connected to spiritual energy, for He is the vine and we are the branches. We are already connected to the life-giving nutrients of the vine flowing onto the branches. We waste precious energy trying to establish a connection when we should focus on living in His presence. Spiritual energy comes from a life of being—a life that is centered upon God and drawing nutrients from the vine. Like spokes on a wheel, when God is central to all that we are and do, He touches every facet of our lives. Spiritual energy comes by living a life centered upon the One whose presence touches our entire being.

Time Energy

The margin of time is our next energy center. Tethered to the tyranny of 24/7 technological access, we find it difficult to escape its grasp for the things that matter. Bombarded with email, instant access to the Internet, and real-time texts and social media updates, the priorities that should matter fade into the background. We are addicted to busyness, and the tail is wagging the dog.

Time management has helped me pursue the significant—those things that relate to my goals. I don't subscribe to satellite or cable television because I won't allow it to derail me from my goals. Saying "no" to the things that chop at the root of what matters most is essential. We all have the same amount of time in a day. The difference is what we do with the minutes allotted to us. To pursue the things that matter means saying "no" to other good endeavors. It may be necessary to prune our activity tree if it has gotten out of hand. Life isn't about doing everything; it is about doing the right things—the things that matter. What matters to you? What will you stand for? What has God placed upon your heart? These are the right things.

When the tiny light on your phone indicates an incoming email or text, do you stop everything in order to check it out? Are you able to pull yourself away from the allure of technology? Do you sleep with your cell phone next to your bed so you don't miss a thing? If so, you have a problem. Take a break from your gadget addiction and be present with those around you. One of the greatest gifts you can give to loved ones is the gift of yourself—of being present. Reassure those you love that they have your undivided attention, free from the attachment to technological interruptions.

I plan breaks into my day as a way of creating margin. I am also trying to simplify my life, not only by pruning needless activities that consume my energies, but also in the things I possess. How many pieces of clothing do I need? How much furniture and knick-knacks can one possess? To find more margin, I am cutting back, paring down, and simplifying my life (well, I am planning to keep my guitars!). It is freeing, stress-reducing, and results in greater energy reserves. I am more content with less.

Financial Energy

Financial energy is the last area to address. When we do not have enough to make ends meet or we live beyond our means, energy is drained. I know firsthand what it's like to barely squeak by. My first pastorates were this way and, quite frankly, it wasn't much fun. In order to earn enough income to properly care for my family, I either had to secure a better-paying job or increase my knowledge and skills so that I was more marketable. I ended up doing both. I have lived with little, and I have lived with financial margin. I much prefer the latter, for it makes life more pleasant. Instead of spending precious energy struggling to make ends meet, financial margin provides peace of mind and allows you to focus on other important matters.

All too often, however, the opposite occurs. We secure enough funds to be content but confuse our wants with our needs. Contemporary culture glorifies immediate gratification. Why save? Why wait until you can pay for things? Why constrain your cravings? Just put it on the plastic card, go in debt up to your eyeballs, and live beyond your means. Spend your life behind the eightball and expend your energies playing catch-up. There is a snowball effect to unmanaged debt—amassing more and more financial obligation along the way. It isn't profitable for you, but it is certainly beneficial for lending institutions. If they can get you to overspend and pay only the minimum payment each month, they may keep you in the hole for the rest of your life.

Borrowing is not wrong, but unmanaged debt is a killer and drains our energy. We experience less stress and more energy when we live within our means, decrease our spending, separate needs from desires, increase income, create savings accounts, and live within a reasonable budget. Our culture of affluence, achievement, and appearance doesn't promote such things; instead, living without restraint is encouraged. Creating financial margin takes discipline and time, for it requires that we be mindful of our desires and our needs and that we operate with restraint and reason. Only then will our financial energy be restored.

Both standing and sitting are hallmarks of our journey through life. Standing bestows meaning to our existence. We stand for what matters, what is right and good, and the courage of conviction motivates us. Sitting bestows the energy reserves necessary for our journey. We desperately need times of rest—opportunities to replenish our reserves so there is margin between the energy needed and the energy available. Sitting provides the margin needed to stand.

Wisdom for the Journey

Life is about forward movement and requires both energy and direction—standing and sitting. Take time to sort out, monitor, and adjust what matters to you so that you are not chasing after every interesting distraction that crosses your path. Navigating life is far easier when you know what is important to you, for it provides the stability and direction needed to reach the finish line. Neglect moments of rest at your own peril. Think of sitting as fuel for the journey—a method of replenishing the necessary energy reserves that propel you forward. Standing and sitting are both essential elements for a meaningful journey.

– chapter fifteen –

Gaylen's Journey

Singer and songwriter Gaylen Paul has been a familiar name to me since 1984 when I recorded my own album in Minneapolis. It has only been recently, however, that I became personally acquainted with Gaylen and his story. Gaylen's journey, like most of us, has had its share of ups and downs, joys and disappointments, and struggles and victories. His story, however, extends beyond the typical bumps and bruises we expect from the sojourn—his journey involved the sting of addiction, betrayal, suicidal thoughts, the heartbreak of divorce, bad choices and bad behavior, and an inordinate amount of pain and suffering. Mixed in with all of this was fruitful ministry and a continued glimmer of hope in a kind and loving God.

Littered with Danger

We often think that life is like a rocket blasting straight up into outer space and finally landing in heaven—just straight-up growth until we reach our final destiny. Life is far from that, and we know it. If we were to chart the journey for most of us, the graph would look more like a poorly designed rollercoaster ride. Rather than a nice, straight, linear path of progress, our trajectory

223

resembles a plate of tangled spaghetti. Life can become rather messy, and the journey we travel is fraught with pitfalls, potholes, crevices, ravines, quicksand, dead-ends, and deep rivers. Much to our chagrin, we often fall into the same pothole over and over again. Once we learn to avoid it, life seems to go along pretty smoothly—until we are thrown another curveball that knocks us off our feet and hurls us into another dilemma.

A linear life rarely occurs, so we might as well throw that idyllic picture out the window; instead, we must come to grips with the fact that life is littered with danger, filled with highs and lows, and encompasses complicated and conflicting feelings. When examining the life of others, we can easily shake our head in disgust and quickly point out where they went wrong and what they should do to fix things. That, however, is nothing more than spiritual arrogance. One thing is certain—no matter how messy life gets, it is in the journey that we meet God. We search for Him in the perfect, but we discover His presence in the imperfect, in the lowly, and in the realm of pain and suffering. That is when God becomes real to us and we experience firsthand His moving in our life. God is found in the winding journey of life rather than in the halls of perfection.

Gaylen's journey certainly isn't a direct shot to the moon; rather, it is a circuitous route filled with recurring pitfalls. One pothole befell him over and over again—his addiction to alcohol and its ruinous effect upon his life. Still, he journeyed on when he would rather have given up. Still he journeyed on when he didn't know why. Still, he journeyed on despite the pain and suffering. It is when we deal with the truth about ourselves that God is able to do His best work in our heart. Gaylen faced his biggest obstacle, and in so doing, met God in ways he could not have imagined. Through the arduous journey, Gaylen has been able to turn his scars into treasures—reminders of God's good work in his life.

Gaylen is a gifted singer, songwriter, and recording artist. He is also a husband, a father, and fellow sojourner on this path of following God. I am not much for the rehashing of one's gory life details, for that, in my opinion, is not the real story; it is merely the scaffolding upon which transformation occurs, or the pathway from which the real story flows. Our journey shapes and molds us in many ways, and life's bumps and bruises becomes the conduit for transformation—the very purpose of the journey.

Suicidal Thoughts

Growing up in a rough area of St. Paul, Minnesota, teenage-Gaylen could be found drinking, partying, and dancing with friends at the local bars. It was all very innocent and, after all, everyone else was doing it. Yet, something was deeply troubling Gaylen on the inside, so much so that he began to seriously contemplate suicide while working alone at his warehouse job. He was tired of having church shoved down his throat and could no longer stomach the religious hypocrisy he saw in his mother and family. Maybe it was simply better to end it all.

At this point, Gaylen sensed the Lord saying to him, "If you are going to throw your life away, give it to Me instead." This wasn't an audible voice but a voice from within—an impression that seemed to come from his maker. Responding to this inner prompting in 1976, Gaylen replied, "Take it." That amazing, life-changing moment brought about an overwhelming sense of peace within his heart. It was unlike anything he had ever experienced—as if God had sought him out, found him, loved on him, and became present and real. That day, Gaylen was changed. Instead of ending his life, he desired to live it for God. To that end, he stopped drinking and partying, and he turned his entire focus toward God and Christian music.

Success Arrives

As a self-taught piano and guitar player, Gaylen grew up in what may arguably be considered the golden age of Christian music where artists like Evie, Dallas Holm, Larry Norman, Keith Green, Petra, Tim Sheppard, Leon Patillo, Andrea Crouch, The Imperials, Amy Grant, and the like were influencing a generation of young people for God. Keith Green became the clarion voice of many in that era, and Gaylen learned to play piano just like him. Now, with more than 1,500 songs to Gaylen's credit, the influence of Keith Green can be heard in his many compositions. This was a wonderful time in Gaylen's life as he began following the way of Christ. A burning desire raged within for the things of God. He was hanging out with new Christian friends, enjoying tremendous Bible studies, and sharing his newfound faith with zeal. Life couldn't be better, and he was the happiest he had ever been. Little did he know that his happy bubble was about to burst and the inferno within was about to be snuffed out.

Word spread about his music abilities, and soon his concert ministry took off. He was performing all across the upper Midwest, and the concert halls, churches, and coffee houses were packed out on a regular basis. While on this spiritual high, his first album titled *Yesterday's Gone* was completed in 1980. It wasn't long before Gaylen was introduced to a powerful and famous international evangelist who invited Gaylen to travel with him across the United States. This was another one of his mountaintop experiences. He was ministering to large crowds of people and not only influenced their lives, but his own life was touched in tremendous ways, too. Life was good. God was good. Gaylen couldn't get enough of it. Suicide was no longer on his mind, for his life had changed—all for the better.

Total Collapse

Upon his return to Minnesota in 1984, he was asked to perform a local church concert in Minneapolis. The entire evening was one incredibly powerful experience. With the boldness of a lion, he spoke words from the heart—words he sensed the church leaders needed to hear. Unfortunately, his message was ill-received, and yet, the truth of what he addressed would later be confirmed as the congregation eventually split over the issues Gaylen picked up on that evening. After the concert, a confrontational meeting occurred with the Lead Pastor who was unhappy with Gaylen's concert message.

The following day, calls came in from pastors all across the Midwest cancelling his concerts at their churches. Overnight, his entire concert schedule for the next year was completely wiped out. Unbeknownst to Gaylen, the disgruntled Lead Pastor happened to be the superintendent of all the churches in the upper Midwest for that denomination, and he took it upon himself to warn all of the other pastors about Gaylen—labeling him a heretic. Heretic, really? Those are fighting words, archaic words from eons ago, purely designed, in this situation, to stir up others and cause disruption. Gaylen had been labeled, destroyed, and cast out. On that day, he crossed the wrong person, who initiated the collapse of an entire ministry. Gaylen was unable to schedule one concert—anywhere, and it was devastating. No one would touch him, for his reputation had been destroyed overnight. After all, he was now a "heretic."

The most painful aspect of this difficult situation wasn't the canceling of concerts or the free-flow of gossip, but the fact that many of his close friends stopped associating with him. They knew him, and yet they believed the gossip. That hurt. Since the rumors came from the sacred lips of church leaders, it had to be true, didn't it? Even Gaylen's wife was at a loss in how to offer support. This wasn't anything she had ever experienced before. They were both unprepared for this eclipse in their life. It was a moment of total abandonment—a feeling of being lost and alone—as though God had left them in the dust. The following year was filled with hardship. The world they once knew and loved had crashed and burned. Every morning Gaylen woke up in emotional pain, struggling with feelings of complete abandonment and worthlessness.

One morning, Gaylen's wife asked him, "Why were you crying in your sleep last night?" The anguish was so deep that Gaylen didn't even realize it had happened. "Was this the kind of pain that Jesus felt when others abandoned him?" Gaylen wondered. The words of John 15:18 came to mind: "If the world hates you, you know that it has hated Me before it hated you."

A Newfound Friend

A woman in Gaylen's church, whom he greatly respected, informed the couple that God was finished with Gaylen and had put him on the shelf. Those were sure encouraging words, wouldn't you say? Gaylen returned home and fixed himself a hot-toddy with brandy. Surprisingly, the alcohol gave him a pretty good buzz, and for the first time in months, he felt his pain slip away. It was a wonderful feeling, and from that day forward, Gaylen was hooked. When all others had abandoned him, Gaylen finally found a friend who was always available—a friend who always made him feel better. Hitting the bottle had a way of melting away his pain, if only temporarily. It would be years before he realized the high price his comforting friend would exact of him—a completely destroyed life.

A few months after discovering the rapturous effects of brandy, Gaylen signed a recording contract with a record company in Los Angeles that needed new songs for the albums of up-and-coming Christian artists. Galyen wrote songs and shipped them off to Los Angeles to be sung by others—and he composed hundreds of them, some good and some bad. The record company, however, refused to allow Gaylen to record his own album. He was back to writing songs, which was a good thing, for it kept him busy, lifted his countenance, and provided a sense of purpose, yet he wasn't doing what he really wanted to do. With little money to his name, Gaylen decided to record a second album, and in 1984, he started his own label—HomeWork Records. In the midst of all of this, Gaylen was drinking heavily and spending more and more time with bottled amber liquid.

In 1985, Gaylen opted out of his Los Angeles recording contract, and with donations from family and friends, raised enough funds to begin work on the album. Recording an album was an expensive endeavor back in 1985, unlike the pervasive home recording studios of today. Back then, it was an all-or-nothing commitment to record your own songs. It took a great deal of time, money, and sweat equity to see it to completion.

During the day, Gaylen worked construction jobs and recorded in the studio. Most every night he was getting drunk. Alcohol was controlling his life, and he couldn't stop returning again and again to nurse his addiction. With a new album underway, Gaylen began performing concerts again, and even though God's hand was still upon his music and ministry, the addiction was slowly destroying him from the inside out. With tortuous feelings, Gaylen saw himself as the worst kind of hypocrite. Here he was, singing publicly about the joy of the Lord while having a hangover on stage. He sincerely loved the Lord and truly believed in the merits of his singing and speaking ministry, but he hated being a phony. He was, in fact, saying one thing and doing another—the very essence of hypocrisy.

Gaylen remembers performing a concert for a small Christian retreat, and all he could think about was finishing the concert, packing up, and returning home as quickly as possible to enjoy the comfort of a bottle of brandy. The concert was merely a necessary interruption to his drinking problem. It was brandy that consumed his thoughts, and he longed for the relief his friend could bring. Gaylen rushed through his repertoire of songs and as he was singing his last number, he noticed a woman in the front row weeping uncontrollably, deeply touched by the song. Gaylen was shocked that even in his miserable state of mind, God was still using him to touch the lives of others. It was at this moment that Gaylen realized, for the very first time in his life, that his ministry wasn't about him.

After three long years of studio work, his second album, *The Only One*, was completed in 1988. It took all that he had just to record it, and he now needed $7,500 to reproduce it. With no more cash available, the only thing left to do was to pray and ask God to send someone to help. During one of his concerts, a woman introduced herself, and after a lengthy conversation, Gaylen and his wife invited her for dinner. During their time together, she told the story of her recent loss—the death of her husband. It was a sad story, and at the same time, a loving and glorious testimony of God's grace. She informed Gaylen that her husband had left her a large sum of money. Was this a coincidence? Was she the answer to his prayer? Gaylen resisted the urge to tell her about his financial situation. He may have had a secret problem with alcohol, but he hadn't sunk that low! It just wasn't right. They said their goodbyes and went home.

Later that evening, the woman contacted Gaylen and asked, "Do you need money?" For a few seconds Gaylen was speechless, but he went on to tell her about his album that was finished but awaiting reproduction. She inquired further, "How much do you need to reproduce it?" Knowing that it was a lot of money, Gaylen gathered up the courage to tell her. Without hesitation, she told Gaylen to stop by her home the next day, and a cashier's check for $7,500 would be waiting for him.

Gaylen was in awe. Could this be happening to him—the man whose ministry was supposed to be on the shelf—the man with a secret addiction to alcohol? This sort of thing had never happened to him before; instead, they were merely stories that others told. Gaylen's prayer had been answered in a marvelous way. After an incredible incident like this, you would think that he might unearth an inkling of self-confirmation or that it might lead him to give up his old friend, brandy. Deep down, however, he still felt worthless. Maybe he feared success again, or maybe he didn't want to endure another bout of someone sabotaging his ministry. Whatever the reason, his lack of self-confidence ran deep as he kept returning to the bottle to prop himself up.

The Wandering Years

"What is wrong with me?" Gaylen thought to himself, "Why am I still hurting, and how can I fix it?" He realized that he badly needed help and yearned to talk with someone about it, but sharing his embarrassing situation terrified him. He was, after all, a Christian leader performing concerts and speaking publicly. It wasn't acceptable for someone like him to have an alcohol addiction or any other type of weakness and still be allowed to minister, as though we need the approval of others to pursue what we feel called to do. Understandably, he didn't feel comfortable going to pastors for help. Sharing his addiction with Christian friends was risky, for they would judge him—some already had. His wife was already worried about him, and she was overwhelmed with raising their three children in the midst of an alcoholic father. Feeling alone and inadequate, Gaylen retreated back to his comfort zone—his familiar bottle of brandy. In many ways, he was totally dysfunctional and the alcohol helped to ease the pain—at least temporarily.

In 1991 Gaylen's album *The Only One* won the Minnesota Music Award for "Best Gospel Recording." In the Upper Midwest Battle of the Bands, Gaylen's band won third place. Success was finally coming around again. From the outside, everything looked fine and dandy.

On the inside, however, disarray brewed. Gaylen was a mess. His drinking had escalated to the point where he would get the shakes, known as DTs (detox tremors), whenever he stopped drinking to go on small weekend concert tours. He didn't know what detox tremors were at the time, and it frightened him. He would later become very familiar with them. Concert after concert, he lived in a constant state of denial. He loaded up on breath mints, gum, or whatever he could do to mask the taint of alcohol from either the previous night's drinking or the morning binge to ward off the shakes during a concert.

Gaylen comes from the more charismatic stream of religious experience, and a woman known for her gift of prophecy came to the church Gaylen was attending. Since the last so-called prophetess told him he was all washed up, he was understandably a bit reluctant to attend the meeting. In an attempt to go unnoticed, he sat in the back of the church. The prophetess began pointing her finger at specific individuals to come forward and receive a word from the Lord. Realizing that something was about to happen, Gaylen sank lower into his chair hoping to disappear, all the while popping breath minds into his mouth—just in case. Sure enough, her eyes landed squarely on him, and to Gaylen's horror, she pointed her finger at him and said, "Get on up here. God has a word for you!" Under his breath, he muttered, "I am so done for!" He knew some of the people she had already spoken over, and the word she had for them was spot-on. Gaylen thought he was toast, but he said to himself, "If this is going to deliver me from my bondage to alcohol, go ahead God, let me have it, right here in front of everybody!"

When the finger-pointing prophetess finally reached Gaylen on stage, she gazed at him with a puzzled expression. "Can she smell the alcohol on my breath?" Gaylen wondered. They stood there looking at one another until the prophetess again pointed her finger. Gaylen was thinking, "I am ready, just let me have it for crying out loud!" Looking into his eyes and still pointing her finger, she loudly proclaimed into the microphone, "God is getting this one ready for the front lines!" Gaylen thought, "What? Front lines? This woman is definitely nuts and certainly isn't any kind of prophet! She doesn't have a clue what I've been going through or where I am in my walk with the Lord. If she did, she surely wouldn't have said that. Front lines, what a joke!" She obviously didn't know what she was talking about—or did she?

It was time for Gaylen to seek professional help for his alcohol problem, and he knew it. No longer could he control it or hide it, and he was unable to stop drinking on his own. In his efforts to reach out, Gaylen was admitted to inpatient treatment on three separate occasions, out-patient treatment twice, and attended hundreds of Alcoholics Anonymous meetings—all to no avail. These programs work for many, but they weren't working for Gaylen.

The reason Gaylen wasn't getting well, he was told, was because he didn't seriously work on the Twelve Steps of Alcoholics Anonymous. Deep down, Gaylen desired to overcome his addiction, but he couldn't get past step one—admitting that he was powerless over alcohol. If he didn't believe in the truth of step one, they said, there would be no progression through the next eleven steps of the recovery process. Gaylen felt caught in the middle. There was the church, on one hand, that seemed full of judgment and condemnation. Its lack of compassion for struggling leaders prevented him from reaching out for help with recovery.

The secular world, on the other hand, encouraged him to declare himself an alcoholic with a disease that he would be powerless over for the rest of his life. Gaylen was on the horns of a dilemma: does he embrace a status of powerlessness or stand for his belief that God, who has power over everything, can deliver him from anything? An internal wrestling match ensued over this perceived contradiction, and it created a stumbling block in his attempts to progress through the Alcoholics Anonymous recovery program.

The Grip of Addiction

Feeling lost, frustrated, and alone in his battle with alcohol, Gaylen's life was spinning out of control. Along with a drinking problem that was getting worse, his attitude and behavior became abusive. Gaylen began blacking out on a regular basis, and when he came to the next morning, he had very little memory of the abusive things he had said and done. His wife of fifteen years finally had enough and told Gaylen to move out. She could no longer tolerate his drinking and abusive behavior, and he refused to watch him destroy his life and his family's life. Their destructive arguments were negatively affecting the children, and they didn't deserve any of it. The grip of addiction, left unchecked, is devastating—ripping apart everything in its path, especially those things we cherish the most. The emotional pain Gaylen inflicted upon others is something he deeply regrets, and he has apologized to his children and ex-wife many times, in addition to writing letters to each of them. Amends have been made, but the damage was already done.

Gaylen was broken, lonely, separated from his wife and children, no longer engaged in ministry, and killing himself with alcohol. He was through with Christian music and never wanted to step inside another church as long as he lived. He despised church—it was nothing more than man-made religion and brought him nothing but pain. He gave his life to the cause and look where it got him. God, on the other hand, wasn't finished with Gaylen.

When his wife filed for divorce, Gaylen was laid waste. He not only lost his spouse, but he missed his family and his home, too. He was brought so low that he lost all sense of purpose. He was a shell of a man whose life consisted of empty space. In his mind, God had abandoned him, and he had no one to blame but himself. Gaylen would later come to realize that God had not forsaken him. When everyone else had given up on Gaylen, including Gaylen himself, God was still there using the chaos in his life to weave a beautiful tapestry that others would someday view as the handiwork of the Holy One.

While Gaylen was at his lowest point, God brought a beautiful woman into his life who snatched him from the brink of death and nurtured him back to health. They fell deeply in love, and for the first time in a long time, Gaylen was experiencing feelings of happiness and beginning to enjoy life again. His self-confidence grew and though he wasn't drinking as much, the addiction still would not loosen its grip on his life.

Those in the recovery program encouraged Gaylen to view his alcoholism as a gift. Though he struggles with the concept of something so damaging being a gift, he now sees that in many ways it can be, even if for the mere fact that his story is written on these pages so others can find hope. In recalling the many ways he wounded others, he doubts they would view his addiction as a gift. His daughter still struggles with childhood memories of verbal abuse, arguments, and nights when the police came to the door. Alcoholism isn't easy for anyone involved, and yet, in typical God-like fashion, He has the ability to bring forth beauty from ashes.

Gaylen had come to the end of his rope so many times that he lost count. History has a way of repeating itself for alcoholics, and here was Gaylen with a beautiful new wife repeating the damaging actions that had ruined his first marriage. He tried to sober up and endured many nights of detoxing, shakes, and night terrors, but the grip of addiction would not let go. For those of us who have never experienced the addictive sway of drugs and alcohol, it is difficult to imagine its incredible power over one's life.

In one sense, we can look at all that Gaylen was given and how he squandered much of it to the power of addiction. God blessed him with good gifts, a music ministry, a treasured wife, three children, and then a second beautiful wife and stepchild. Gaylen felt like he was taking these gifts for granted. But, try as he might, he couldn't beat alcohol. Why was he repeating the past and going down the same well-traveled road as before? Though he cried out to God in prayer, he couldn't stop drinking.

The Coming Crash

Scared and feeling like he was racing faster and faster down a steep hill with no brakes, Gaylen realized he was fast-approaching an inevitable crash. Finally, after nearly twelve years of marriage to his second wife, the crash occurred. She, too, had finally had enough of his antics and was about to leave. The lies, excuses, hidden secrets, self-destructive behaviors, and the horrible cycle of dysfunction alcoholism creates for everyone involved became too much to deal with. She was unwilling to stand by and watch Gaylen drink himself to death. No more ultimatums and no more chances—she was done: "I'm letting you go and putting you in God's hands. I still love you so much, and I will always love you, but I'm letting you go."

Gaylen's precious wife had saved him from the brink when they first met, and she tried hard to save him now. Over and over she gave what she could to help him heal, provide hope, and offer him a reason to live, but nothing seemed to work. Finally, the day arrived when she knew in her heart that her best strategy was to let him go. If there was any chance to save Gaylen, it would come by way of releasing him, as hard as it was to do.

Denial is a deadly thing. How many walls do people have to hit before they surrender? Gaylen was once again in a familiar predicament, alone in an apartment, separated from his wife, and feeling lost, miserable, and desperate. Gaylen wondered why God wasn't answering his prayer and taking away the alcoholism. Would the Lord ever respond to his earnest seeking? Did even God find him worthless to the point of giving up on him? He was at an all-time low.

In retrospect, Gaylen realizes he was one tough nut to crack. Stubborn as can be, life's lessons didn't come easy for him. Six months after the separation, Gaylen was recovering from a second knee surgery. Because of the operation, he was miserably detoxing, since he was without alcohol for a couple of days. He was a mess—incredibly lost and dejected. Hobbling to the next room, he managed to get on his knees before God. Sick of constantly messing his life up and tired of the pain and suffering, he began pleading for something that he had never asked for in the past. If God would restore his broken marriage, he would never drink again. Gaylen was bargaining with God, and though he felt it was wrong, he was desperate, and desperate people do desperate things. He realized that he might be setting himself up for failure by making promises he couldn't keep, but it was a last ditch effort. His addiction to alcohol had destroyed his entire life. There was nothing left. If God didn't act, hopelessness is all that remained.

Freedom Found

Gaylen made it through the difficult days of detoxification fairly well, and as the days went by, he realized that he didn't need a drink of alcohol. There it was—one whole day, then the next day, and finally several days had gone by. This was new and exciting. Gaylen hadn't gone a day without alcohol in well over twenty-five years. This wasn't normal. He went ten days with no desire to drink. This was impossible. Was this a miracle? Had God finally freed him from the prison of addiction?

Ten days after his desperate prayer, Gaylen's wife came to check on his recovery from knee surgery. She seemed to be in an odd frame of mind, and she looked at Gaylen with an intense stare. She had something to tell him—she had come to a decision. Gaylen was devastated, thinking that she was finally going to tell him the marriage was over for good and that she was filing for divorce. Bracing himself for the impending news, he felt as though he deserved it and couldn't really blame her for seeking closure and moving on with her life. Everything had finally come full circle, and he was ready to receive the final blow.

With solemn poise, she stated, "I've decided to invite you back to our home." Wow! Had Gaylen heard correctly? "What do you mean?" he uttered in shock and disbelief.

"I don't want a divorce. I want you to come back home," she remarked. A few days ago, she explained, God told her that He had healed Gaylen and was bringing him back home to her—back home for good. She trusted God and was faithful to His leading. She was asking Gaylen to come back home! Humbled and elated, Gaylen's heart overflowed with gratitude. God had done the seemingly impossible, and Gaylen was in total awe. He was delivered from his addiction and hasn't had a drink since. His marriage was saved, and He sensed God's love back in his life.

For over twenty-five years, Gaylen was addicted to alcohol. For over twenty-five years, Gaylen never went a day without craving a drink. Each day he yearned for the buzz that allowed him to escape his fractured reality. He exchanged one reality for another—one that engulfed him, destroyed him, and brought down everything around him. Addiction is a very hard taskmaster.

What has been shared here is merely the tip of the iceberg. It is difficult to put into words the power of addiction and the terrifying experiences it brings, especially over a twenty-five-year period. When God met Gaylen's deepest desire the day he hobbled to his knees in prayer, the urge to drink was gone—totally and completely. From Gaylen's viewpoint, there is no way to explain his complete turnaround other than an act of God's grace. What five treatment centers and countless Alcoholics Anonymous meetings couldn't do, God did in one ten-minute prayer.

Why would God decide to answer this prayer while seemingly ignoring all of his other cries for help? We may never know. Maybe Gaylen had finally reached a point in his journey when there was absolutely nothing left but God. It took an arduous trek for Gaylen to finally get where God wanted him to be—open and primed to receive. When the student is ready, the teacher appears.

If we focus entirely upon the elements of Gaylen's journey, we may miss the real story of change the journey produced. In other words, there is a difference between the road we travel and how those travels impact us. Journey and transformation are intricately linked together; and yet, they are different. One is the pathway and the other is the result; one is the means and the other is the outcome. It is in the journey that we experience God, and it is the journey that God uses to change us from the inside out.

In speaking with Gaylen about his odyssey and its effect upon him, I couldn't help but notice the wheat principle at work. The wheat principle, as you recall, comes from John 12:24 where Jesus purportedly states: "Truly, truly, I say to you, unless a grain of wheat falls into the earth and dies, it remains alone; but if it dies, it bears much fruit." It is the idea that as old ways of thinking, seeing, acting, and being are buried in the ground to die like a seed of wheat, new understandings and new ways of seeing rise up. It is in the letting go that we are freed to approach things differently. This happened to Gaylen. It is called transformation—a change from within that allows one thing to morph into something different and better.

Humility and Character

In my chapter titled "Forgotten Virtues," I mention two foundational virtues worth pursuing—humility and character. Gaylen encountered both. My mind keeps going back to Gaylen's concert at a small Christian retreat where he realized for the first time in his life that his ministry wasn't about him. One is tempted to say, "Really? It took you that long?" After recording an album, traveling across the nation with a well-known evangelist, and experiencing a full concert schedule, he is just now figuring this out? It wasn't rocket science.

Before we put on a smug Christian attitude, we do well to remember our own struggle with humility and character. Gaylen had the guts to acknowledge his misplaced focus. In essence, he is saying, "This is where I was, and this is where I am now." That is transformation at work. Gaylen acknowledges a spirit of arrogance about him in his younger days and that he looked upon the church with indignation during his wandering years. Gaylen recalls his guest appearance on a local television show along with another now-famous Christian musician and singer. Gaylen's presence prompted more phone calls than the other guest, and Gaylen now says, "I thought I was something."

Before long, however, Gaylen's music ministry would crash and burn as he entered the "wandering years"—the desert of brokenness, of which the author of Proverbs 16:18 predicts, "Pride goes before destruction, and a haughty spirit before stumbling." How many times have we stumbled over ourselves because of pride, arrogance, and thinking we were something? If we are honest with ourselves, there is an awful lot of "me" in our artificially inflated self-perspective. We are pretty good at dressing it up in Sunday clothes and giving it that pious look. In reality, however, it is nothing more than self-interest parading around in religious garb. That's what Gaylen did. He paraded around in the religious garb of "ministry," when all along it was self-promotion that often fueled his ego. Been there, done that.

But things have changed for Gaylen. Once you've been thrown to the curb—once you have been brought low—you begin to see with new eyes. Gaylen now names it for what it is and courageously walks a new path of service and empathy. Life is no longer about him. Ministry is no longer about self-promotion. It is the empathy factor that Gaylen now loves to talk about, and I hear the enthusiasm in his voice. He has learned a life-changing lesson about other-centeredness. When the seed of wheat is placed into the ground, by choice or by the hand of God, what springs forth is something entirely new, different, and transformed. Once we begin to see things differently, we wonder why we didn't see this way before and can't imagine reverting back to our old way of being. It is the transformative wheat principle at work.

Forgiveness

Having traveled through the wasteland of brokenness, I figured Gaylen may have struggled with forgiveness, and he did, but just not in the way I imagined. I asked if he felt the need to forgive God, thinking he would jump on that bandwagon without hesitation. Much to my dismay, he didn't. In his mind, it was his own actions that caused so much grief, not God's. Gaylen loved God deeply and wanted nothing more than to please his Creator. It wasn't God who needed forgiveness; Gaylen needed to forgive himself.

Self-forgiveness is perhaps the most difficult forgiveness to extend. It was Gaylen's behavior that caused such pain in the lives of his family members. His first wife left him, for the turmoil he triggered was too much to bear. His second wife separated for a time, citing similar reasons. Gaylen's children were wounded by his actions and may have their own forgiveness issues to deal with.

The anguish he caused others strikes at Gaylen's heart so deeply that it becomes a continuing obstacle to forgiving himself. He has engaged in multiple conversations with those he harmed, even writing letters to them in an attempt to ease their hurt and mitigate his own pain. But Gaylen has changed and his sensitivities now realize the destructive nature of his past behavior. In days gone by, Gaylen didn't see his harmful ways in the same light. Forgiving himself isn't easy, but it is a journey, and he continues making progress. It is what I call "second-chance loving," the art of extending to ourselves the second chance we so willingly extend to others.

Years ago when my children were young, we undertook a road trip out West to visit my grandmother in Wyoming. On the way home, my son was playing with an annoying little toy in the back seat. On multiple occasions I asked him to stop, but he refused. That toy kept annoying me until I finally had enough. I reached around my seat, grabbed the toy, broke it in half, and tossed it out the window. My son began to cry, and though I had succeeded in silencing his irritating little toy, the self-aggravation was deafening. The outward irritation was gone, replaced with an internal breaking of the heart for me and my boy. For some reason, that is one of those incidents that I recall time and time again. I can't seem to shake it, and I find myself at times lying awake in the middle of the night with tears streaming down my face as I recall the incident.

I relate this occurrence, not because it mirrors the kind of agony alcoholism produces, for it doesn't, but because of the sensitivity it produced. I know, in my own little way, what it means to wrestle with self-forgiveness, but the greater transformation which I experienced in the toy incident, and which Gaylen experienced on a larger and deeper scale, is that our spirits are much more sensitive to the hurt our actions cause others. To see wounded individuals creates a heartache in its own right, but to be the cause of their injury is a pain all its own. Fortunately, God softens the heart, enlarges its capacity to love, and sensitizes our spirit to the needs of others so we live with greater empathy. Whether the stressful action is as simple as breaking the irritating toy of a child or breaking the heart of those you love through addiction, the transformation is that we now seek to become instruments of His grace rather than pathways of pain.

Surprised by God

Experiencing our Creator is the thrill of my heart, and something I relentlessly pursue. In my experience, the path of conventional religion doesn't seem to get us very far in our effort to intimately experience the Divine. Instead, I find God in surprising places. Strange as it may seem, it was while Gaylen contemplated suicide that he experienced a surprise encounter with God and felt unspeakable joy. It was Gaylen's financial need of $7,500 for duplicating a newly recorded album that God surprised him with a surprising donor to fill the gap. After a failed marriage, God surprised Gaylen with a nurturing and kind woman who would be a forever blessing. Sick and tired of church and religion, it was through the sermons of a local pastor that God surprised Gaylen with His presence and comforted his soul. Wounded and broken, Gaylen would sit in the back of the church with tears in his eyes. Through the journey of addiction and loss, Gaylen was surprised to find the freedom he so desperately longed for. God moves like the wind, wherever and whenever He wills. He is not constrained by our demands, expectations, or preferred pathways. He is the God who surprises.

It is through crises that God often reveals Himself. When our faith is on the brink, we discover the surprise of His presence in real and genuine ways. Our once fragile bumper-sticker religion turns into something much deeper and more meaningful—something Gaylen made certain that I caught about his journey. His faith has been transformed into a richer, freer, and deeper relationship with his Creator.

In my chapter titled "Surprised by God," I note two primary pathways for experiencing the kind of intimacy with God that brings about radical transformation—solemn seeking and suffering. It was the suffering part that brought Gaylen to his knees. By losing his marriage, his ministry, his joy, his purpose, etc. he was stripped of all that mattered to him. Even his second marriage reached a point of near disaster as Lynn separated for a time while releasing Gaylen over to the Lord, for there was nothing else she could do to turn him around. In the end it was just Gaylen and God, and Gaylen discovered that God was enough. Life does that to us—strips us of all the fluff we think is important so that we can get alone with our Creator. It is when we are alone with God that He does His best work in our heart and surprises us.

Suffering taught Gaylen that God can be found in imperfect, flawed human beings. God reveals Himself through our failures and screw-ups. God showed Himself to Gaylen through an imperfect church, through imperfect people, through imperfect circumstances. Suffering has a purifying effect upon our heart and helps us see things from a new perspective. Gaylen wouldn't wish his pain on anyone, but he would be hard-pressed to ever give up the resulting wondrous effect upon his life. If there were a way to get the end result without the painful process, I could go for something like that. Unfortunately, there is no other way. It was through an arduous journey that God revealed Himself to Gaylen so that others may see the good work of God's grace in his life.

Lost Hope

It didn't escape my attention how often Gaylen felt abandoned and forgotten by God as the events of his life unfolded. When his ministry collapsed, he was lost and alone. When told that God was finished with him, he felt worthless. Singing about the joy of the Lord while living a secret life of hypocrisy made him feel ashamed. When his wife filed for divorce, he viewed himself as a failure. When God was slow to answer his prayers, he felt confused. When numerous attempts at rehab didn't work, he felt deflated.

Disillusionment can be a huge obstacle in our pursuit of God. Gaylen may have felt abandoned, but he never blamed the Lord. Instead, he eventually recognized his own problems, failures, and hypocrisy. This takes courage to admit, especially when it is far easier to make excuses and blame others. Many of us would have given up long ago had we been in Gaylen's shoes, but he admitted his own need and held steadfast to a strong belief in God's ability. I am amazed, quite frankly, at how Gaylen kept on going after getting knocked to the ground so many times. Others may have been screaming, "Stay down. The fight isn't worth it. Give up," yet, Gaylen kept getting up to fight another round. It was on that day, when he was about to lose Lynn, the love of his life, that he fell upon his knees in one final attempt to tug at the heart of God: "Move God. Please move. I can't stand the thought of another loss and another failure." I wonder if it is in moments like these that we fully grasp what Jesus meant when he asked us to become dependent on God like little children.

Though lost hope had shot its full quiver of arrows into his heart, Gaylen continued clinging to the only hope he knew—hope in a compassionate and caring God. Without that hope, what else do we have? Gaylen knows what it means to become destitute in spirit, to continue rising when it is far easier to stay down for the count, and he maintains firsthand knowledge of a child-like dependency upon the Father. That is transformation.

Stand

We learn many things throughout our journey, and over time we discover a great deal about what matters. Now that Gaylen has progressed to the point of significant hindsight, I asked him what he stands for these days. He mentioned several things, but something caught my attention that revealed to me that he had indeed experienced the wheat principle in his life. Gaylen said he had learned to take an "internal stance." Going through the motions is one thing, but standing from the inside adds an internal marker to the whole idea of standing. He now stands for what he calls "morality in his heart." He desires to take a stand for the right things—all the time.

Do you see what has transpired? Life is no longer about external causes; rather, it is about internal motivations—spurred on by intrinsic and eternal values. When the heart is changed, all else changes. If you want to change your perspective on life, change your heart. For instance, Gaylen now stands for loving the unlovable, which he thought he once was, only this time around, he does it from the heart—from the inside, with a pure an honest desire. Beautiful! That is transformation.

Stains of Glory

I know an acrylic artist who paints coffee and tea stains on canvas. She places them in beautiful settings so they become marks of beauty. What was once considered an ugly blemish destined for quick removal by washrag, has now been transformed into a valuable piece of artwork that is admired by many. Her artwork is a metaphor for life itself—for the journey.

Luckily for us, we serve a God of second chances, One who is filled with love and compassion for His creation. Though we are at times noting but blemished stains on the kitchen counter destined for washrag removal, God, the ultimate artist of life, takes our many failures and mistakes—our dirty little stains—and turns them into treasured works of art so others can marvel at His handiwork. Gaylen knows exactly what I am talking about, and I have a sneaky suspicion that you do, too. In essence, God can turn our scars into treasures.

Gaylen wrote a song titled "I Cleave to You" that is recorded on his 2018 album *Church Without Walls*. As I listened to it, and I listened to it multiple times, it seems to not only sum up his journey to this point, but it also seems like a fitting way to close this book.

I Cleave To You

I cleave to you, when my heart is broken
I cleave to you, when my soul needs to rest
I cleave to you, my words are left unspoken
I cleave to you, with tears on your breast

I cleave to you, when life just gets too crazy
I cleave to you, when I just can't fight
I cleave to you, when my mind's so tired of racing
So I cleave to you, with all of my might

I cleave to you, when fear has tried to shake me
I cleave to you, when I feel I can't go on
I cleave to you, when time has tried to break me
So I cleave to you, and sing you this song

I cleave to you, and tell you that I love you
I cleave to you, and ask you to stay
I cleave to you, only heaven is above you
And only God can take you away

I cleave to you, when our time on earth is over
I cleave to you, and tell you that I'm here
I cleave to you, here and now forever
I cleave to you, there's nothing to fear

Written and composed by Gaylen Paul © 2018
As recorded on the album *Church Without Walls*
gaylenpaul.com

CPSIA information can be obtained
at www.ICGtesting.com
Printed in the USA
LVHW021244040920
665076LV00016B/695